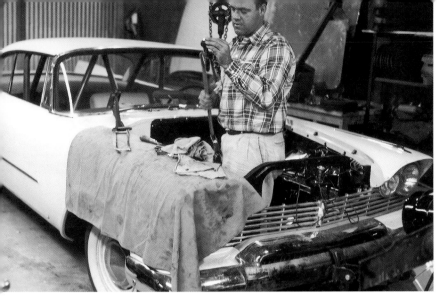

Hot Rod Magazine
All the Covers

Drew Hardin and the Editors of *Hot Rod Magazine*

First published in 2010 by Motorbooks, an imprint of MBI Publishing Company, 400 First Avenue North, Suite 300, Minneapolis, MN 55401 USA

Motorbooks titles are also available at discounts in bulk quantity for industrial or sales-promotional use. For details write to Special Sales Manager at MBI Publishing Company, 400 First Avenue North, Suite 300, Minneapolis, MN 55401 USA.

To find out more about our books, visit us online at www.motorbooks.com.

ISBN-13: 978-0-7603-3817-9

Editor: Chris Endres
Designer: Martine Forte Sticha
Jacket Designer: Sandra Salimony

Printed in China

Drew Hardin's 30-year automotive journalism career includes 14 years at Petersen Publishing, where he was editor of *Hot Rod* from 1994 to 1996 and later served as the magazine's editorial director. His current projects include freelance magazine, book, and marketing assignments covering a wide range of topics, from muscle cars to 4x4s, motorcycles, and "green" vehicles.

Contents

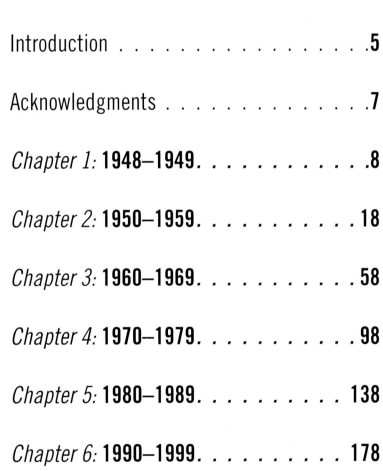

HOT ROD OF THE MONTH

Sitting in the driver's seat is Eddie Hulse, who, a few moments after this picture was taken, drove number 668, to set a new SCTA record for Class C roadsters. Hulse, a native Californian, nosed out Randy Shinn, a long-time top honor holder for the RC Class. Shinn's old record was 129.40 in a channeled Mercury T.

Foreword

Hot Rod magazine has often been vaunted as an American success story. Launching the magazine from his Hollywood apartment, founder Robert E. Petersen created a voice that would almost single-handedly turn an outlaw hobby into a huge, mainstream industry. Along the way, *Hot Rod* has changed the nature of the industry simply by following what the readers were doing with their cars. In reviewing the six-plus decades of magazine covers that ensued, it's easy to see the trends that readers created and followed; the cars and the graphic designs mirror the arc of pop culture itself.

In the seminal years, *Hot Rod* was about dry lakes race cars and the occasional custom car. As the 1950s wore on, the emphasis shifted to street-going hot rods and drag racing cars, and by the middle of that decade, the covers revealed that the publishing executives had awakened to the advertising benefits of new-car editorial coverage. When *Hot Rod* editor and National Hot Rod Association (NHRA) founder Wally Parks moved the drag racing U.S. Nationals to Detroit in 1959, the spark of competition lit a fire within the Big Three, leading to the creation of the factory muscle cars that dominated *Hot Rod* covers throughout the 1960s.

Other 1960s experiments included trucks, boats, and dune buggies. But many consider 1972 the moment that things turned for the worse. By then, insurance regs and later the gas crunch forced new topics on *Hot Rod* covers:

mileage tips, Pintos, Vegas, and vans. Even the staffers of the time consider it the dark ages.

Thankfully, the street machine craze soon hit, with guys hopping up the muscle cars that were then 10-year-old affordable used cars. That led to Pro Street cars and then a "Dare to be Different" motto, both of which sent newsstand sales soaring in the 1980s. When those fads ran their course, *Hot Rod* created the next boom in 1992—the Fastest Street Car in America Shootout. Overall, the magazine pushed for cars that were really driven or raced rather than just polished, and that period's legacy is the annual cross-country trek called Power Tour, a subject that has landed on *Hot Rod* covers annually since 1995.

In the 2000s, the rebirth of the factory muscle car sent Camaro, Mustang, and Challenger covers into stratospheric sales, though at the close of the first decade of the new millennium, it's those original '40s- and '50s-styled rods, customs, and racers that are once again proving the hottest topic.

We'd call it a full circle, but we know there's no end to the loop. What's the next big hot rodding trend? You'll find the answer on the covers of *Hot Rod* magazine.

David Freiburger
Editor in Chief
Hot Rod magazine

Introduction

More than 60 years after the fact, Alex Xydias' eyes still gleam at the memory. "To be on the cover of *Hot Rod* magazine? It was such a thrill."

Xydias was looking back in time at the January 1949 issue of *Hot Rod* with his So-Cal Speed Shop belly tanker on the cover. The magazine was just a year old, but even then, being on the cover of *Hot Rod* was something special.

The thrill Xydias felt when he first saw that issue a half century ago has been shared by hot rodders, customizers, drag racers, engine builders, and many others whose high-powered accomplishments earned a place on *Hot Rod*'s covers during the past six decades. No one is blasé about being on the cover of *Hot Rod*. Even media-jaded celebrities are excited to be featured under the familiar red and white logo. Dale Earnhardt Jr., no stranger to the camera, said his cover shoot for the December 2007 issue was the fulfillment of a childhood dream.

Name-dropping Xydias and Earnhardt in one paragraph speaks to the tremendous scope of events *Hot Rod* has chronicled over the years. The magazine's history is the history of post–World War II automotive performance, from the early speed pioneers on Southern California's dry lakes through the formation of organized drag racing to today's Drag Week; from Detroit's earliest muscle cars to the twenty-first-century grandkids of those behemoths;

from Ford flatheads and early Chrysler Hemis to twin-turbocharged, 1,500-horsepower big-block Chevys; from the Barris brothers to Boyd, Troy, and Chip. Sure, there were some head-scratchers along the way. Much of the 1970s now looks like an exercise in "What were they thinking?" But the editors were doing what they could during those dark days of oil embargoes and emissions regulations to keep hot rodding's creative juices flowing and to keep readers wanting *Hot Rod* magazine.

That's a challenge every editor has faced. How do you entice someone to pick up and then spend their hard-earned green on your magazine? It's all about the cover. A magazine's cover is where art and commerce butt heads as the single most important sales tool an editorial staff has. And just as automotive performance has evolved over the past 60 years, so have the magazine's covers.

Right out of the gate, Robert E. Petersen, who co-founded *Hot Rod* with Robert Lindsay, had an eye for compelling cover subjects. It's no accident that Regg Schlemmer's modified T, with a smiling Eddie Hulse at the wheel, was on the first issue's cover. Schlemmer, a relative newcomer to lakes racing, seemingly came out of nowhere with a car that Hulse drove to 136 miles per hour, setting a record nearly 7 miles per hour faster than the previous mark in an era when records inched up a mile per hour at a time.

Schlemmer's roadster shocked a lot of lakes-racing veterans on that October day in 1947, and they'd no doubt want to read about how it went so fast.

Hot Rod wasn't in business long before other magazines went after the same readership. Petersen himself was responsible for some in-house competition when he started *Motor Trend* in 1949 and *Honk!* (which would become *Car Craft*) in 1953. Outside the Petersen stable, the publishers of *Road and Track* launched *Hop Up*, in its "little book" format, in 1951. A couple of years later came the first *Rods and Customs*, which dropped the plurals in the title with its second issue.

Given the competition from those new magazines and more, it's not surprising that *Hot Rod*'s staff felt the need to enhance its covers for added eye appeal. The first color photograph appeared on the April 1951 issue, and the first cover blurb in the skyline (also called the roof) position, at the very top of the cover above the logo, was put there in March 1952. That piece of cover real estate has only grown more important over time, as newsstands have become more crowded and retailers stack competing magazines on top of one another on the rack.

By the late 1950s, cover designs got fairly crowded with words and images, and for the most part they stayed that way for the next five decades. As you'll see inside, photography trends would change, as would the favored typefaces, their coloration, and the sure-fire cover words that "worked," according to the circulation directors. But busy covers were, and still are to a degree, perceived as better covers, with

more hooks to snag potential newsstand buyers. Today, conventional magazine sales wisdom says that you have scant seconds—five, maybe as many as ten—to catch a magazine shopper's eye. So your cover blurbs have to be big, bold, and to the point. If you get the shopper to pick up your magazine, you still have only a 50-50 chance that he or she will actually buy it.

That's where the content comes in. A cover will get you in their hands, but what's inside the magazine has to deliver on the promises made on the cover, and then some. Wally Parks, who took over the editor's role from Petersen and Lindsay with the October 1949 issue, set the bar incredibly high for those who followed him. Parks deftly juggled multiple agendas—cleaning up hot rodding's then thuggish reputation, promoting safe cars and safer races—while expanding *Hot Rod*'s editorial scope to include topics still in the magazine today: technical and how-to stories, coverage of drag races, and (controversially, at the time) new car road tests. In his spare time, Parks also started a small drag racing organization called the NHRA, but that's a whole other story.

The press run for *Hot Rod*'s first issue was a tiny 5,000 issues. On the strength of the work by Parks and his staff, including ace lensmen Eric Rickman and Bob D'Olivo, technical wizard Don Francisco, and the multi-talented (illustrator/cartoonist/photographer/writer) Tom Medley, circulation exploded in just a few short years. By mid-1952, on the now famous cover showing Dick Flint's roadster stopped short in front of UCLA co-ed Harriet Haven, the editors proudly proclaimed, "Over HALF-MILLION copies this issue." And by the time editor Jim McFarland wrote his 20th-anniversary retrospective for the January 1968 issue, "The print order was 1,044,000!"

If there was a downside to this level of success, it came in the form of pressure put on the editors to keep the magazine growing. Editors didn't always have a free hand to decide what went on the cover. If anything, they had to deal with a growing number of voices with an opinion on what should be on the front page. Circulation directors would oversee cover concepts prior to publication to make sure the editor was delivering the right words and images in the right places on the cover. Those meetings didn't always end in the editor's favor, but if you could get the circulation guys to back you on a concept, great things—like extra pages, posters, additional distribution—could happen.

And then there were the advertisers. Whether it was to woo a new advertiser or keep an existing one happy, the cover was sometimes used as a bargaining chip. In hindsight, many of those covers are easy to spot now. For that matter, some of them were easy to spot *then*, as they weren't necessarily on target with the readership's interests.

There were some hard-fought battles among those who had a stake in what went on *Hot Rod*'s cover. There still are. Ask any editor, present or past, and he'll have stories about locking horns with circulation, his publisher, or both. (We share some of those inside.) Yet despite the in-fighting, despite the dark days of the 1970s, *Hot Rod*'s circulation continued to grow until it reached its peak in 1989. That year's July issue, with Billy Gibbons' radical *CadZZilla* custom Cadillac on the cover, was the best-selling *Hot Rod* of all time, with total sales of about 1.16 million copies. And those were sales numbers, not the total print run. Ironically, Editor Jeff Smith had to fight to get the concept approved, as it broke several cardinal rules of conventional newsstand sales wisdom: The car was dark purple but looked almost black; it was a Cadillac; it was a custom (not a hot rod or muscle car); and, in Smith's opinion, its most dramatic angle was from the rear. In the end, management caved (a rarity, but it happens), and the readers were drawn to it, just like the first buyers of *Hot Rod* were to Schlemmer's fast roadster in 1948 and the So-Cal belly tanker a year later.

At our breakfast meeting, Alex Xydias looked up from that January 1949 issue and sighed. "You know, Pete came out to the lakes in 1947 and showed us his plans for the magazine. He wanted me to buy an ad for So-Cal, and I told him I'd wait, to see how the magazine turned out. He never let me forget that."

Acknowledgments

I was privileged to work with many past and present *Hot Rod* editors while researching this book. Their recollections provided valuable insight into a publication that in many ways has changed a great deal and in many others hasn't changed much at all over the course of 60 years. Current editor in chief David Freiburger was an immense help with his keen ability to interpret and digest the magazine's extensive history and put it into a framework I could use for the cover chapters. Thanks to former editors Jim McFarland, Lee Kelley, Leonard Emanuelson, Pat Ganahl, Jeff Smith, Steve Campbell, Ro McGonegal, current editor Rob Kinnan, and former publisher Harry Hibler for your time and your stories. I also want to thank John Dianna, who promoted me to *Hot Rod* editor and put me, undeservedly, in the company of these great men. A big thank you goes to Alex Xydias, founder of the So-Cal Speed Shop, hot rodding pioneer, and a true gentleman who is always so generous with his memories. I owe you for that breakfast, Alex. And finally, though it is cliché for a writer to thank his wife and family, I truly could not have done this without the love and support from Kerry, Emily, Katie, and Tristan.

—Drew Hardin

Chapter 1

1948–1949

Wally Parks had a problem. Well, more accurately, hot rodding had a problem. In the years right after World War II, young men who drove hopped-up cars were generally viewed by the public as a menace, flaunting local traffic laws and causing accidents that generated lurid headlines in local newspapers. As the president of the Southern California Timing Association (SCTA), a racing organization that held speed trials on the dry lakes in the high desert, Parks knew that he and his fellow racers were by no means criminals. He needed a way to burnish their image and the image of hot rodding in general. Parks and the SCTA hit on the idea of staging a car show at the Los Angeles National Guard Armory "to let the public know we weren't flakes," Parks later said. To sell booth space, Parks hired a young PR rep named Robert E. "Pete" Petersen, who was drumming up business for his fledgling Hollywood Publicity Associates agency.

While promoting the show, Petersen and fellow agency member Robert Lindsay saw an opportunity to launch a magazine for the lakes racers and other guys interested in making their cars go faster. Petersen took his ideas to speed shops and lakes meets, received some solid advertising support (there were more than 30 ads in the first issue), and put together a 24-page, 9x12-inch-format magazine with a 25-cent cover price. At first he considered naming it *Autocraft* but decided instead to use the more controversial term *Hot Rod*. Hey, if you're out to clean up hot rodding's image, you might as well be up front about the magazine's content.

The design of the first *Hot Rod* cover, with Regg Schlemmer's T roadster framed by red banners top and bottom, mimicked the look of *Throttle*, a lakes- and track-racing magazine that had been published for a year prior to the war. By *Hot Rod*'s second issue, though, the banners were changing colors; and for the May issue art director Al Isaacs broke the mold completely by moving the magazine's name out of the top banner and into a red flag in the upper left corner. That logo has evolved over time, as the lettering style has changed with design trends, but the cover's basic format has stayed remarkably similar to that May 1948 iteration.

Cover layouts remained pretty consistent—a single, full-bleed photo of lakes racers, hot street roadsters, a coupe or two, and even a hot rod truck—until the fall of 1949.

The September issue was the first to use multiple images, while a major graphic redesign for the October 1949 issue reflected big changes at the magazine. The *Hot Rod* logo got much bigger, and white space top- and bottom-framed the cover photo, in this case the remarkable So-Cal Speed Shop streamliner, which had smashed speed records at the first speed meet at the Bonneville Salt Flats. With this issue, Petersen and Lindsay turned *Hot Rod*'s editorial management over to Parks, who could now fully utilize the magazine's pages as a way to recast hot rodders in a more positive light.

Hey, if you're out to clean up hot rodding's image, you might as well be up front about the magazine's content.

Stu Hilborn's fuel-injected streamliner ran 136 miles per hour on the dry lakes when the car appeared in *Hot Rod* in April 1948. Just a couple of months later Hilborn's 'liner is the first to break 150 miles per hour.

Robert Petersen and Wally Parks were instrumental in convincing the governor of Utah to allow hot rodders on the Bonneville Salt Flats. The first meet was in 1949, and rodders to this day make the pilgrimage to Bonneville in search of speed.

HOT ROD *Magazine*

VOL. 1, NO. 1 • • • PRICE 25c   WORLD'S MOST COMPLETE HOT ROD COVERAGE   JANUARY 1948

HOT ROD OF THE MONTH

Sitting in the driver's seat is Eddie Hulse, who, a few moments after this picture was taken, drove number 668, to set a new SCTA record for Class C roadsters. Hulse, a native Californian, nosed out Randy Shinn, a long-time top honor holder for the RC Class. Shinn's old record was 129.40 in a channeled Mercury T.

Keeping the Car Out Front! by George Riley — Page 10

January

What do you put on the cover of your very first magazine about hot rods? How about the fastest car at the most recent lakes meet? Regg Schlemmer, a relative newcomer to the SCTA, brought his Class C 1927 T roadster to the October 1947 meet at El Mirage and "smashed past records with its initial competitive run at the lakes." Driven by Eddie Hulse (who is sitting in the car for the cover photo), Schlemmer's track-nose T averaged 136.05 miles per hour, easily eclipsing the previous record of 129.40 miles per hour set by Randy Shinn. Hulse's speed was also fastest of the meet, with Shinn a close second at 131.77 miles per hour.

"*B*ehind the record of this car are 20 years engine experience and six weeks of relentless day and night work on the part of owner-builder Schlemmer," says the magazine. "The roadster checked in at El Mirage with Mercury engine, Navarro heads, Evans manifold and a Smith cam and running 3.27-1 gears. For ignition he is running two four-cylinder Wico mags. 668's body is a '27 T channeled over a special built tubular frame. Body work on the car, done by El Slaven, is a job of which any body man would be proud."

The magazine informs the reader that Schlemmer, whose dry lakes racing days go back to the 1930s, plans to open a speed shop in South Gate, California, "where he will build both boat and auto engines for speed enthusiasts." Those plans may be accelerated by the ad he has bought in the issue, joining the likes of Navarro Racing Equipment, Riley Racing Carburetors, Smithy Muffler Manufacturing, Bell Auto Parts, the Carson Top Shop, Sta-Lube, the Winfield Carburetor & Manufacturing Company, Sharp Speed Equipment, Blair's Auto Parts, Barris' Custom Shop, and the Weber Tool Company as some of *Hot Rod*'s very first advertisers.

Schlemmer's T is just one of many notable hot rods appearing in this first issue. The center spread contains 16 photos of lakes and track racing highlights, featuring Tom Beatty, Phil Weiand, Phil Remington, Manuel Ayulo, Dick

1948

Craft, Don Brown, and other notable rodders. Bill Burke's *Sweet Sixteen* belly tanker (with Wally Parks behind the wheel) gets a full-page photo, as does Dick Vineyard's *Little Beauty* roadster, a "top flight CRA [California Roadster Association] track job," says the magazine.

The issue also includes a story called "Keeping the Car Out Front," with tips on what racing mechanics should pay attention to during and after a race. The author is George Riley, well-respected for his two- and four-port cylinder heads.

Filling out the issue's 24 pages is a story on the upcoming Hot Rod Exposition at the National Guard Armory, a lengthy piece of fiction called "Someone to Watch Over Me," race results from recent speedway and lakes events, cartoons by Tom Medley, a profile of the CRA, and the very first "Parts with Appeal" page, with 19-year-old model Jane Norred holding a new compact fuel pump. Petersen and Lindsay know a thing or two about getting a young hot rodder's heart pumping.

The center spread of the first *Hot Rod* features lakes racers, track roadsters, midgets—and one coupe—from around Southern California.

April: Stu Hilborn's streamliner is Hot Rod of the Month. A photo with the hood open shows the flathead V-8 fitted with an Eddie Miller intake manifold and four Stromberg carburetors. On the hood is Hilborn's fuel injection manifold. "With this equipment, an unofficial time of 136 mph was reached."

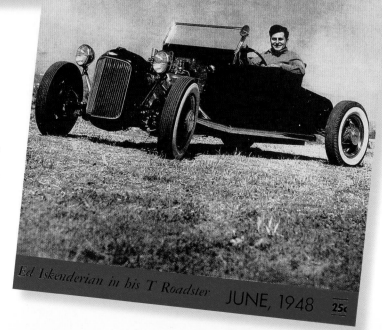

June: Yes, that's the Camfather, Ed Iskenderian, smiling from the driver's seat of his T/V-8 in the first of many such poses to follow. "Ed bought the whole '24 T from which the body was made for only $4. That was in 1939. Just try to buy it now."

HOT ROD *Magazine*

VOL. 1, No. 2 • PRICE 25c • WORLD'S MOST COMPLETE HOT ROD COVERAGE — FEBRUARY, 1948

Overhead Valves by Wayne—Page 10

February

March

May

July

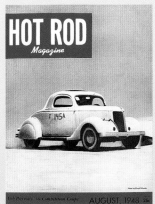

August

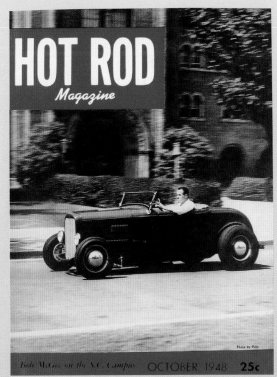

October

September

November

December

February: Keith Landrigan's LaSalle-powered roadster, a record-setter "both in time trials and on the highway."

March: Don Blair's 1927 T "recently clocked 124.88 mph at a Russetta timing meet."

May: Bert Letner's 130-mile-per-hour Elco Twin under the new *Hot Rod* magazine title flag.

July: Rudy Ramos has "great expectations for his combination lakes-track roadster."

August: Bob Pierson's 117-mile-per-hour 1936 coupe "represents an important phase in hot rodding."

September: First Midwest cover: Dick Frazier's T sets the half-mile record of 21.37 seconds.

October: Bob McGee's "pleasure job" 1932 roadster cruises in front of USC.

November: Dick Vineyard wins a championship in Ed Walker's track T at Culver City Speedway.

December: Harold Daigh averages 143.19 miles per hour at the SCTA's rain-delayed October meet.

1948

October

HOT ROD
Magazine

TOP RECORD BREAKER IN
BONNEVILLE SPEED TRIALS

OCTOBER 1949

TWENTY-FIVE CENTS

Hot Rod and hot rodding take a major evolutionary step. Just a couple months shy of its second birthday, *Hot Rod*'s cover has a new look, with white space providing strong contrast to the redesigned title flag and the image below it. Bigger changes take place inside: Petersen and Lindsay announce that Wally Parks, the SCTA's former business manager "and a long-time advocate of hot rod interests," will take over editorship of the magazine. "As editor, writer, artist and layout man of the Association's monthly timing meet programs, Parks has been exposed to his share of printers' ink."

The issue's cover image represents rodding breakthroughs on several fronts. After months of planning and countless meetings, the SCTA holds its first speed trials on the Bonneville Salt Flats, which, until now, had been the province of speed-record attempts by the likes of Ab Jenkins, Malcolm Campbell, and John Cobb. The Southern California hot rodders who turn out for the event have to do some tuning to adjust to the salt's 4,200-foot altitude, but they also find the hard-packed surface and long course ideal for top-speed runs.

Alex Xydias and Dean Batchelor surprise even themselves with the speeds they achieve in the *So-Cal Speed Shop Special*. Early in the meet, with a V-8/60 for power, the streamliner sets an average speed of 156.39 miles per hour. But after swapping that engine for an Edelbrock-built Mercury flathead, "the car breezed through the traps at a speed of 185.95 mph, which at that time was over 20 miles an hour faster than any other car had ever run in dry lakes competition." A day later, the car turns 193.54 on a northbound run and 185.95 on the return, for an average of 189.745 miles per hour.

"By far the most outstanding car, not only in performance but in its striking appearance as well, the little flat streamliner was the smoothest running machine on the course," says the magazine. "In the traps on the return record run, at close to 190 mph, both front tires lost their treads. The car continued on its way straight down the course and was brought to a smooth stop by driver Dean Batchelor."

The first Bonneville meet draws about 60 entries, a number that's "not at all disheartening" to the SCTA. "The fact that this first attempt at staging a National Meet on unfamiliar ground would be a strange venture to all led the SCTA to be cautious in building it up in advance," says the magazine. But with the success of this first meet under their belts, "The Bonneville National

1949

Speed Trials should become one of the nation's greatest annual events."

Speaking of great annual events, the issue contains a full-page ad for the first annual National Roadster Show, to be held in Oakland, California, in January. "More than $5,000 in trophies and merchandise awards" will be handed out at the show, including the 8-1/2-foot ("world's largest") trophy for America's Most Beautiful Roadster.

Hot rodders hit the salt for the very first time, and the *So-Cal Special* streamliner gets oh-so-close to 200 miles per hour.

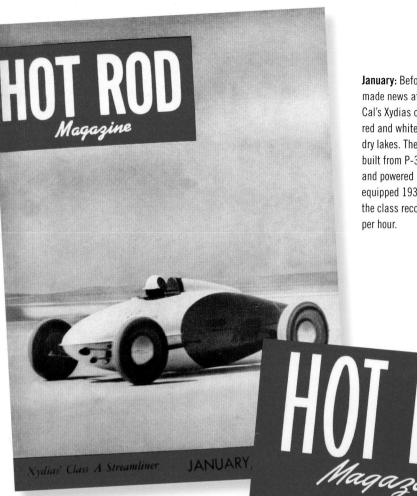

Xydias' Class A Streamliner   JANUARY,

January: Before his streamliner made news at Bonneville, So-Cal's Xydias campaigned this tidy red and white belly tanker at the dry lakes. The Class A streamliner, built from P-38 drop tank halves and powered by an Edelbrock-equipped 1939 Ford V-8/60, holds the class record of 130.155 miles per hour.

HOT ROD
Magazine

JACK CALORI'S HANDSOME
STREET AND LAKES COUPE

NOVEMBER 1949

TWENTY-FIVE CENTS

November: Lakes- and track-racing roadsters have dominated *Hot Rod*'s covers, with an occasional competition coupe or street roadster thrown in the mix. Jack Calori's "Unusual California Coupe" is different. It's a custom, "rebuilt to combine comfortable transportation with accessible high speed," that was clocked at 114.50 miles per hour on the lakes.

February: Johnny Hartman's Chevy six-cylinder roadster "does an excellent job representing the overhead interests."

March: Spurgin, Giovanine, and Rufi "make an obsolete four-barrel out-perform anything in its class."

April: Fran Hernandez's 122-mile-per-hour 1932 Ford is only the second coupe on *Hot Rod*'s cover.

May: Jim Berger's T, with Frontenac heads, is Roadster—not Hot Rod—of the Month.

June: The George-Pestana 1927 T is Track Roadster of the Month. Note the logo's new drop shadow.

July: Bill Kenz' twin-engine "Odd Rod" pickup lays the groundwork for his streamliner to come.

August: The "World's Fastest Hot Rod" is Bill Burke and Don Francisco's 151-mile-per-hour belly tank.

September: The first multiple-image cover features Wes Cooper's roadster over four-bangers of the past.

December: Howard Johansen's twin-tank streamliner gets a push from Jim Woods' roadster at the lakes.

February

March

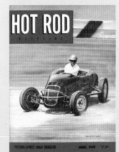

June

1949

April

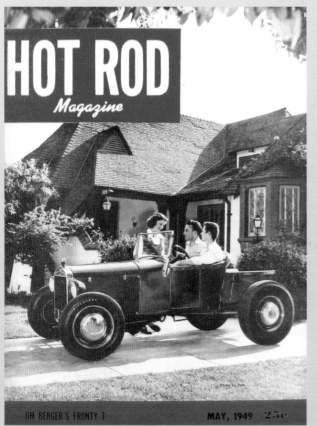

May

July

August

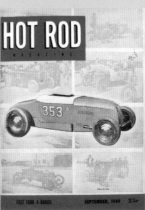

September

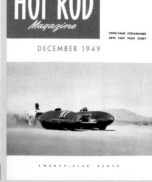

December

Chapter 2
1950-1959

There wasn't a single decade more critical to the evolution of automotive performance—and *Hot Rod* magazine—than the 1950s.

Editor Wally Parks would put his imprint on the young sport of drag racing when he announced the formation of the National Hot Rod Association (NHRA) in the May 1951 issue. With its emphasis on safety and cooperation between racers and local politicians, the NHRA fit nicely into Parks' mission to promote hot rodding's positive image. The new association grew quickly, staging its first sanctioned drag race at Pomona in 1953. A year later, Parks dispatched the Drag Safari—four guys in a station wagon towing a trailer full of timing equipment—to show rodders in the rest of the country how to properly stage a drag race. In 1955, the NHRA held its very first national meet in Kansas, and the NHRA U.S. Nationals are still held in the Midwest, though the venue changed a couple of times before settling in Indianapolis.

For those who liked "show" along with their "go," the Grand National Roadster Show first opened in Oakland, California, in 1950. Its towering America's Most Beautiful Roadster trophy remains a pinnacle of car building achievement.

Two underhood icons were born in the 1950s: Chrysler's first Hemi engines in 1951 and Chevrolet's overhead-valve small-block V-8 in 1955. *Hot Rod* produced in-depth analyses of both engines, recognizing them for their power-making potential—traits that have kept these engines at the forefront of automotive performance ever since.

Conventional wisdom says the Detroit muscle car was born with the 1964 Pontiac GTO. Yet the seeds of Detroit muscle were sown in the 1950s with cars like the Plymouth Fury, Olds 88, and Pontiac Bonneville—all "rod-tested"

by the magazine. Detroit became so important to *Hot Rod* (and vice versa) that stockers were frequent cover subjects in the middle and late years of the decade.

New car testing was just one new addition to the magazine's content in the 1950s. Readers also started to see technical how-to stories and the first use of dynamometers to measure engine output. All three are still important to *Hot Rod*'s editorial package today.

Color—of a sort—was introduced inside the magazine when the first rotogravure pictorial section appeared in 1953. This special process allowed pages to be printed using colored inks, and the editors created a whole new style of minimal-text/photo-heavy car feature for those sections.

New car testing was just one new addition to the magazine's content in the 1950s.

Yet the magazine's most dramatic visual change was the color cover photograph that appeared on the April 1951 issue. Suddenly, the first three issues of the year looked like they came from another, darker era, not just a few months ago. Color cover photography sparked a burst of design creativity that forever altered the face of *Hot Rod*. In the coming months Art Director Al Isaacs would for the first time utilize illustrations, engine photos, multiple images, tightly cropped photos, and other design elements that would make up *Hot Rod*'s look for decades to come.

Chevrolet's new overhead-valve V-8 was an immediate hit with hot rodders. Eric Rickman documents one of the first small-block swaps in December 1955.

Just four years after Wally Parks announced its formation, the NHRA holds its first national meet, "The Big Go," in Kansas in June 1955.

BOB PIERSON WITH 142 MPH
RECORD-HOLDING COUPE

APRIL 1950

TWENTY-FIVE CENTS

April

The matter-of-fact cover story inside this issue gives *Hot Rod* readers the basics about Dick and Bob Pierson's heavily hammered 1934 three-window coupe, but its significance goes far beyond the short captions that accompany Tom Medley's photos and Rex Burnett's detailed cutaway illustration.

Let's start with the fact that it's a coupe, in an era when almost all hot rods are built from roadster bodies to make them as light as possible. Coupes are considered too heavy to make serious speed; in fact, the Southern California Timing Association doesn't even have a coupe class (yet), so the Pierson Brothers earn their early speed records with the Russetta Timing Association.

Then there's the shape. Bob Pierson works at Douglas Aircraft and understands aerodynamics, so the car is laid out with a narrow frontal area, a belly pan, and an incredibly low roofline. Edelbrock's Bobby Meeks is the one who figures out the radical chop, laying the A-pillars back so far that forward visibility nearly disappears.

The Piersons first run the car at the lakes in primer, but it's best known for the red-to-white-to-blue livery seen here. Its well-finished looks also set it apart from many of the other rods on the lakes, which are typically works in progress whose owners care more about going fast than looking good.

It takes more than good looks to earn a Russetta record, though. Meeks carefully assembles a 59-A flathead with Edelbrock heads, pistons, and three-carb manifold sporting Stromberg 48 carburetors converted to run alcohol. (Edelbrock's nitro experiments are still to come.) The camshaft is an Ed Winfield grind, while the ignition is from Kong Jackson. "In setting their record of 142.98 mph the Pierson Brothers were running 2.94 gears in the [Halibrand quick-change] rear end, with 7.50x18 tires." Soon, they'd run even faster on the Bonneville salt.

This issue also includes a story by Editor Wally Parks called "Controlled Drag-Races," introducing *Hot Rod* readers to speed contests "being conducted weekly on abandoned airstrip runways." One of the "smoother operating systems" Parks has seen "has been conducted near Santa Ana, California, where an isolated practice landing field has been the scene of experimental meets." Though uncredited in the story, those meets are the work of drag strip pioneer C. J. "Pappy" Hart.

Hot rodding safety was always a concern of Parks, and this story is no different. The lead photo shows a half-dozen cars taking off at once, though Parks' caption warns this is "not the recommended method for these events." Later in the story he writes, "Naturally the more attention that is paid to safety in these events, the better chances are to produce an accepted sport."

The man who will found the NHRA predicts, "As the sport progresses, it will undoubtedly outgrow the 'choose off' method of selecting contestants. Qualifying runs would provide an easy means of effectively matching various types of cars, especially if points or awards were to be offered for fast qualifiers."

1950

How revolutionary was the Pierson Brothers coupe? It set dry lakes speed records before the SCTA even had a coupe class.

HOT ROD Magazine

DECEMBER 1950
TWENTY-FIVE CENTS

518 B

COMPETI
Pictoria

December: Jimmy and Tommy Dahm's SCTA B-Modified roadster (with Jimmy behind the wheel) is brightened up with some color— the first such treatment on a *Hot Rod* cover. "This well built and fine performing car is an example of the type of equipment that can be built by the average hot rodder."

September: Breaking the magazine's design mold, Art Director Al Isaacs "has dreamed up a new cover adaptation, of which we are all very proud," writes Parks. Don Waite's 1927 T "has set the fastest known clocked speed for all types of American roadsters: 160.71 mph."

HOT ROD Magazine

SEPTEMBER 1950
TWENTY-FIVE CENTS

* Don Waite and his Record Holding Modified Roadster

In This Issue:
● NORTHERN CALIFORNIA REVS UP
● FORD 4-BARREL SPEED SECRETS
● 160 MPH REAR-ENGINE ROADSTER

UNIQUE MODEL T BATHTUB
HOUSES V-8 POWER PLANT

MARCH 1950

TWENTY-FIVE CENTS

March

January

February

May

June

January: Ray Bowles' 1925 T is the Best Appearing Car at the Pasadena Reliability Run.

February: Roy Prosser in the Spalding Brothers' Chevy 6 at Carrell Speedway in Gardena.

March: "With more under the hood than meets the eye, this T is capable of fast speeds."

May: Ray Brown and Alex Xydias prep Brown's rear-engine lakester for pre-season runs.

June: Guy Wilson (69) and George Amick (18) go wheel-to-wheel on El Monte's quarter-mile oval.

July: A former Ralph Schenck streamliner gets a push to the starting line at El Mirage.

August: Three years in the making, Eddie Miller's lakester is almost ready for Bonneville.

October: Streamliners break the 200-mile-per-hour barrier at the second Bonneville Nationals.

November: Herman Russell gets his Bonneville start; in the corner is the 210-mile-per-hour *So-Cal Special*.

July

August

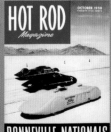

BONNEVILLE NATIONALS

October

210 MPH

National Champion

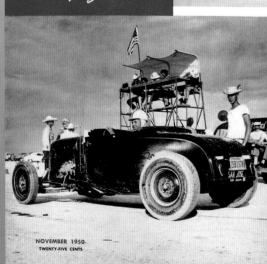

NOVEMBER 1950
TWENTY-FIVE CENTS

November

1950

HOT ROD

MAGAZINE

APRIL 1951
25c

NOW—16 MORE PAGES!

DRAG STRIPS DEVELOP PHENOMENAL SPEEDS!

April

As *Hot Rod* enters its fourth year of publication, Art Director Al Isaacs is feeling some freedom to break the bounds of what has been a fairly rigid cover format. The April issue is significant for its first color cover photo, but 1951 also sees the first use of an engine as a cover subject and not one but two illustrated covers, including the first (and only) cover appearance of our favorite cartoon rodder, Stroker McGurk.

The April issue has a number of firsts. The editorial package is bulked up with 16 additional pages, allowing Editor Wally Parks to introduce new features. One, "Touring the Hot Rod Shops," begins a long-standing, on-again/off-again magazine staple that rewards advertisers with fresh editorial exposure. The extra pages also give Parks room to bring back "Parts with Appeal."

The photo Parks selects for *Hot Rod*'s first color cover is Tom Medley's shot of Jack Morgan's 1934 roadster and Skip Hudson's 1929 A/V-8 at the Santa Ana drag strip. The canary yellow paint on Morgan's hot rod makes it a natural for color film, but there's more going on in this photo than just a couple of pretty cars.

Morgan's roadster would be a standout even without its bright color. The 1934 body is channeled 5 inches over a stock 1934 frame, but what really sets it apart is its 1937 truck grille, an unusual treatment that would inspire rodders—including Jim "Jake" Jacobs—for years to come. The car isn't just a looker, either; on the dashboard is an SCTA timing tag certifying the car's 127.65 mile-per-hour run. As Hot Rod of the Month, Morgan's roadster is rendered in a Rex Burnett cutaway illustration that reveals details like the slip-in mufflers in the chromed 4-inch exhaust pipes.

Hudson's A is colorful, too, though it's not featured in the magazine. Hudson and Dan Gurney entered the roadster at the 1950 Bonneville Nationals, where Gurney drove it over

130 miles per hour. According to rodding historian Dean Batchelor, Hudson got into so much trouble street racing that he had to sell the car to keep the Riverside police from impounding it.

The location of Medley's cover photo is no accident, either. A feature story inside the issue called "Clutch Artists and Their Mobile Missiles" talks about the "phenomenal speeds" racers are hitting at the nation's drag strips. "At the Orange County Airport, Calif., where organized drag racing has reached a high peak, there have been car speeds clocked as high as 127 mph at the end of the quarter mile." Though many of the cars "bear little resemblance to the common concept

1951

of the automobile"—early diggers did look a little weird at times—"there are plenty of souped-up late model sedans and coupes that turn impressive speeds" of nearly 100 miles per hour. "The average speed for a good new model stock car, in this distance, is around 70 mph."

OD' OF ONTH

JACK MORGAN'S CHANNELED '34 ROADSTER
Photos by Medley

Jack Morgan, of Santa Ana, Calif., likes 1934 Ford roadsters—likes them so well in fact, that he has rebuilt three of them within the past few years. The first two were painted red, but this one, his third, is a bright canary yellow. Without a doubt, this is one of the most attractive street roadsters ever seen on the west coast. In addition to the '34 body's roominess and solid construction, Jack appreciates its

clean, flowing lines—a feature which he makes the most of in his reconstructions. In spite of the fact that this car's body has been channeled over the frame, it has a smooth riding quality seldom found in roadsters. Largely responsible for this feature, no doubt, is the fact that the frame is still in its original state—stock '34. Well planned, careful construction have obviously paid off in this product of skill.

● ront view shows unusual effect adapting 1937 Ford truck shell in place of the original '34. are mounted directly to shell.

● ABOVE—The 1934 roadster body has been channeled 5 inches over a stock '34 frame. Structural braces were added to body and body was welded solidly to frame. Brakes are hydraulic.

● LEFT—Brass plated instrument panel was fashioned from a 1932 Ford coupe panel, filled in. Single unit instrument cluster has 160 mph French Ford speedometer. SCTA tag certifies 127.65 mph.

● ABOVE—The chromed front axle has been dropped and filled. Stock '34 front spring has had the main leaf eyes reversed. Front shock absorbers are stock '41 Ford.

● ABOVE—Complete new firewall was made of .051 hardened aluminum. Engine is a '46 Mercury with 3½-inch bore and ⅛ stroke. Exhaust headers, made by Morgan, lead into 4" pipes.

HOT ROD MAGAZINE

● ABOVE—The all aluminum hood has one-piece top, hinged on the right, with side panels that are secured with Dzus fasteners. Doors have been shortened 5 inches at bottom to clear exhausts.

● LEFT—Special engine equipment includes Smith heads, Cyclone three carburetor manifold, camshaft ground by Potvin, a Potvin converted Ford ignition, Weber alloy flywheel, and Auburn clutch.

● BELOW—The windshield has been shortened 1½ inches with new safety glass installed. Original seat cushions and interior have been upholstered in black Fiberlite by Berry of Santa Ana.

See Next Page

Jack Morgan channeled his hot rod's roadster body over its stock frame, giving it a "smooth riding quality seldom found in roadsters."

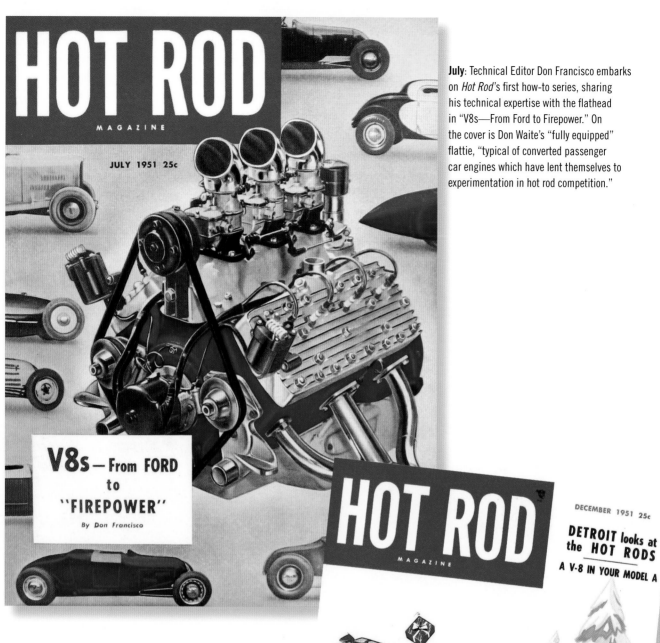

July: Technical Editor Don Francisco embarks on *Hot Rod*'s first how-to series, sharing his technical expertise with the flathead in "V8s—From Ford to Firepower." On the cover is Don Waite's "fully equipped" flattie, "typical of converted passenger car engines which have lent themselves to experimentation in hot rod competition."

December: Tom Medley's Stroker McGurk finally gets his one and only shot at cover stardom, and inside he introduces a Christmas buyer's guide of hot rodding parts, from oil-bath air cleaners to Dynatone mufflers. Of course Stroker's a member of the brand-new NHRA, proudly displaying his windshield sticker.

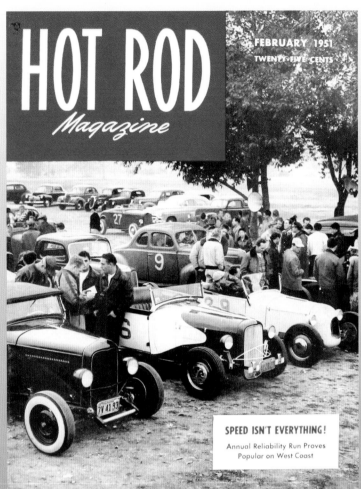

SPEED ISN'T EVERYTHING!
Annual Reliability Run Proves Popular on West Coast

February

1951

January: Local television broadcasts the Motorama car show, bringing cred to the hot rodding movement.

February: Pasadena's popular Reliability Runs prove that "speed isn't everything."

March: *Hot Rod* celebrates rodding's early days showing a 1934 downtown Los Angeles parade.

May: Frank Hubbard renders rodders emerging in the spring; Parks announces the formation of the NHRA.

June: 200-mile-per-hour midget planes are "as ingenious and spectacular as their four-wheeled counterparts."

August: Don Ferara's roadster at the Indio Date Festival; the NHRA is on the grow.

September: Kenz 'liner, Squaglia's Most Beautiful T/V-8, and nitromethane, the "poor man's supercharger."

October: Red and gold Rounthwaite coupe runs 146 at the lakes, 119 at Santa Ana.

November: Members of the LA Rams stop practice to admire Don Williams' chopped, channeled coupe.

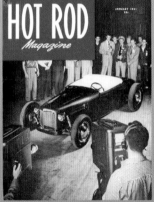

January

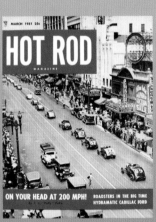

March

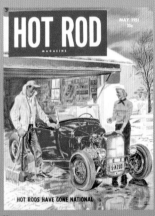

May

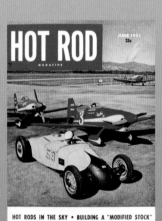

June

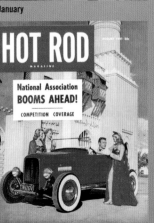

August

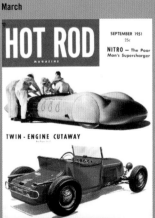

September

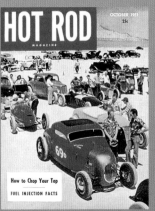

October

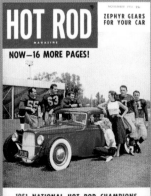

November

HRM TESTS 8-WHEELED "MOUNTAIN GOAT" JEEP

HOT ROD
MAGAZINE

MAY 1952 25¢

OVER **HALF-MILLION** COPIES
THIS ISSUE

**66% MORE HP
FOR OLDSMOBILE "88"**
By Don Francisco

May

Forget all the hot roadsters, hopped-up engines, cool customs and fast street cars on issues before or since. *This* is the quintessential *Hot Rod* magazine cover.

A full year and a half before Hugh Hefner publishes his first *Playboy*, *Hot Rod* is the young man's magazine of its day. This photo, taken by Felix Zelenka, encapsulates everything that makes a young man's heart beat faster. It's hard to know where to look, at lovely UCLA co-ed Harriet Haven or Dick Flint's low-slung A/V-8 roadster. Flint's passenger, Bob Roddick, is barely contained between the two, a pompadoured, loafer-wearing symbol of the entire generation growing up in the exuberant years following World War II. Before Hefner put Marilyn on his first cover, this was sex appeal in the 1950s.

Flint, a college student, built his roadster over a period of five years and "an investment of approximately $3,500 in time and materials," roughly double what you'd pay for a brand new Ford or Chevrolet sedan in 1952. "Consequently it gets loving care." But not all the time. The Merc flathead behind that unique, hand-formed aluminum nose is built with Edelbrock heads, a three-carb manifold and a Winfield cam. A member of the Glendale Sidewinders, Flint runs the roadster at SCTA lakes meets, where it has been clocked at 143.54 miles per hour.

Flint displayed the car at the National Roadster Show in Oakland (which is also covered in this issue). While he didn't come away with the America's Most Beautiful Roadster trophy, he did win a top award for originality. The car's lasting appeal—and the relative obscurity of that year's AMBR winner, Bud Crackbon's roadster pickup—makes us wonder if the judges had it wrong.

While there's only one story in the issue called "New Horizons in Engine Development," that description could really be applied to two of them. The article with that title is about the Chrysler FirePower V-8, written by James C. Zeder, Director of Engineering and Research for Chrysler Corporation. The FirePower V-8 is the now-year-old Hemi, and Zeder writes of the engine's "history within our organization, its features, good and bad, and its potentialities for the future." He somehow misses the whole Top Fuel thing in his prognostication, but he does get this right: "In the battle of the combustion chambers, the spherical segment chamber has demonstrated unquestionable supremacy."

And then there's Don Francisco's story about Ak Miller's Olds hop-up. Miller would become a regular presence in the magazine; here he pours the foundation for his performance reputation by souping up a 1949 Olds 88 Club

1952

Sedan using a full-race Weber cam, a solid-lifter valvetrain, higher compression, Belond headers, bigger Strombergs and lower rear end gears. That would all be standard stuff today, but in 1952 these mods lift the max horsepower from 91.5 to 154, showing "the possibilities of the many new overhead-valve V-8 engines now on the market, and forecast what the future holds," Francisco writes.

• Side view shows clean lines produced b dropping hood and nose. Bump is for generator.

• Rear end gears are 3.27 to 1. Dual exhaust system has by-passes for use in competition.

• Cutaway drawing by Rex Burnett shows structural arrangement of Flint's roadster. Front and rear shocks are Hartford friction type. Headers and exhaust system are homemade, quiet for street. Although body is channeled, floor remains in original position.

HOT ROD MAGAZINE
COPYRIGHT

• Flint did all of mechanical work on car himself. Special pump mounted on head directs water to side of block, aids cooling.

• Engine is 1940 Mercury with 3 5/16 bore, 4½ stroke. Extras include Edelbrock 9 to 1 heads, 3-carb manifold, Winfield 1A cam.

35

HOT ROD MAGAZINE   MAY 1952

Rex Burnett's cutaway drawings give readers an "inside" look at a hot rod's components.

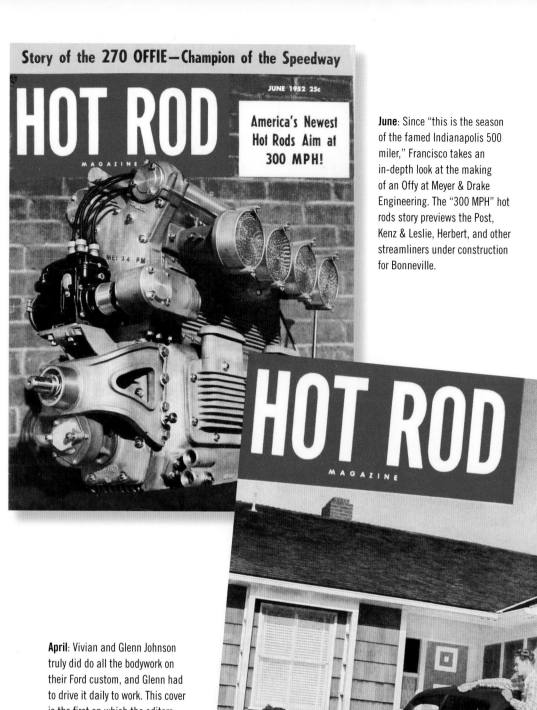

Story of the 270 OFFIE—Champion of the Speedway

HOT ROD
MAGAZINE

JUNE 1952 25c

America's Newest Hot Rods Aim at 300 MPH!

June: Since "this is the season of the famed Indianapolis 500 miler," Francisco takes an in-depth look at the making of an Offy at Meyer & Drake Engineering. The "300 MPH" hot rods story previews the Post, Kenz & Leslie, Herbert, and other streamliners under construction for Bonneville.

HOT ROD
MAGAZINE

THIS ISSUE—470,000 COPIES
APRIL 1952 25c

ROAD TESTING THE NEW
S.C.O.T. SUPERCHARGER
By Don Francisco

April: Vivian and Glenn Johnson truly did do all the bodywork on their Ford custom, and Glenn had to drive it daily to work. This cover is the first on which the editors display their print run. Note that it grows from 470,000 to "over half-million" between April and May.

WE CHANNELED AND CHOPPED OUR CAR AT HOME

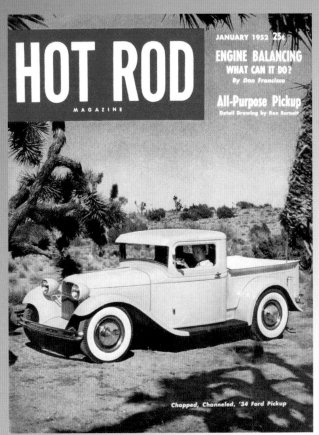

January

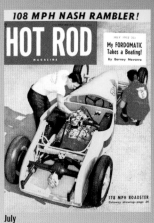

July

March

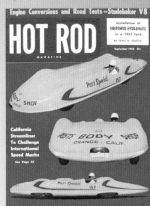

August

September

January: Roy Desbrow's chopped and channeled "all-purpose" pickup is Hot Rod of the Month.

February: This Merc flathead powers Earl Bruce's "most customized" 1940 Ford coupe.

March: *Hot Rod* explores alternative fuels way before there's even a hint of global warming.

July: Fred Carrillo and Robert Betz's Merc-powered T roadster is clocked at 178 at Bonneville.

August: Ted Miller built his 152-mile-per-hour 1927 T roadster in his spare time at home.

September: Eric Rickman's first cover credit is for Harold Post's land-speed-contending streamliner.

October: Ray Schlachter's aluminum-block blown flathead makes 140 horsepower with 3 pounds of boost.

November: City of Burbank streamliner sets new speed record of 229.77 miles per hour at Bonneville.

December: Chet Herbert works on his 'liner; the "City-Sponsored" drag strip is in Pomona. Heard of it?

October

November

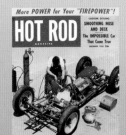

December

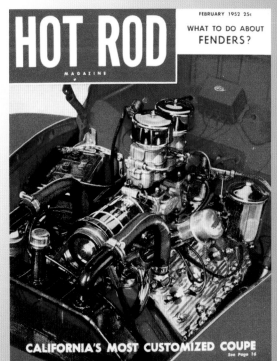

February

1952

MORE PAGES! • MORE PHOTOS! • MORE FEATURES!

HOT ROD
MAGAZINE

TRUE FACTS about HORSEPOWER

By Don Francisco

MARCH 1953
25c

Hot Rod of the Month—
FIREPOWER Street Roadster
See Page 34

March

Just two years after its introduction, Chrysler's FirePower V-8 is making serious noise in the hot rodding community. Gordon Potter's Model A roadster is one of the first—and finest—examples of a Hemi-fied hot rod, hopped up with four Strombergs, a Herbert 3/4 cam, Scintilla Vertex magneto, and Potter's own intake, headers, and pistons. On alcohol the roadster is clocked at 153.51 miles per hour at Bonneville; running gas, it tops 145. The cover photo, shot by Felix Zelenka, shows Potter with Zelenka's nephew, Mike Delnick. Careful, kid.

Elsewhere in the issue, Technical Editor Don Francisco writes up Chuck Potvin's dyno test of the 299-inch, Hilborn-injected Chrysler V-8 used in Harold Post's streamliner. Equipped for the dyno "exactly the same as it was at Bonneville, with the exception of the air rams shown on the fuel injector," the engine makes 312 horsepower at 5,300 rpm on straight methanol. The injector stacks were good for "approximately 4 horsepower and seemed to make the engine run smoother."

1953

This issue is the first with *Hot Rod*'s trademark rotogravure pictorial section. The printing process reproduces photographs in fine detail and accommodates ink colors other than black, so the roto sections become filled with large photos and short, punchy captions. Potter's roadster opens the section, which also features a "glamorized '51 Mercury" that displays an "abundance of distinctive restyling." Built at the Barris Kustom Shop for owner Bob Hirohata, this Merc would become one of the most iconic custom cars ever created.

Chuck Potvin's 299-inch FirePower Hemi makes 312 horsepower at 5,300 rpm "on straight methanol fuel."

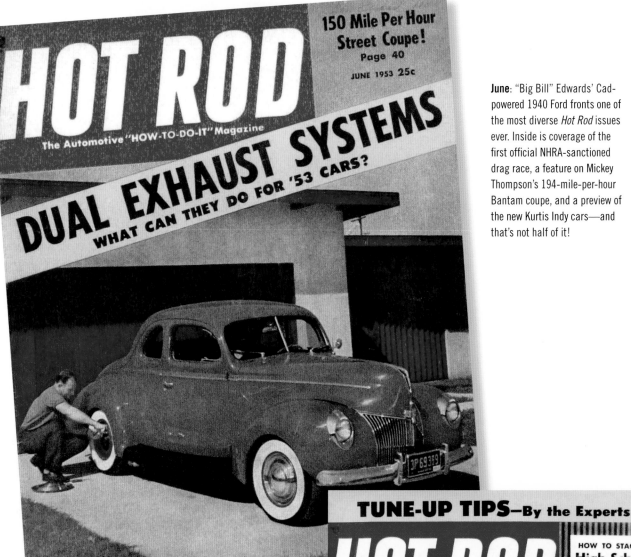

150 Mile Per Hour Street Coupe!
Page 40

JUNE 1953 25c

HOT ROD
The Automotive "HOW-TO-DO-IT" Magazine

DUAL EXHAUST SYSTEMS
WHAT CAN THEY DO FOR '53 CARS?

Building a Hot Rod S

June: "Big Bill" Edwards' Cad-powered 1940 Ford fronts one of the most diverse *Hot Rod* issues ever. Inside is coverage of the first official NHRA-sanctioned drag race, a feature on Mickey Thompson's 194-mile-per-hour Bantam coupe, and a preview of the new Kurtis Indy cars—and that's not half of it!

November: This is the year flatheads battle the overhead-valve engines for fast times at Bonneville, and Photo Editor Eric Rickman captures Ray Brown adjusting the tappets on the Chrysler engine going into the *Shadoff Special* while dyno owner Tony Capanna looks on. Output: 350 horsepower on straight alcohol.

TUNE-UP TIPS—By the Experts

HOT ROD
The Automotive "HOW-TO-DO-IT" Maga

HOW TO STAGE A High School Auto Show

NOVEMBER 1953 25c

FLAT-HEADS BATTLE ROCKER-ARMS FOR ALL-OUT SUPREMACY

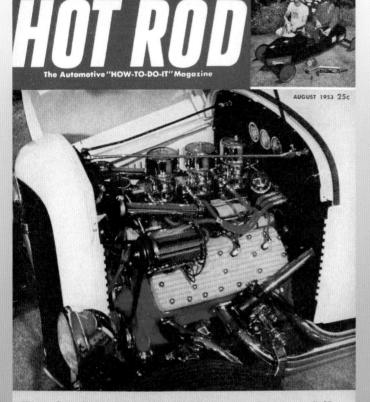

SOAP BOX DERBY SPEED SECRETS

HOT ROD
The Automotive "HOW-TO-DO-IT" Magazine

AUGUST 1953 25c

Previewing America's Hottest Automobiles

August

1953

January: The Hubbard-Palamides Merc-powered Crosley sets a 131.96-mile-per-hour Bonneville record.

February: Original Bean Bandit Joaquin Arnett gets a push; Bandits are racing to this day.

April: Harvey Haller's lakester is Hawaii's hottest; Ray Brock joins the staff as associate editor.

May: GMC power, Chrisman dragster, custom Stude—the "most complete hot rod coverage" motto is true!

July: Frank Bertuccio's pickup, *Cad-iac*, is a custom Catalina; Italian sports car gets Stude power.

August: This flathead sits while its owner serves an army tour; those kids are going downhill fast.

September: Valley Custom builds the *Polynesian* for Jack Stewart; Bob Greene joins the editorial staff.

October: The full-house GMC in Chuck Tatum's 150-mile-per-hour sports rod, which cost $7,000 to build.

December: "All that is hot rodding": lakes jobs, street roadsters, and custom rods.

January

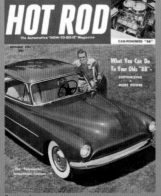

February

April

May

July

September

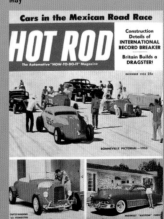

October

December

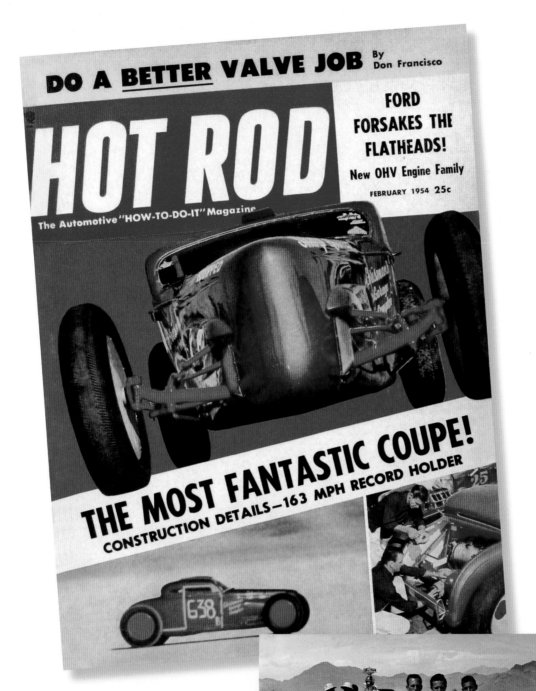

DO A BETTER VALVE JOB By Don Francisco

HOT ROD

The Automotive "HOW-TO-DO-IT" Magazine

FORD FORSAKES THE FLATHEADS!
New OHV Engine Family
FEBRUARY 1954 25c

THE MOST FANTASTIC COUPE!
CONSTRUCTION DETAILS—163 MPH RECORD HOLDER

The Chrisman brothers go through several engines at Bonneville on the way to a class record of 160 miles per hour with an Ardun-equipped Mercury flathead.

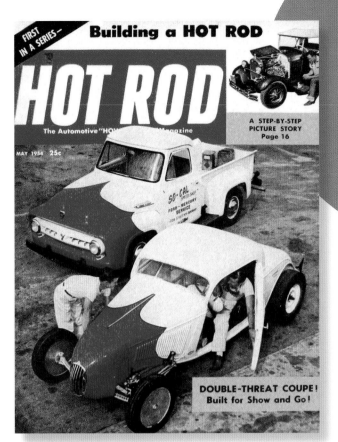

1954

May: Alex Xydias always wanted his So-Cal Speed Shop team to be well turned-out, so when he was racing his "double-threat" three-window coupe, he painted his 1953 Ford F100 tow rig to match. "Double-threat" refers to the records Xydias set at Bonneville and on the drag strip.

July: Petersen's Hollywood connections didn't stop with the starlets featured in "Parts with Appeal." His studio connections put several big-name stars in the magazine, including Dean Martin and Jerry Lewis, who posed for this "rod test" of Jerry Gershenberg's roadster during the filming of *Living It Up*.

"We hesitate to call any car 'the greatest' but there are times when the temptation is might' nigh overpowering," say the editors about Jack, Art, and Lloyd Chrisman's competition coupe, shot on the salt by Eric Rickman.

"The Most Fantastic Coupe" is a marvel of engineering and ingenuity, from its wind-cheating nose (two 1940 Ford hoods welded together) to its "chopped to the limit" 1930 Model A coupe body, which lifts off the frame to provide quick access to the rear-mounted flathead V-8, 1940 Ford transmission, and Halibrand quick-change rear end. All three are built as a single assembly so the "complete propulsion system may be removed from the chassis in a matter of minutes."

It turns out the Chrismans would make use of that feature several times at Bonneville in 1953. Their first 304-inch Merc flathead "scattered itself during a desperation run after turning a speed of 163.63 mph in Class C." A 258-inch Ardun-Merc propelled them to a Class B record average of 160.178 miles per hour. Then another Merc flattie was installed "in an attempt to improve the Class C standing but wasn't too successful." In years to come, the flatheads would be replaced by Hemis as the coupe reached for the 200-mile-per-hour mark, but even at this early stage the editors are justified in calling the beautiful bronze coupe "utterly fantastic."

Elsewhere in the issue, the news that Ford is introducing new overhead-valve V-8s is met with the grim headline, "Ford Forsakes the Flatheads."

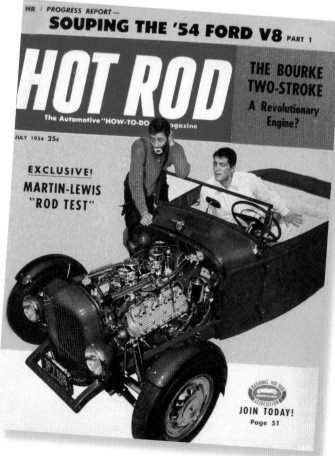

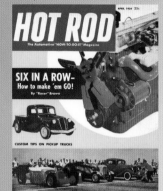

January

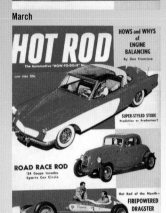

March

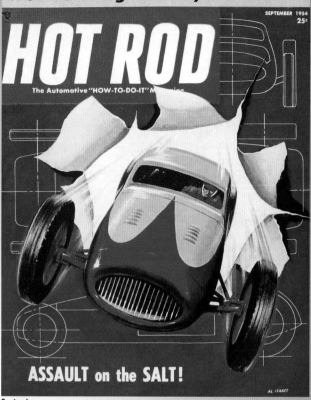

Hot Rodding Your Hydra-Matic!

SEPTEMBER 1954
25c

HOT ROD
The Automotive "HOW-TO-DO-IT" Magazine

ASSAULT on the SALT!

AL ISAACS

September

April

June

August

November

October

December

January: "Operation Drag Strip" pushes for track standards; rodders are victims of "bungled muffler laws."

March: Carroll Gentry had little bodywork experience before he sliced into this custom Ford.

April: Notice a loosening in cover design? Multiple images are now the norm.

June: Parks continues to put late-model customs in *Hot Rod* despite criticism from purist rodders.

August: The nailhead's big bore and short stroke "are just made for a supercharger."

September: Art Director Al Isaacs' composite of the rods ready for "action on the salt."

October: An odd crop on Dick Kraft's sports rod; part one of a supercharger primer.

November: Dragging action from Paradise Mesa Strip, shot by Bob D'Olivo.

December: Frank Iacono's GMC reaches 121 miles per hour—"not bad for an old six-holer!"

1954

Analyzing the Chevrolet V8
By Racer Brown

HOT ROD
The Automotive "HOW-TO-DO-IT" Magazine

JANUARY, 1955 25c

DRAGNET'S "BIG ROD"

1955

Jack Webb's presence on *Hot Rod* is more than just another example of Petersen's Hollywood connections bearing circulation-enhancing fruit. Having Bob D'Olivo photograph the top cop from *Dragnet*, "TV's most eyeballed crime detection show," admiring Tommy Pollard's roadster is a strong salvo in Wally Parks' battle to bring respectability to the rodding community. The photo is more than just a one-off publicity shot; Webb is filming a *Dragnet* episode that involves rodders (wrongly) suspected in a hit-and-run, only to be cleared because their "precision-built machine" couldn't be the shoddy car that did the deed. The NHRA gets huge national exposure when its offices are duplicated on the show, complete with huge NHRA logo posters plastered on the set's walls.

In hindsight, though, the cover's top blurb is even more significant than Webb's show. Chevrolet has just released its new overhead-valve V-8, an engine that will have an enormous impact on the entire automotive performance community. The editors can't know that yet, but their in-depth analysis, written by Technical Editor Racer Brown, indicates they are well aware of the new mill's potential.

January

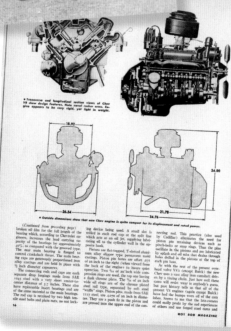

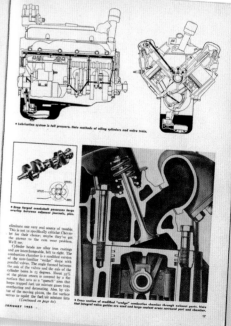

Detailed illustrations and diagrams give *Hot Rod* readers their first look at Chevrolet's new overhead-valve V-8.

The examination starts with the cylinder block, an "alloy iron casting that appears to be stiff, sturdy and capable of withstanding far more than the advertised power output without imposing stresses that would cause distortion or warpage." Brown is impressed that Chevrolet chose to release both gross (162 horsepower) and net (137 horsepower) power ratings, the latter obtained under dyno conditions more reflective of the real world. "Making the advertised and actual power figures known and available to the buying public is an act for which Chevrolet is to be highly commended. No one else does it."

The story then walks readers through the new engine in minute detail, from crankshaft to carburetor. Brown spends several paragraphs explaining "Chevrolet's (and Pontiac's) new approach to valve actuation": the stamped-steel rocker arms that are "secured to the cylinder heads by individual studs" instead of "pivoting about the axis of a conventional rocker arm shaft." He also lauds the upgrade to a 12-volt electrical system and is complimentary about how the reciprocating assembly is balanced "as an assembly, assuring vibration-free operation." Illustrating the story are photos, power charts, and many cutaway illustrations revealing the V-8's design features, including the "novel" rocker arms and the wedge-shaped combustion chambers.

In the story's very last column, Brown gets to the good stuff: the high-performance package "for go-fast enthusiasts" that consists of a Carter four-barrel carburetor, special intake manifold, and dual exhaust. Available through Chevrolet dealers, the option package will raise gross horsepower to 180 for "about $95." Plus, "cams, oversized pistons, exhaust headers and other goodies will be available very soon to complement the special factory kits for potentially the best Chevrolet engine yet." These items, in combo with Chevy's line of transmissions, optional rear end ratios, and the 1955 Chevy's "completely new and more stable chassis, should transform the formerly docile 'Stovebolt' into a real fire-breathing monster. Look out, 88s!"

October: From this angle it's tough to recognize, but the rod on top is Norm Grabowski's T pickup, the car that launched the whole T-bucket craze and became the *Kookie T* on TV's *77 Sunset Strip*. Below it is Jim Miller's Ardun-powered roadster pickup, which didn't become quite as famous.

December: Don Van Hoff's maroon coupe is beautiful, but there's news-making stuff inside, including coverage of the first NHRA National drag meet in Great Bend, Kansas, and *Hot Rod*'s first new-car road test. This trend will blossom into a full-court Detroit press in the coming months.

February: Neumayer and Reed's belly tank on the salt; flames by "Rodder's Dali" Von Dutch.

March: Racer Brown analyzes Pontiac's new OHV V-8; Chuck Porter's Ford pickup is Cad-powered.

April: This late-model Cad V-8 sports Hilborn injection and "flame thrower" Spalding ignition.

May: Working on the City of Burbank 'liner's Merc flathead with OHV conversion.

June: A turbine-powered Indy car years before the Granatelli brothers ran with the idea.

July: Racing is a family affair. Helen Root qualifies the roadster; husband Bart handles eliminations.

August: The Losinski dragster solves the suspension problems that plague racers as speeds increase.

September: "Big Bill" Edwards' Cad-powered "flyin' barn door" of a pickup runs 151 miles per hour.

November: Dick Hallen works on Tom Medley's A/V-8; "Fastest Cars" are from Bonneville.

1955

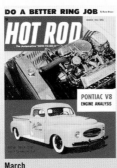

March

April

May

February

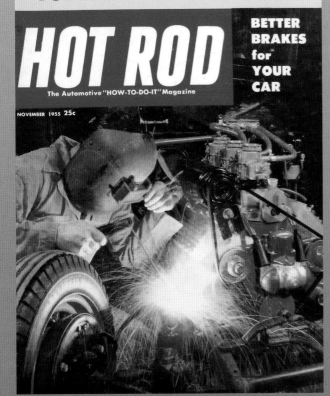

November

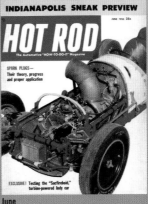

June

August

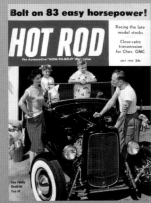

July

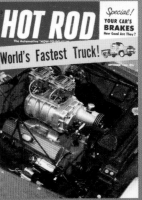

September

SEE THE
181-mph
Glass Slipper
Page 32

HOT ROD

The Automotive "HOW-TO-DO-IT" Magazine

JANUARY 1956 25c

EXCLUSIVE
PROGRESS REPORT

220-HP CHEV STREET ENGINE!

January

1956

Just 12 issues ago, *Hot Rod*'s Technical Editor Racer Brown had his first look at Chevrolet's new overhead-valve V-8 as a 160-horsepower stocker. Now he really has something to sink his teeth into: a thorough testing by Vic Edelbrock of hot rod parts for the Chevy.

"It all started when the Edelbrock Equipment Company acquired a brand-new crated '55 Chev engine, complete with all the accessories," Brown writes. "At the time, not too much was known about the Chev's potentialities, and less yet was known in which category the engine was best suited; that is, for street, drags, straightaway, track or marine use." Vic Sr. opts to go the marine route, figuring if the engine lasted under those conditions, it would work "for less strenuous purposes."

After tearing down and rebuilding the engine, Edelbrock subjects it to more than 250 full-load, full-throttle runs on his Clayton 300 engine dynamometer (a piece of equipment so new to the readers that Brown spends a full page explaining how it works). His ultimate goal is to test more than 20 camshafts to find one "that would allow an engine speed in excess of 7,000 rpm together with good power output but without prohibitive valve spring pressures," Brown writes. As a result, "two cams gave the desired results," and "a very excellent street cam was uncovered," though Brown won't reveal the names of the cam grinders involved "to prevent any thoughts of discrimination."

Prior to swapping the cams, Edelbrock makes some changes to bring up the V-8's power and give him a stable platform for the cam tests. Because the stock valve springs float the valves at 5,200 rpm, he swaps in stiffer Corvette springs. The stock intake manifold and its single Rochester two-barrel carburetor are replaced with a three-pot Edelbrock manifold and triple Rochesters, a change that nets 20 percent more power at 4,500 rpm. Bill Million, co-owner of Hedman Muffler and Manufacturing, is commissioned to build a set of 1.5-inch headers to better scavenge exhaust gases, and they net another 6.3 percent gain in power at 4,500 rpm. Next the heads come off for some mild porting, valve pocket work, and combustion chamber polishing, which net a nearly 2 percent gain in power (now at 176 at 4,500 rpm).

At this point the first cam goes in, a Corvette grind that pushes horsepower to 192 at 4,500 rpm and hits its peak of 205 horsepower at 5,300 rpm. But it's the seventh test that "was most satisfactory from all standpoints," Brown writes. Maximum power is 229 horses at 5,850 rpm, low speed power is "better than average," and valve float doesn't set in until 7,800 rpm. For those looking for a similar grind, Brown lists the cam's full specs.

In sum, "The Chevrolet V-8 engine is a very rugged and thoroughly dependable power plant," writes Brown. "When modifications are properly administered, the engine is amazingly responsive. Does all this kindle the fires of enthusiasm, imagination and inspiration?"

Vic Edelbrock Jr. readies a 265-inch Chevy V-8 for a pull on Edelbrock's Clayton 300 engine dyno.

Rodders Test GOLDEN HAWK

HOT ROD

The Automotive "HOW-

APRIL 1956 25c

Beginning:
**BUILDING a
FLATHEAD the
RIGHT way**

by Don Francisco

MORE PAGES!

April: Former Technical Editor Don Francisco is back (and on the cover) with his memorable series: How to build a flathead Ford V-8 "the right way" so it's "mild enough for the street, but strong enough to 'stand on.'" Traditional rodders use his expertise to this day.

2 TESTS: PLYMOUTH V8-DODGE "500

HOT ROD

DAYTONA
BEACH START
PURE

Part 2—
**BUILDING
A FLATHEAD
ENGINE**

MAY 1956 25c

on-the-spot coverage:
STORMING THE BEACH at DAYTONA
NASCAR's Speedweeks

May: There are no fewer than three Chrysler-oriented stories in this issue—the cover story on a Plymouth Fury that set records at Daytona Beach, plus road tests of the Dodge D-500 and Plymouth Belvedere, called "The Best Plymouth Yet." *Hot Rod* is certainly courting Detroit in a big way.

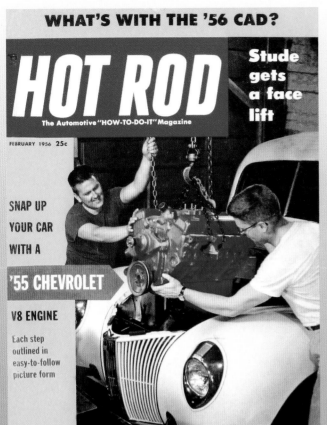

WHAT'S WITH THE '56 CAD?

HOT ROD
The Automotive "HOW-TO-DO-IT" Magazine

Stude gets a face lift

FEBRUARY 1956 25c

SNAP UP YOUR CAR WITH A

'55 CHEVROLET

V8 ENGINE

Each step outlined in easy-to-follow picture form

February

VRINGING OUT THE '56 FORD

HOT ROD
The Automotive "HOW-TO-DO-IT" Magazine

MARCH 1956 25c

HOW TO HOP IT UP

March

TESTING A NEW TYPE SUPERCHARGER

HOT ROD
The Automotive "HOW-TO-DO-IT" Magazine

BIG GEARS for your FORD

RODDERS WIN in Mobilgas ECONOMY RUN

JUNE 1956 25c

HRM REPORTS:
'56 INDY PACE CAR—HOTTEST DRAG SEDAN

June

THUNDERBIRDS: STREET, STRIP and STRAIGHTAWAY!

HOT ROD
Automotive "HOW-TO-DO-IT" Magazine

Know Your VALVE TRAIN
Part 1—by Racer Brown

HOW-TO-DO-IT An OHV Ford in your 'FORTY

JULY 1956 25c

DRAGGIN' DREAMBOAT

July

POWER STEERING—Pros and Cons

HOT ROD
motive "HOW-TO-DO-IT" Magazine

GEARING FOR TOPS and TORQUE

VALVES A Necessary Evil?

AUGUST 1956 25c

August

February: Bob Greene's 1940 pickup gets the magazine's first small-block V-8 swap.

March: Overhead-cam conversion for "Full House MG" ups power by 50 percent … to 75.

June: Another Chrysler makes the cover, this time the Indy Pace Car DeSoto.

July: Dave Marquez's Ardun-powered "draggin' dreamboat" proves "a showpiece can be a gopiece."

August: Bill Breece's Olds-fired Deuce is a show winner capable of 90-mile-per-hour quarters.

September: An injected Buick makes 315 horsepower in a Kurtis sports car; Chrysler lands another test.

October: An all-Detroit cover: An injected Mercury prototype and a 'Vette with factory race options.

November: This Romeo Palamides digger has yet to make a pass; hey, another Chrysler test!

December: TV's *The Life of Riley* features rods; stars pose with Jim Griepsma's 1934 coupe.

ROD TEST: CHRYSLER'S OUTSTANDING "RACE CAR"

HOT ROD
The Automotive "HOW-TO-DO-IT" Magazine

STOCK CARS CHALLENGE PIKES PEAK

SEPTEMBER 1956 25c

A HOT BUICK V8 ENGINE FOR COMPETITION

September

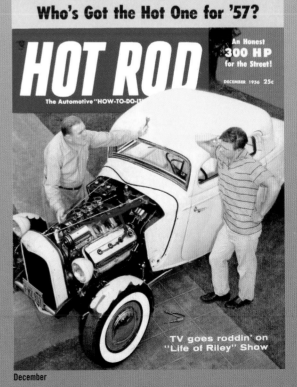

Who's Got the Hot One for '57?

HOT ROD
The Automotive "HOW-TO-DO-IT"

An Honest 300 HP for the Street!

DECEMBER 1956 25c

TV goes roddin' on "Life of Riley" Show

December

ROD TESTING the "STOCK" CORVETTE

HOT ROD
The Automotive "HOW-TO-DO-IT" Magazine

152 MPH PROTOTYPE MERCURY

October

REVOLUTIONARY '57 PLYMOUTH

HOT ROD

How-to-do-it
CHEVROLET V8 installation in AERO WILLYS

World's Fastest ¼-milers in Action

De Soto
DRAGSTER

FULL DETAILS

November

1956

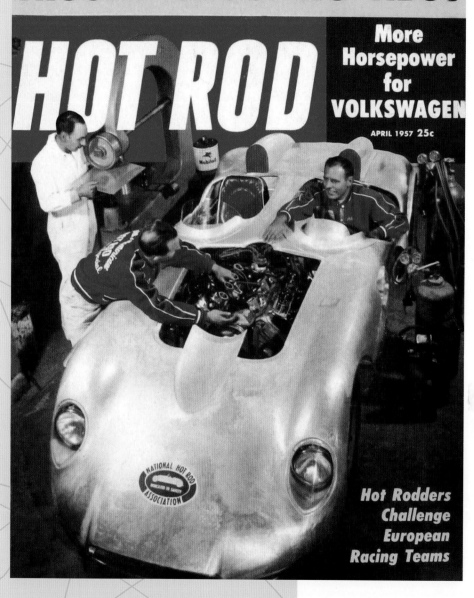

TROUBLE SHOOTING — ABC's

HOT ROD

More Horsepower for VOLKSWAGEN

APRIL 1957 25c

Hot Rodders Challenge European Racing Teams

April

I nventive rodder Ak Miller would provide *Hot Rod* with editorial grist for years. One of his most valiant efforts is building a crude but sturdy Olds-powered T roadster, dubbed *El Caballo*, to run against the high-dollar American and European machinery in the Carrera Panamericana Mexican road races in 1953 and 1954. For 1957, Miller was going to step up his Carrera efforts with this sleek, aluminum-bodied sports car. But when Mexican officials cancelled the race, Miller and co-pilot Doug Harrison "raised their sights to the Italian Mille Miglia," writes Managing Editor Bob Greene. Jack Sutton's alloy body shell is patterned from an Italian Osca competition car and fits over a modified Kurtis frame that cradles a 392-inch Chrysler Hemi fitted with Hilborn fuel injection.

Bob D'Olivo photographs (from left) Sutton, Harrison, and Miller for the cover just days before a garage fire "ruined much of the fine bodywork, consumed the Hilborn injection system, the tires and much of the brake system and incidental items," Greene writes. Repairs are made and the car competes in Italy, but without the success Miller and Harrison enjoyed in Mexico.

Surprisingly, one of *Hot Rod*'s most important project cars doesn't even rate a mention on the cover. Research Editor Ray Brock writes about "Suddenly ..." the 1957 Plymouth that Brock and Wally Parks would enter into the 1957 Speedweeks trials at Daytona. Parks gets the idea after hearing that Tony Capanna (who appeared on the November 1953 cover) had built a 389-inch Chrysler

1957

V-8 capable of producing 448 horsepower on alcohol "with well over 500 horses available at a gentle tip of the nitro can." Parks orders a Savoy to house the motor, but delays push the car's delivery back until just two weeks before the team would have to leave for Florida. A full-scale thrash ensues, with Bob Hedman building headers, Tom Sheddon of Belond Muffler bending tube for the roll cage, and Ak Miller banging out a belly pan from aluminum sheets.

"A last-minute telegram from NASCAR informed us that racing fuel would not be allowed," Brock writes, but Capanna quickly adapts the Hilborn injectors to run gasoline "and the engine responded by registering 420 horsepower at 5,000 rpm."

After a largely uneventful tow to Daytona, last-minute mods are made: Firestone provides a set of Bonneville tires, and Plymouth supplies new 2.92 rear end gears. Beach conditions are poor on the first day of the trials, but

on the second, "lead-footed Wally Parks" gets his shot on the course. Making an easy pass against a stiff headwind, the Savoy clocks 153.453 miles per hour; the return, with an assist from the wind and Parks leaning on it a bit harder, is measured at 166.898 miles per hour, for a two-way average of 159.893. "We'd proved that luck doesn't always favor the big moneyed outfits," writes Brock. "Our backyard project, consisting of a borrowed chassis, a borrowed engine, and approximately $400 in expenses had gotten the job done."

A fire at Ak Miller's garage nearly destroys the aluminum-bodied sports car Miller is building for the Mille Miglia.

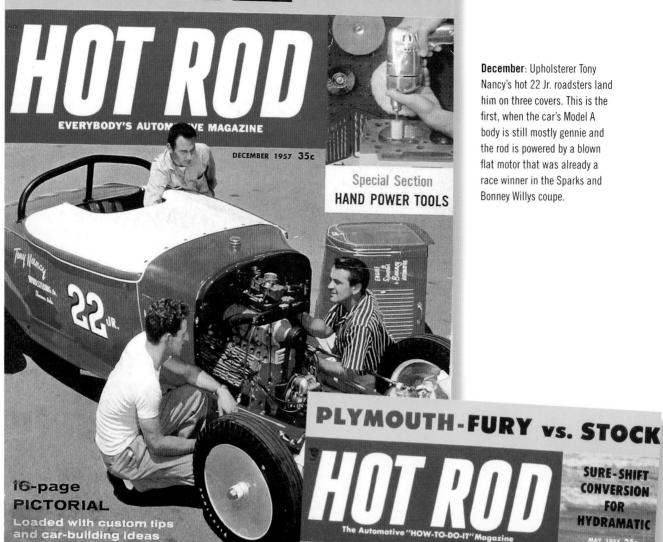

HRM TESTS ALL NEW '58 CHEVY

HOT ROD

EVERYBODY'S AUTOMOTIVE MAGAZINE

DECEMBER 1957 35c

Special Section
HAND POWER TOOLS

16-page
PICTORIAL
Loaded with custom tips
and car-building ideas

December: Upholsterer Tony Nancy's hot 22 Jr. roadsters land him on three covers. This is the first, when the car's Model A body is still mostly gennie and the rod is powered by a blown flat motor that was already a race winner in the Sparks and Bonney Willys coupe.

PLYMOUTH-FURY vs. STOCK

HOT ROD

The Automotive "HOW-TO-DO-IT" Magazine

SURE-SHIFT
CONVERSION
FOR
HYDRAMATIC

MAY 1957 25c

May: A month after telling *Suddenly*'s tale, Brock is back with coverage of Daytona's Speedweeks, featuring a beauty shot of the 1957 Plymouth pace car on the cover. (A factory-entered, Lincoln-powered T-Bird beats *Suddenly*'s top speed.) Two more Plymouths square off in a "Fury vs. Stock" double feature road test.

DAYTONA SPEEDWEEKS PICTORIAL

WHAT'S NEW ABOUT THE EDSEL?

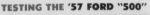

HOT ROD
EVERYBODY'S AUTOMOTIVE MAGAZINE

OCTOBER 1957 35c

DETROIT'S FIRST BIG '58 ENGINE

AMERICA'S TRUE SPORTS CAR — THE HOT ROD

WORLD'S QUICKEST HOT ROD ?

Dragster Clocks 168 mph in ¼ mile

October

1957

January: Late-model Chevys are big with custom fans; Lindley dragster nears 160 in the quarter.

February: Brock demonstrates engine-gearbox adaptors for "stock to hot" swaps.

March: "How Hot Is the Hawk?" The blown Stude is "hard to beat."

June: Pontiac is Detroit's hottest "stock rod"; "Competition Corvette" is Duntov's finned Corvette SS.

July: "Styled for Speed," Bill Stroppe's Mercury Mermaid runs 159 miles per hour at Daytona.

August: Tommy Ivo's first magazine appearance with his Buick-powered T, built for "kicks and cups."

September: Do we have to tell you that Ted Cooper's exhaust plumbing didn't work?

October: Thirty years before Pat Ganahl tries it, Eric Rickman shoots the first swimsuit cover.

November: If you think the injected Ardun is wild, check out the eight straight pipes.

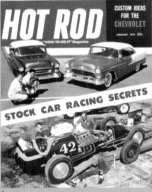

TESTING THE '57 FORD "500"

HOT ROD
CUSTOM IDEAS FOR THE CHEVROLET

STOCK CAR RACING SECRETS

January

TEST REPORT: NEW OLDS '88

HOT ROD
ENGINE ADAPTORS
NEW POWER for YOUR CAR

February

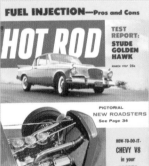

FUEL INJECTION — Pros and Cons

HOT ROD
TEST REPORT:
STUDE GOLDEN HAWK

PICTORIAL
NEW ROADSTERS
See Page 34

HOW-TO-DO-IT
CHEVY V8 in your SPORTS CAR
MG & Jaguar

March

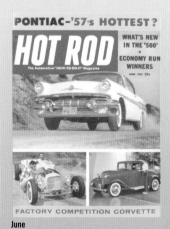

PONTIAC — '57's HOTTEST?

HOT ROD
WHAT'S NEW IN THE '500'
ECONOMY RUN WINNERS

FACTORY COMPETITION CORVETTE

June

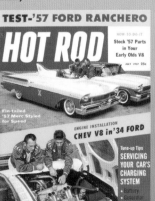

TEST — '57 FORD RANCHERO

HOT ROD
Stock '57 Parts in Your Early Olds V8

ENGINE INSTALLATION
CHEV V8 in '34 FORD

Tune-up Tips
SERVICING YOUR CAR'S CHARGING SYSTEM

Fin-tailed '57 Merc Styled for Speed

July

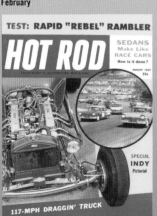

TEST: RAPID "REBEL" RAMBLER

HOT ROD
SEDANS Make Like RACE CARS
How is it done?

SPECIAL INDY Pictorial

117-MPH DRAGGIN' TRUCK

August

STOCK CARS UP PIKES PEAK

HOT ROD
EVERYBODY'S AUTOMOTIVE MAGAZINE

LOWER YOUR CAR the right way
Home Tune-up
IGNITION DISTRIBUTOR Servicing

NOW — MORE PAGES!

HOW-TO-DO-IT
FOUR-BARREL CARBURETOR Overhaul

September

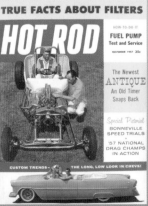

TRUE FACTS ABOUT FILTERS

HOT ROD
HOW-TO-DO-IT
FUEL PUMP Test and Service

The Newest ANTIQUE
An Old Timer Snaps Back

Special Pictorial
BONNEVILLE SPEED TRIALS
'57 NATIONAL DRAG CHAMPS IN ACTION

CUSTOM TRENDS — THE LONG, LOW LOOK IN CHEVS!

November

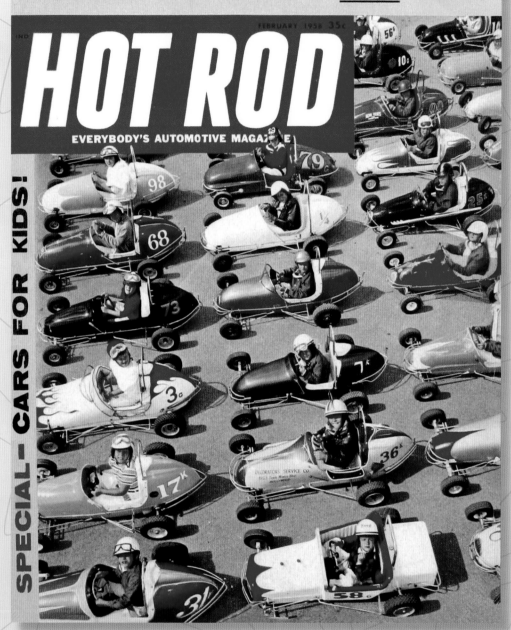

February

In today's ultra-competitive magazine newsstand market, where shouting cover lines compete with dramatic photography to catch a potential buyer's attention, this sort of cover design would never be allowed to happen. Yet the sea of colorful quarter midgets and their happy drivers is compelling on its own. In fact, the cover wouldn't have anywhere near its impact if the "Cars for Kids!" blurb ran across the photo rather than carefully next to the magazine's spine.

Eric Rickman photographed these young racers, who are members of the Glendale (California) Quarter Midget Association. The cover leads to a nine-page feature about the surge in popularity of these tiny terrors and a roundup of the various kit and turnkey models available to "eager cub drivers."

It's not just the kids who are into it, either. "Old-guard speed equipment manufacturers have once again felt the thrill and the challenge reminiscent of the pioneer dry lakes days, evidenced by wee hours at the drawing board and lathe," writes Managing Editor Bob Greene. "Already offered are high torque cams, high compression pistons and heads, roller bearing cranks, beefed gearboxes and hot ignition systems." Among the speed part makers shown in the story are ignition master Kong Jackson, former *Hot Rod* tech editor turned cam manufacturer Racer Brown, and rodders C. W. "Scotty" Scott and Earl Evans. Even Chrondek gets into the act with a special electronic timer for the quarter midget set. The Ansen Automotive Anscraft QM is typical: The $395 turnkey model has chrome, paint, Naugahyde upholstery, and striping. The $335 kit version is less well equipped.

1958

Pontiac's Hot One is the all-new 1958 Bonneville, which puts "proven power in a sleek, low body with a new frame and suspension for '58." Technical Editor Ray Brock samples several versions, including a tri-power-equipped, 310-horse model that takes 7.6 seconds to get from 0 to 60 and runs the quarter-mile in 16 seconds flat at 88 miles per hour. "Mileage figures with triple setup were very good with 15 mpg in city and mountains, 18 mpg at highway speeds."

Also in this issue, Jerry Unser, driving a 1957 Ford with "Hot Rod Magazine Spl." lettered on the front fender, wins the final USAC race of the 1957 season at Riverside and with it the season championship. Unser's coupe is powered by a 312-inch V-8 fitted with a McCulloch centrifugal supercharger. The race's three fastest qualifiers are supercharged 1957 Fords; two Mercs follow them.

The happy kid at upper left is Gary Medley, Tom Medley's son, trying on a Tiny Mite Sprint for size.

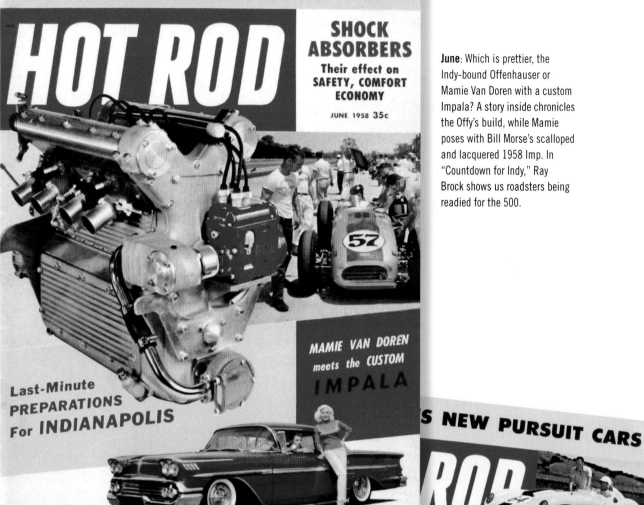

'58 THUNDERBIRD ROAD TEST

HOT ROD

SHOCK ABSORBERS
Their effect on
SAFETY, COMFORT
ECONOMY

JUNE 1958 35c

57

Last-Minute
PREPARATIONS
For INDIANAPOLIS

MAMIE VAN DOREN
meets the CUSTOM
IMPALA

June: Which is prettier, the Indy-bound Offenhauser or Mamie Van Doren with a custom Impala? A story inside chronicles the Offy's build, while Mamie poses with Bill Morse's scalloped and lacquered 1958 Imp. In "Countdown for Indy," Ray Brock shows us roadsters being readied for the 500.

S NEW PURSUIT CARS

ROD
MOTIVE MAGAZINE

64

How To Do It—
SUPERCHARGERS
Servicing and
Tune-up Tips

BODY SECTIONING
Do-It-Yourself

CUSTOM OR '59?
see page 42

BONUS PICTORIAL
"$17,000 HOT ROD"
•
BOATS
Testing the
Hi-Horsepower
OUTBOARDS

October: Richard Peters and his *Ala Kart*, built (and photographed) by George Barris. "The controversial roadster pickup was built expressly to win the Oakland Roadster Show Sweepstakes," reads the story's subhead. It did—twice. Inside: tips on body sectioning and Don Francisco checks out Mercury's new Police Special.

January: A 454-inch Hemi in a 1955 T-Bird equals a 12-second, 114.54-mile-per-hour quarter-miler.

March: Build yourself a roadster, just like sailor Bob Smith's flathead-powered 1927 T.

April: Neal East's Olds-fired five-window is the centerpiece of a "wild Ford trio."

May: Brock tests the Packard Hawk "supercar"; Carol Austin poses with Joe Zupan's custom Ford.

July: Eric Rickman gets the lowdown on a streamlined rail from Daddy's Auto Body.

August: This wild-looking Chrysler Hemi is built for a drag boat, not a (dry) lakes racer.

September: East meets West: Sam Parriott's Kurtis-Cad and Norm Wallace's 1932 roadster.

November: Blown and injected small-block makes 430 horsepower in a Lee's Speed Shop dragster.

December: First featured in 1950, this "Movietown Model T" now belongs to actor Skip Torgerson.

1958

January

May

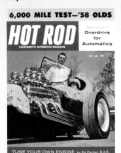

July

March

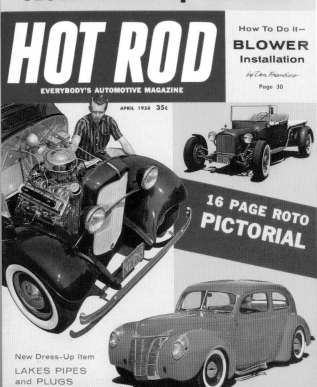

April

August

November

September

December

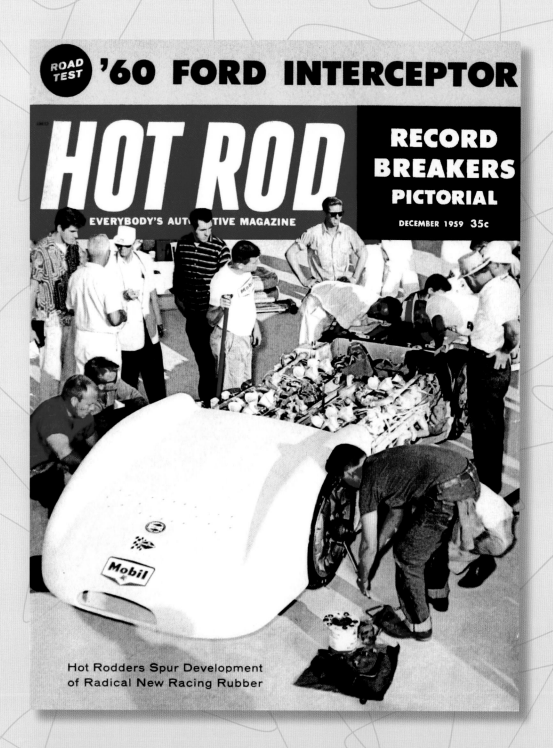

ROAD TEST '60 FORD INTERCEPTOR

HOT ROD
EVERYBODY'S AUTOMOTIVE MAGAZINE

RECORD
BREAKERS
PICTORIAL

DECEMBER 1959 35c

Mobil

Hot Rodders Spur Development
of Radical New Racing Rubber

December

The cover description on the issue's table of contents page sets the stage: "The man, the car, and the crew most likely to succeed the World's Fastest: Mickey Thompson spreads his pit on the table-smooth lake bed that was later to teach him a trick or two before letting his *Challenger* I garner 16 new records."

Hot Rod alerted readers to Mickey Thompson's radical, four-engine land-speed-record challenger by showing it under construction in the September 1959 issue—before it was named *Challenger*. Ed Iskenderian, that master of understatement, featured the *Challenger* prominently in his ad in the October 1959 issue and called it the "world's fastest hot rod"—before it ever hit the salt.

In hindsight we know Isky was right on. At the 1959 Bonneville speed trials, Thompson and the *Challenger* set a meet record with a two-way average speed of 330.5 miles per hour. His fastest one-way speed was 362.3. All were short of his 400-mile-per-hour target—which he would hit a year later—but they were impressive enough to make Thompson's Pontiac-powered streamliner "the star of the meet" and land him on the December issue cover courtesy an Ektachrome transparency shot by Bob D'Olivo.

(Ironic historic footnote: In 1960, Thompson's 400-mile-per-hour run was made a week after the Bonneville meet, so it was not included in the magazine's event coverage. It was Ed Iskenderian, again, who scooped the magazine's writers by putting Thompson's 406.6-mile-per-hour effort at the top of his November 1960 ad.)

The "trick or two" alluded to on the contents page is described in more detail in a photo caption: "To slow the Pontiac-powered four-engined streamliner after many high-speed runs, two five-foot ribbon parachutes were ejected from the tail by an explosive charge. Early chute tests with shorter static line resulted in slide. Longer line solved his problems."

Accompanying the Bonneville coverage is a five-page story about the Goodyear LSR tires Thompson uses and their development for the *Challenger*. At the end of the story, Goodyear announces a line of LSR tires will be available in time for the 1960 Bonneville trials. "These will be the answer to the prayers of most builders of streamlined vehicles," writes Griff Borgeson.

The Interceptor cover line refers to Ray Brock's road test of a 1960 Ford Starliner. He calls it "Ford's Optional Super Stock" because of the top-speed potential from its 360-horse, 352-inch V-8. "We just got back from Detroit where three days were spent behind the wheel of a 1960 Ford two-door hardtop Starliner that toured Ford's five-mile high-speed track at Romeo, Michigan, at an average speed of 152.6 miles per hour." The same car, driven by Cotton Owens to test tires for Firestone, would average 142 miles per hour over 40 laps on Daytona's high banks.

Mickey Thompson makes some shake-down passes at Edwards Air Force Base before taking *Challenger I* to Bonneville in the hunt for 400 miles per hour.

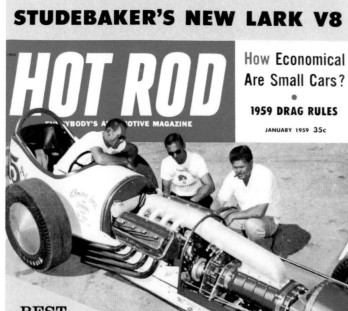

STUDEBAKER'S NEW LARK V8

HOT ROD

THE YBODY'S AUTOMOTIVE MAGAZINE

How Economical
Are Small Cars?
•
1959 DRAG RULES

JANUARY 1959 35c

BEST
ENGINEERED
DRAGSTER–
Chrisman and Cannon's Award Winner

plus Ike Iacono's GMC-6
see page 39

January: The Chrisman Brothers/ Frank Cannon *Hustler* would become a drag racing legend. Here it's already setting records at Southern California strips, including a 163.33-mile-per-hour mark on fuel at Riverside, 152.80 using gas at Long Beach. "Best E.T.'s: 9.42 (fuel) and 9.92 on gas at Long Beach."

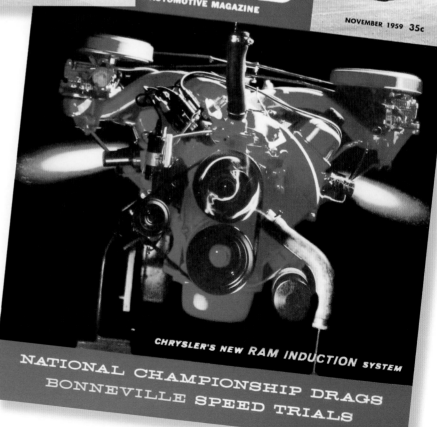

NG THE NEW DODGE DART

T ROD

'S AUTOMOTIVE MAGAZINE

NOVEMBER 1959 35c

CHRYSLER'S NEW RAM INDUCTION SYSTEM

NATIONAL CHAMPIONSHIP DRAGS
BONNEVILLE SPEED TRIALS

November: Dodge introduces the 1960 Dart and its optional D-500 engine, "a 361-cubic-inch V-8 identical to the Golden Commando Plymouth engines for 1959 but fitted with an exotic looking and able performing intake manifolding which Dodge calls Ram Induction." Tests show the long manifolds boost torque as much as 10 percent.

'59 MERC ROAD TEST

How-to-Modify CHEVY'S BIG V-8 by Don Francisco

HOT ROD — EVERYBODY'S AUTOMOTIVE MAGAZINE

APRIL 1959 35c

CAPITAL CUSTOM — page

COMPETITION CLUTCHES AND FLYWHEELS

RARE '36 FORD—page 61

April

FORD'S Ranchero vs CHEVY'S El Camino

TIRE TREADS Key To 'Handling' Problems

How To Win At The Drags see page 36

FUEL INJECTION Latest Systems Explored

February

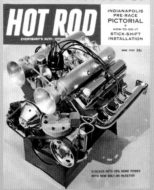

OLDS' HOTTEST FOR '59

INDIANAPOLIS PRE-RACE PICTORIAL

HOW-TO-DO-IT STICK-SHIFT INSTALLATION

STOCKER GETS 25% MORE POWER WITH NEW BOLT-ON INJECTOR

June

TESTING THE '59 BUICK

MORE GO through simple IGNITION modification

SHOW ROD $3000 lavished on 30-year-old Ford roadster

HOW-TO-DO-IT A CHRYSLER FOR YOUR MERCURY

ROAD ROD Ancient in year only is this Olds-powered 'T'

March

TEST: FORD'S 430-INCH T-BIRD

Chevrolet's FACTORY HOT ROD Exclusive Cutaway NEW DEVIN SPORTS CAR

TROPHY-TAKER See Page 47

Newest Developments in DRAGGIN' BOATS

Experimental OLDS

July

February: "New Fields in Fuel Injection" are represented by the injected Cad in Webb Callahan's 1934 Ford.

March: "Ancient" roadsters "make more exciting copy than ever in this space age."

April: A 1955 Plymouth and a 1936 Ford roadster demonstrate late 1950s custom trends.

May: A fuelie-powered Deuce roadster shares cover space with "all that mahogany planking."

June: Bolt-on fuel injection—tested on a 1958 Edsel engine—adds 60 horsepower.

July: "Roadster fever" as expressed by Paul Buckingham's T and Harley Earl's experimental Olds.

August: Joe Brienza's Cad-powered 1934 roadster is a cut-down East Coast show winner.

September: Never mind the digger and boat; read about Mickey T building his 400-mile-per-hour *Challenger*.

October: Two months' work and $3,000 went into building the Grasshopper T roadster.

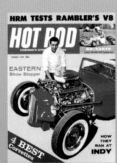

HRM TESTS RAMBLER'S V8

EASTERN Show Stopper

4 BEST Corvettes

HOW THEY RAN AT INDY

August

PONTIACS GUN FOR 400 MPH!

SPECIAL SECTION POWER BOATS How the Hot Ones Get Their Speed

PIKES PEAK On-The-Spot Coverage

September

2000-HP GOLD CUP BOATS

BIG VALVES for CHEV V8's

Construction Details— SUPERCHARGED SHOWPIECE

EASY BOLT-IN: CHEV V8 IN A STUDEBAKER

October

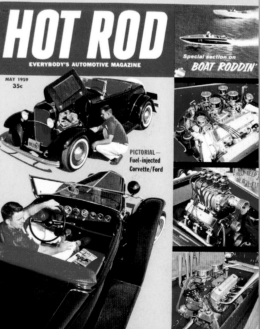

PONTIAC 410 HP ENGINE

HOT ROD — EVERYBODY'S AUTOMOTIVE MAGAZINE

MAY 1959 35c

Special section on BOAT RODDIN'

PICTORIAL— Fuel-injected Corvette/Ford

May

1959

Chapter 3
1960–1969

While the 1950s laid *Hot Rod*'s foundation, the magazine—like the rest of our culture—went through enormous changes in the 1960s. Just four months into 1960, Wally Parks traded the editor's desk for an editorial director position; and in 1963 he left Petersen altogether to run the NHRA. Bob Greene filled the position after Parks, and he would be followed by Ray Brock, Jim McFarland, and Don Evans. Each had a unique window on what would be a mind-blowing period in the speed industry.

Mickey Thompson kicked things off when he finally broke the 400-mile-per-hour barrier in his four-engine *Challenger* in 1960. Three years later, Craig Breedlove set a 407-mile-per-hour record in the jet-powered *Spirit of America*, and two years after that he blew through the 600-mile-per-hour mark in *Sonic 1*.

Things were even more frenzied on America's drag strips. The NHRA had banned nitromethane in 1957, but the sanctioning body rescinded the rule in 1963 after watching too many paying customers defect to independent tracks and the competing AHRA. Detroit also became interested in drag racing, the result, many believe, of the 1959 NHRA Nationals being held in the Motor City. Purpose-built drag cars started to emerge from the Big Three, and the Super Stock wars were on. Things got really wild when drag racers relocated the wheels under their stock-bodied cars in a quest for traction, and those altered-wheelbase match racers were just a step away from full-blown funny cars.

Detroit's attention wasn't just directed at drag strips. A "youth market" of new car buyers was emerging, and

Pontiac went after them with the 1964 GTO, giving birth to the muscle car as we know it today. Not to be outdone, Ford introduced the Mustang in April 1964, and it was an immediate sales smash. Soon after, every U.S. automaker was pumping out big-cube or pony car products—or some combination of the two, as was the case with the Cobra Jet Mustang and Camaro SS396.

Hot Rod was in the perfect position to ride the muscle car wave. Ray Brock had built solid relationships in Detroit years before, and he was now able to deliver the best Motown had to offer for the magazine. Ironically, Brock did almost too good a job, as some of the more traditional rodders on staff bristled at how much Detroit iron was landing in the magazine.

The parallel growth of drag racing and Detroit's influence changed *Hot Rod* to its core. The roadsters and coupes

Hot Rod was in the perfect position to ride the muscle car wave.

that had been the magazine's mainstays disappeared from covers by mid-decade, replaced by tire-smoking rails and funnys, exotic skunkworks engines, wild customs, and new muscle cars. *Hot Rod*'s new focus pushed Eric Rickman, Bob D'Olivo, and other Petersen shooters to produce some landmark cover images, including Connie Kalitta's dragster in Ford's wind tunnel in August 1965 and the back-to-back 1966 knockouts of Don Nicholson's Eliminator funny car in April and the *Hurst Hairy Olds* "see-through" shot in May.

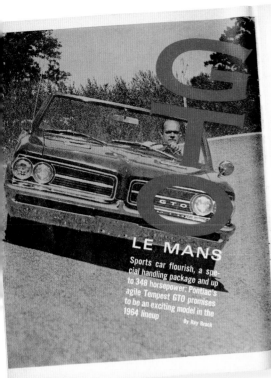

GTO

LE MANS

Sports car flourish, a special handling package and up to 348 horsepower: Pontiac's agile Tempest GTO promises to be an exciting model in the 1964 lineup

By Ray Brock

GM's Pontiac Division has earned a reputation in recent years of building stylish, spirited cars which appeal to man and woman, young and not-so-young. The fact that Pontiac closed out the '63 model sales year in third place proves the popularity of their cars. One model, the Grand Prix, was in such demand that it was back-ordered nearly all of the model year.

Changes in the full-size Pontiac line for '64 are not extreme but the Tempest line has an entirely different makeup which should make it more popular than ever before. There is one particular Tempest model for '64 which attracted our eye on a recent trip to the GM proving grounds and, unless we miss our guess, this might be the '64 model dealers will sell faster than Pontiac can build.

It's called the LeMans GTO. The initials stand for Grand Turismo Omologato and in case you don't understand Italian, the English translation would be Grand Touring Homologated. In European sports car circles, grand touring classification stands for an enclosed coupe and the homologation terminology means that the model in a regular production model, not just a limited-production option designed for racing or rallys. Pontiac violates the accepted grand touring classification slightly by offering a convertible model as well as a two-door coupe in their GTO series.

The GTO option is based on LeMans Tempests but extra items included in the GTO option are considerable. Most obvious differences are a number of items of special trim, both exterior and interior. GTO in block lettering replaces "Pontiac" on the grille and "Le Mans" on the rear fenders and deck lid. Tri-colored (red, white and blue) GTO crests are affixed to the front fenders just behind wheel openings.

A special hood stamping is used for GTO models with simulated twin air scoops and cast aluminum grilles in the hood depressions. This distinctive hood plus the six, count 'em, GTO identification trim pieces on the car's exterior leaves little doubt that this model is a new breed of Tempest. Interior trim is virtually the same as Le Mans with front bucket seats and an optional console between the buckets. A GTO crest appears on the dash panel and an engine-turned aluminum panel surrounds the instruments.

1964 Tempests are larger and differ many ways mechanically from their '63 counterparts. The '64 Tempest is based on a 115-inch wheelbase, and is 203 inches long, giving three inches more wheelbase and 9 inches more length than last year's models. A conventional GM-style suspension is used with the curved driveshaft and torque tube; transaxle and rear swing axles of '63 were discarded. A conventional semi-floating, Hypoid rear axle unit is used for '64 with four rubber-bushed, stamped steel links positioning the axle and a pair of coil springs for suspension.

Front suspension is by conventional unequal-length A-arms and coil springs. A link type stabilizer bar fastens between the two lower control arms. All steering linkage is mounted ahead of the front wheels. Frame, suspension components and all other running gear on the '64 Tempests are of the same design as those used on the '64 Olds F-85's, Buick Specials and Chevrolet Chevelles.

Since the GTO is styled and named as a sports type, numerous chassis modifications are employed which distinguish the GTO from regular Tempests. First of all, spring rates both front and rear are higher and shock absorber valving is more positive. The result is a firmer ride than the regular models offer. A larger diameter, stronger stabilizer bar is used with the GTO chassis package. Wider based wheels and larger tires are also part of the GTO option. Regular Tempests use a 14-inch wheel with 5-inch wide rim but for improved stability, the GTO 14-inch wheel has a six-inch rim width. 7.50 x 14 tires are

(Continued on following page)

Standard powerplant with GTO option is a 389 V8 with either four-barrel or optional triple two-barrel carburetion.

Taillights on GTO are similar to Grand Prix, concealed by chrome strip when not on. GTO emblem is used 4 times.

Distinctive features of GTO include simulated hood scoops, standard nylon black-wall tires with thin red stripe. Wheels used on GTO have 6-inch rim width, springs and shocks were selected for good handling.

Technical Editor Ray Brock tests the 1964 Pontiac Le Mans GTO, which is targeted at the emerging youth market. The term "muscle car" wouldn't be coined for another few years.

Don Nicholson's flip-top *Eliminator I* revolutionized funny car design in 1966.

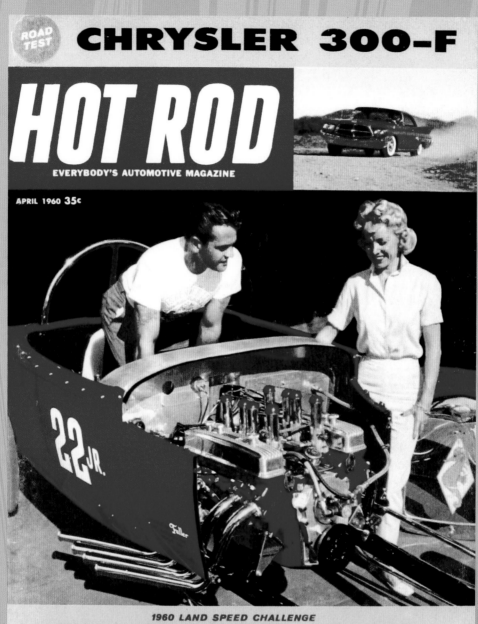

ROAD TEST

CHRYSLER 300-F

HOT ROD

EVERYBODY'S AUTOMOTIVE MAGAZINE

APRIL 1960 35¢

22 JR.

Fuller

1960 LAND SPEED CHALLENGE
6900 Horsepower JET ROD

April

Three years after first appearing on *Hot Rod*'s cover, Tony Nancy is back with another 22 Jr. This is the more iconic pose, with Tony looking buff for Eric Rickman's "new Swedish Hasselblad camera." While he previously used flathead power, the Model A now sports an injected Buick V-8 in the chrome-moly tube frame, all visible through the car's Plexiglas grille panel. Much of the sheet metal was replaced by aluminum so that the A tipped the scales at just 1,550 pounds. The bored, stroked, and injected nailhead propelled the car to a record 10.74 ET at 130.57 miles per hour in just its sixth pass at the San Fernando drag strip.

1960

Technical Editor Ray Brock performs the road test of Chrysler's 300F, "an extra-special hot sedan for the man who wants style, luxury and performance in one package." Brock's limited-edition Letter Car is powered by the 375-horsepower version of Chrysler's 413-inch V-8. It's fitted with the distinctive Ram Induction intake system that put Carter four-barrel carburetors on the ends of 30-inch intake runners feeding opposite cylinder banks. The "mild supercharge" coming from that ram-air intake design helps move the 4,600-pound hardtop through the quarter-mile in 16 seconds at 90.9 miles per hour—"just plain rapid movement for a car weighing so much," Brock writes.

The "6900 Horsepower Jet Rod" story previews a land-speed-record car that is the brainchild of Dr. Nathan Ostich, a physician and Bonneville racer who dreams of running 500 miles per hour on the salt. With help from Brock, Ak Miller, and other friends, Ostich is building a rocket on wheels, using a surplus GE turbojet engine as power, a cylindrical body shaped by tests at Cal Poly's wind tunnel and tires designed by Firestone "for a safe operating speed of 600 mph." The car would later be named the *Flying Caduceus*, and Brock chronicles its maiden—and disappointing—voyage at Bonneville in the October issue.

Also in this issue, Brock comes back from Daytona with his report on Speedweeks 1960, which saw top-speed runs on the hard-packed sand and NASCAR Stock Cars negotiating the still-new tri-oval racetrack. Brock laments the condition of the unfinished pit area and how "crews still had to work on their cars out in the open with sand for a floor and the pits were still sand, not asphalt or concrete. Dirt is the worst enemy of a racing engine and with the loose sand and windy conditions of the Daytona track, it is a wonder any of the engines lasted long enough to make the race, let alone run for 500 miles." Junior Johnson's 1959 Chevy wins the 500-mile main event with a top speed of nearly 150 miles per hour.

This issue is the last with Wally Parks at the helm as editor. Starting with the May issue, Parks is promoted to editorial director, and Managing Editor Bob Greene is made editor.

Editors call the superior craftsmanship that went into the 22 Jr. roadster "The Tony Nancy Touch."

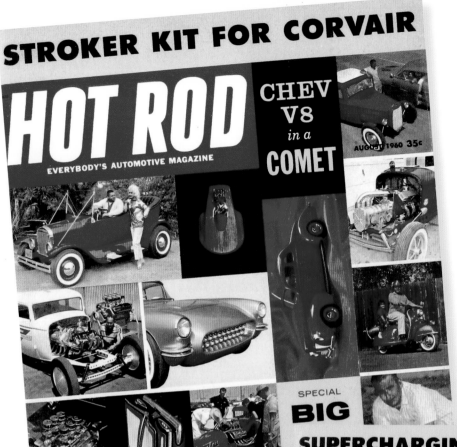

STROKER KIT FOR CORVAIR

HOT ROD

EVERYBODY'S AUTOMOTIVE MAGAZINE

CHEV V8 in a COMET

AUGUST 1960 35c

SPECIAL

BIG

August: Greene calls this a "crazy-quilt cover," illustrating the scope of hot rodding circa 1960. Inside is coverage of the Indianapolis 500 ("138.767 mph—new record race average") and speed records set by Mickey Thompson, plus tips on how to "poke and stroke" a number of popular engines.

July: Not only did he lay on the 30 coats of lacquer covering the car, George Barris photographed the build of Chuck Krikorian's Cadillac-powered 1929 Ford on its way to winning the America's Most Beautiful Roadster trophy at the 1960 Oakland Roadster Show.

SUPERCHARGING the COMPACTS

HOT ROD

EVERYBODY'S AUTOMOTIVE MAGAZINE

JULY 1960 35c

How to do it—
INSTALL A V8 IN YOUR FALCON
by Ray Brock

"America's Most
BEAUTIFUL ROADSTER"
...'60 Oakland Roadster Show

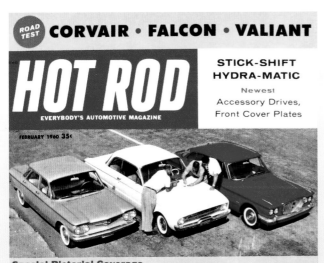

ROAD TEST · **CORVAIR · FALCON · VALIANT**

HOT ROD
EVERYBODY'S AUTOMOTIVE MAGAZINE

FEBRUARY 1960 35¢

STICK-SHIFT HYDRA-MATIC
Newest Accessory Drives, Front Cover Plates

Special Pictorial Coverage
CARS ★ BOATS ★ BIKES ★ KARTS

February

ROAD TEST **SUPER 88 OLDSMOBILE**

HOT ROD
EVERYBODY'S AUTOMOTIVE MAGAZINE

JANUARY 1960 35¢

BOLT-IN Floor Shift Conversions

Plain Talk On FANCY CAMS · Drag Racing's NEW RULES FOR '60

January

ROAD TEST **PONTIAC TEMPEST 425-A**

HOT ROD
AUTOMOTIVE MAGAZINE

MAY 1960 35¢

ENGINE FEATURE— MAKE A 400-INCHER OF YOUR 283 CHEVY
High Horsepower Falcons

May

ROAD TEST **THE HOTTER NEW PLYMOUTH**

HOT ROD
EVERYBODY'S AUTOMOTIVE MAGAZINE

MARCH 1960 35¢

KARTS and COMPACTS in COMPETITION
400 horsepower STUDE LARK

HOT RODDING THE FORD FALCON

March

ROAD TEST **COMET VS. RAMBLER**

HOT ROD
EVERYBODY'S AUTOMOTIVE MAGAZINE

JUNE 1960 35¢

HOT CHEVYS FOR 'INDY'
Latest— VW HOP-UP KIT

June

January: Bill Burke's Harley-powered streamliner gets the push at Bonneville.

February: "Compact cars all," from 1924 and 1932 and the latest from the Big Three.

March: Darryl Starbird's Buick poses with Danny Hilderbrand's Model A.

May: Bill Stroppe (right) with three hot sixes for the Falcon.

June: Bruce Crower (right) takes on the Offys at Indy with a Chevy V-8.

September: "Go and Show" roadsters include the red 1959 Oakland Show Street Roadster winner.

October: George Hurst (dark shirt) looks over the 'Vette engine he put in a Valiant.

November: More show and go, pairing drag race rods with Barris Impalas.

December: A/Roadster action from the 1960 National Championship Drags in Detroit.

A HOT V8 FOR VALIANT

HOT ROD
EVERYBODY'S AUTOMOTIVE MAGAZINE

Modifying the GMC Blower for Racing
JET CAR ASSAULTS WORLD RECORD

October

PONTIAC'S HOT COMPACT 4

HOT ROD
EVERYBODY'S AUTOMOTIVE MAGAZINE

BONNEVILLE America's Fastest Rods
IMPALA CUSTOMS

RESULTS—NATIONAL CHAMPIONSHIP DRAGS

November

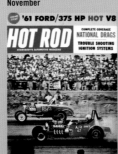

'61 FORD/375 HP HOT V8

HOT ROD
EVERYBODY'S AUTOMOTIVE MAGAZINE

COMPLETE COVERAGE NATIONAL DRAGS
TROUBLE SHOOTING IGNITION SYSTEMS

December

PIKES PEAK RACE PICTORIAL

HOT ROD
EVERYBODY'S AUTOMOTIVE MAGAZINE

HOW-TO-DO-IT **KART** ENGINE HOP-UP
TOP CONTENDERS for '60 NATIONALS
SEPTEMBER 1960 35¢

GO and SHOW RODS

OAKLAND SHOW
Street Roadster Champ

September

1960

December

Tommy Ivo's double life—acting and drag racing—comes crashing together when Eric Rickman photographs Ivo's wild, four-engine dragster on the set of the TV show *Margie*. Ivo's 1920s-era costume inspired the *Hot Rod* editors to call the car *Showboat*, and the name stuck, even though Ivo didn't much care for it. Nor was he happy when the show's producers saw the car and realized their actor was risking his neck at drag strips when he wasn't on the set. They forbade him to drive the car, and until the series ended, he raced under an alias. On the cover Ivo poses with his *Margie* co-star Cynthia Pepper; inside, there's Ivo with a teenaged Don Prudhomme sitting in the car. (Prudhomme painted the dragster.) Even though Ivo was still working the bugs out of the four-wheel-drive rail, which used the left-side Buick V-8s to drive the front wheels and the right-side engines to power the rears, Rickman writes that the car clocked a best ET of 9.14 seconds at more than 170 miles per hour.

Technical Editor Ray Brock brought back pictures and coverage from the 13th Speed Trials at Bonneville. Weather conditions had caused the salt to deteriorate and shorten the course—so much so that land-speed-record attempts by Mickey Thompson's *Challenger* and Dr. Nathan Ostich's *Flying Caduceus* were cancelled—but those who did run found traction excellent on the dry surface. The top speed of the meet—313 miles per hour—was reached by Art Arfons in his Allison-powered streamliner.

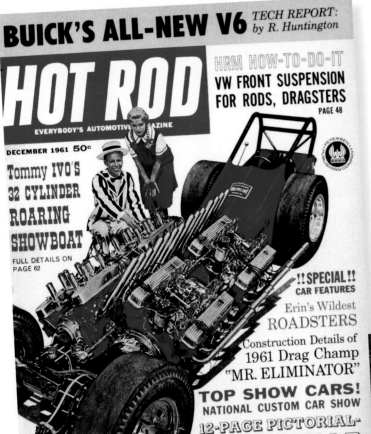

Tommy Ivo (left) and Don Prudhomme pose with Ivo's dragster on the set of Ivo's TV show *Margie*.

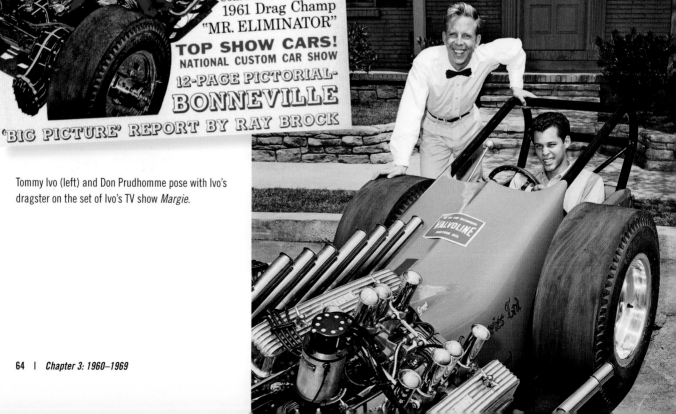

1961

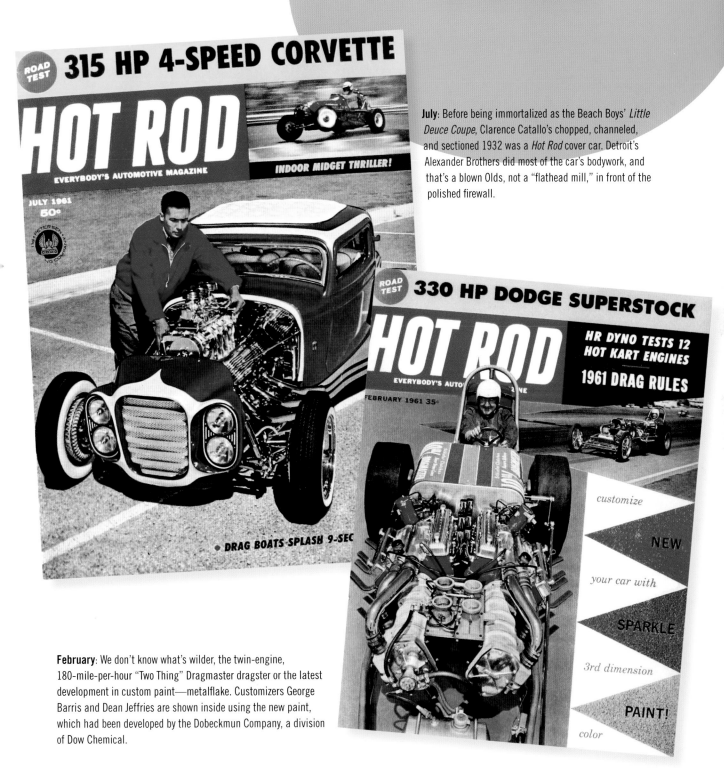

July: Before being immortalized as the Beach Boys' *Little Deuce Coupe*, Clarence Catallo's chopped, channeled, and sectioned 1932 was a *Hot Rod* cover car. Detroit's Alexander Brothers did most of the car's bodywork, and that's a blown Olds, not a "flathead mill," in front of the polished firewall.

February: We don't know what's wilder, the twin-engine, 180-mile-per-hour "Two Thing" Dragmaster dragster or the latest development in custom paint—metalflake. Customizers George Barris and Dean Jeffries are shown inside using the new paint, which had been developed by the Dobeckmun Company, a division of Dow Chemical.

1961

January

January: "What could be a more spine tingling thrill than motoring along with a pretty girl?"

March: Marty Holmann's pioneering T bucket roadster and dune buggies on the Pismo sand.

April: Street and strip hot rods are topped by a test of Chevy's new 409.

May: The Hedrich & McClure rear-engine roadster and coverage of the first Winternationals.

June: That's A. J. Foyt behind the wheel in this Indy 500 preview issue.

August: Two four-wheel-drives on this cover—Mickey Thompson's and Vic Hickey's above it.

September: Dean Moon's *Mooneyes* dragster is his 10-second "Quarter Mile Test Bench."

October: Mickey Thompson's full-dress street Pontiac engine with a new GMC blower.

November: The Nationals move to Indy, and Ford has a new V-8 for the Fairlane.

April

May

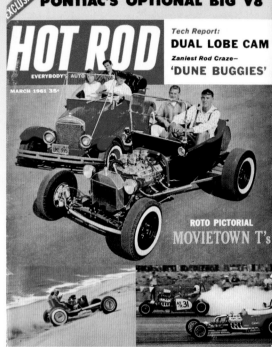

March

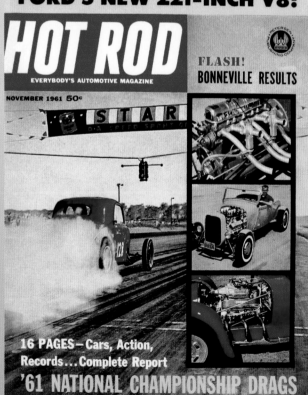

November

June

September

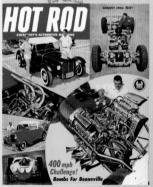

August

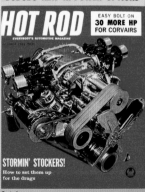

October

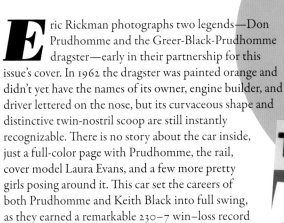

Eric Rickman photographs two legends—Don Prudhomme and the Greer-Black-Prudhomme dragster—early in their partnership for this issue's cover. In 1962 the dragster was painted orange and didn't yet have the names of its owner, engine builder, and driver lettered on the nose, but its curvaceous shape and distinctive twin-nostril scoop are still instantly recognizable. There is no story about the car inside, just a full-color page with Prudhomme, the rail, cover model Laura Evans, and a few more pretty girls posing around it. This car set the careers of both Prudhomme and Keith Black into full swing, as they earned a remarkable 230–7 win–loss record in 1963–1964.

The supercharged Avanti engine in the upper corner "is representative of Detroit's keen desire to produce an exciting assembly line automobile," write the editors, who use a shot of a powersliding Avanti as the lead photo for an article about "The Hot '63s." The blown Avanti 289 wasn't the only excitement from Detroit in 1963. Buick introduced its all-new Riviera, Chrysler would soon release the 426-cubic-inch Max Wedge V-8, and the magazine had already reported on the completely redesigned Corvette Sting Ray in the October issue. Foreshadowing things to come, *Hot Rod* also reveals Ford's Mustang concept car, a two-seat roadster with a 106-horsepower V-4 mounted behind the cockpit.

Jack Chrisman is Top Eliminator at the eighth NHRA Nationals in this issue, driving Mickey Thompson's Pontiac-powered dragster to beat Don Garlits in the final.

1962

November

The Greer-Black-Prudhomme digger two years after its 1962 cover appearance. Ray Brock (left) interviews Don Prudhomme (center) and Keith Black.

405 HP CHRYSLER 300H

BY TECHNICAL EDITOR **RAY BROCK**

HOT ROD

EVERYBODY'S AUTOMOTIVE MAGAZINE

FEBRUARY 1962
50c

DAN GURNEY'S 409 CHEV
ROAD RACING SEDAN

SPECIAL WORLD'S QUICKEST
DRAG BOAT

FEATURES NEW IDEAS IN FLOOR SHIFTS

SECRETS OF ARC WELDING

'62 DRAG RULES

FAIRLANE V8 SPORTS CAR

HOT ROD

EVERYBODY'S AUTOMOTIVE MAGAZINE

DECEMBER 1962 50c
80c IN CANADA

INSIDE PHOTOS DETAILS...

'62 TOP ELIMINATOR
ALUMINUM ENGINE PONTIAC DRAGSTER

Don Francisco reports:

14TH ANNUAL BONNEVILLE
NATIONAL SPEED TRIALS

February: Pete Sukalac shoots the "King of the Rods," Bob Tindle's gorgeous *Orange Crate*. The Olds-powered 1932 Ford Tudor is truly built for show *and* go. It won America's Best Competition Car at the 1961 Oakland Roadster Show and is also capable of low 11-second ETs at the strip.

December: Robert Markley's belly tank made the cover, but this Bonneville meet is historic for other reasons, including the introduction of several now-famous streamliners. Don Francisco opens his story with the tale of New Zealander Burt Munro, whose trip with his Indian Scout "would make a script for a movie."

1962

March

May

June

'62 CORVETTE 327 CUBIC INCHES 360 HORSEPOWER

January

January: Former quarter-midget champ Dean Lowe builds a "bombin' '29" roadster pickup with father Buzz.

March: Richard and Gary Seiden rework Dick Kraft's famous 1925 track T.

April: This 24-page roadster special includes Dick Scritchfield's timeless 1932 highboy.

May: This cover epitomizes *Hot Rod*'s 1960s focus: drag racing, Detroit performance, and show rods.

June: Buzz Pitzen's T roadster is fiberglass, as steel T bodies are already "so rare" in 1962.

July: The nailhead is for Rickman's Comet; turns out the Cougar concept isn't "Tomorrow's T-Bird."

August: Tony Nancy's guns on display again, with his 169-mile-per-hour A/Modified Roadster.

September: Editors call Don Waite's 1929 "the finest example of automotive craftsmanship we've ever seen."

October: Bob Urquhart's DeSoto-powered T roadster is gorgeous; so is the restyled Corvette.

July

August

September

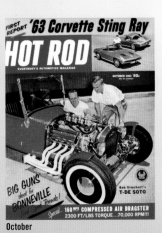

October

April

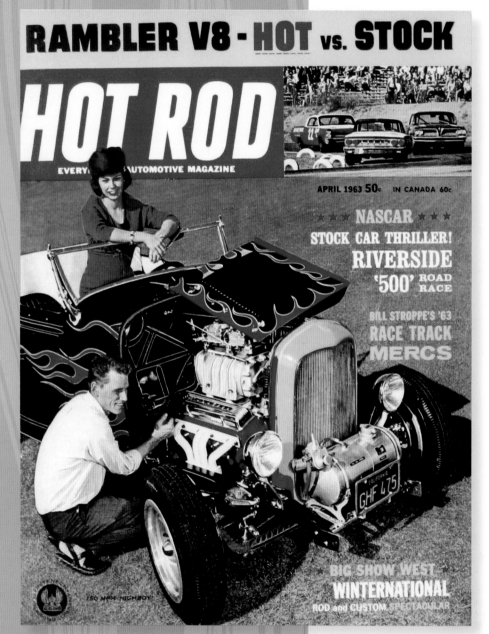

RAMBLER V8 · HOT vs. STOCK

HOT ROD

EVERY... ...AUTOMOTIVE MAGAZINE

APRIL 1963 50c   IN CANADA 60c

★★★ NASCAR ★★★
STOCK CAR THRILLER!
RIVERSIDE
'500' ROAD RACE

BILL STROPPE'S '63
RACE TRACK MERCS

BIG SHOW WEST
WINTERNATIONAL
ROD and CUSTOM SPECTACULAR

150 MPH HIGHBOY

GHF 475

Years after Eric Rickman shot this photo, Tom McMullen would launch his own publishing company and eventually compete with *Hot Rod* on the newsstand. But in 1963 he is an electronics technician with an outrageous—and now iconic—flamed Deuce roadster. The car was famous prior to McMullen's owning it, having appeared on TV's *The Life of Riley*. In McMullen's hands, though, it is transformed with flames (McMullen did the paint; Ed Roth striped the licks and the dash) and a GMC-blown 327-inch small-block Chevy. This is McMullen's street car, but as Rickman notes in the story, it will also run 151 miles per hour at the dry lakes and mid-11-second ETs in the quarter. "That healthy Moon tank above the dropped axle is for speed runs, stock tank for everyday driving." In the years to come, McMullen would sell this car and build two more Deuce roadsters like it. His original Deuce would eventually be restored back to its 1963 incarnation by Roy Brizio Street Rods.

The Bob D'Olivo photo in the upper corner is from coverage of the first Riverside 500 stock car race, later known as the Motor Trend 500. The inaugural race marks the debut of several hot stockers from Pontiac and Ford, with Pontiac seeming at first to dominate the demanding road course. But Dan Gurney and Parnelli Jones, in their "new Ford and Merc fastbacks," shake up the Pontiac crew with impressive qualifying times, and Gurney goes on to win the race and a $13,000 check from Robert Petersen.

April

1963

Hot Rod sticks to the stocker theme with a visit to Bill Stroppe's Long Beach, California, shop to document the build of the 1963 Mercury Marauder fastback piloted by Troy Ruttman to a third-place finish at Riverside. The very detailed story includes photos of Louis Unser checking the true of the Merc's rear end on a lathe and of Stroppe's "ultra-modern engine dynamometer room, complete with elaborate instrumentation."

As a counterpoint to Stroppe's full-house Mercs, Tex Smith writes about a hot sleeper on the drag strip, a Rambler Ambassador raced in D/Stock by Dell-Kraft Rambler of Norwalk, California. The compact runs low 14-second ETs at nearly 100 miles per hour.

This issue also includes coverage of the rod and custom car show held before the Winternationals. Bob Tindle's *Orange*

Crate, revised since its appearance in 1962, again wins the Competition Sweepstakes, while Bill Cushenberry's bubble-domed *Silhouette* wins the Grand Sweepstakes Custom award.

Editor Bob Greene writes with "mixed emotions" that this issue concludes Wally Parks' 14-year association with the magazine. Parks leaves his editorial director position to work full-time at the NHRA, the seeds of which he planted in the May 1951 issue.

HIGHBOY THAT WAILS

First time out at the dry lakes, Tom McMullen's traditionally styled '32 Ford cranked over 150 mph. Not bad at all for a car that performs yeoman duty daily as a street rod

FAR LEFT — When Tom lifts the hood of his roadster exclamations are in order. Horsepressure is the product of a '62 Chevy with 327 cubic inches. Equipment added to help power includes a Herbert cam, Thomas rockers, Ansen blower pistons, Reath boxed rods, Weiand intake manifold and 4-71 GMC blower. Chuck Potvin masterminded the blower drive, Mallory built Mini-Mag.

LEFT — Shades of Stroker McGurk! Tom is a member of the Los Angeles Roadster Club and couldn't figure exactly how to make his tall '32 Ford stand out from the crowd. Finally he chose a paint design long absent from the rodding scene, painted the car himself. Striping is the art of Ed Roth.

BELOW — Posed in front of the Beckman Instrument Co. where Tom is an electronics technician, the car draws admiring glances from Carol Puhlman.

Living room is fitted out in black and white Naugahyde stitched up in manner popular many years ago. Even the dashboard and 26-tooth Lincoln Zephyr transmission carry out the traditional rod theme. American mag wheels, a Halibrand quick-change rear end and homemade headers account in part for the car's performances: 127 mph, 11.59 e.t. in the quarter and 151 mph at the dry lakes. That healthy Moon tank above the dropped axle is for speed runs, stock tank for everyday driving. **HOT ROD MAGAZINE**

cover car

La Habra, California

photos by Eric Rickman

APRIL 1963

Tom McMullen painted the flames on his roadster to help "the tall '32 stand out from the crowd." Ed Roth striped them.

TECH ANALYSIS — '64 CARS

HOT ROD

EVERYBODY'S AUTOMOTIVE MAGAZINE

OCTOBER 1963 50¢ IN CANADA 60¢

WORLD'S FASTEST!
CRAIG BREEDLOVE'S

407 MPH...SPIRIT OF AMERICA

★★★★★★★★★★★★★★

- **220 HP COBRA DEALER BOLT-ON KIT FOR FALCON V8** • **PLYMOUTH— FIRST SEDAN TO CRACK 200 MPH?** • **WHAT'S IN THE CHEVYS THAT RAN THE INDY '500'**

October: Mickey Thompson could not back up his 1960 406-mile-per-hour Bonneville run in the *Challenger*, but Craig Breedlove and the *Spirit of America* average 407.45 miles per hour through the mile on August 5, 1963. Don Francisco's story is complemented by shots Eric Rickman took of the *Spirit* under construction.

INDY 500 - WHAT REALLY HAPPENED!

HOT ROD

RYBODY'S AUTOMOTIVE MAGAZINE

AUGUST 1963 50¢ IN CANADA 60¢

Les Ritchey Speed Secrets —
HOW TO TUNE FOR THE DRAGS
SCTA DRY LAKES OPENER
FAIRLANE V8 IN A HEALEY

SPECIAL COLOR FEATURE!!!
"PHANTOM VIEW"
TEX SMITH'S XR-6
SEE CENTERSPREAD

August: Tex Smith's XR-6 project rod, begun in 1962 as a means of "investigating the uses of modern ideas in hot rod design," poses for Rickman's camera in front of a Lockheed F-104 Starfighter. The fiberglass rod had already won the America's Most Beautiful Roadster trophy at Oakland.

1963

January

PLYMOUTH'S SUPER 426

HRM CAR TEST

HOT ROD
EVERYBODY'S AUTOMOTIVE MAGAZINE

JANUARY 1963 50c
60c IN CANADA

WORLD CHAMPIONSHIP
BOAT DRAGS
★ ★ 7.6 QUARTER - MILE E.T. ★ ★

CHARLOTTE
400-MILE
STOCK CAR
RACE

HOW-TO
BUILD
A
CHARGIN'
STREET ENGINE
STEP BY STEP
with DON FRANCISCO

CALIFORNIA
NDU 786

January: Rickman's first film of rodders Lindebaum and Grant was too dark. The reshoot worked.

February: Radical Corvair mill is fitted with Dell'Orto carbs and "bathed in chrome."

March: Lewis Bridgeforth's metalflake red 1927 T was originally a coupe.

May: Garlits is Top Fuel Eliminator at the Winternationals; he also clocked low ET at 8.11.

June: Mickey Thompson readies a Chevy roadster to take on the Offys at Indy.

July: Walter Kaline's Pontiac-powered T benefits from his owning a chrome-plating shop.

September: Tony Nancy in a staged nighttime leave that took two shoots to get right.

November: Diggers, Stock Cars, streamliners—the special racing issue has it all.

December: Al Coffern offers to help a "fair damsel in distress" in his 1933 pickup.

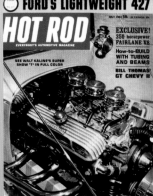

February

March

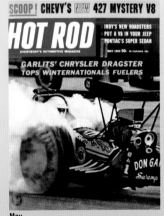

May

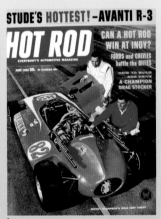

June

July

September

November

December

The cover reads:

327 V8 CHEVELLE EL CAMINO

HOT ROD
EVERYBODY'S AUTOMOTIVE MAGAZINE

APRIL 1964 **50¢**   IN CANADA 60¢

WINTERNATIONALS BIG GO & SHOW
FUEL BOAT DRAGS
NHRA MODIFIED STOCK CLASSES

CHRYSLER'S **"HEMI" IS BACK!**

April

"Don't get too excited fellows," writes Publisher Ray Brock, "but the day you've been waiting for has finally arrived! Chrysler has revived the 'hemi' engine! That's right, the all-time champion on the drag strips—the engine that holds countless records at Bonneville—the *must* powerplant for hot boats—it's been brought back to life in a modern version."

Why all the hubbub? Chrysler stopped making Hemis in 1958, so all those championships and records Brock gushed about in his cover story were accomplished using "old" engines. Having a new source of Hemi power had to thrill members of the Mopar faithful.

At the time of this cover story, Chrysler plans to offer three versions of the Hemi: one with single-four-barrel carburetion for NASCAR-USAC competition and two dual-four-barrel versions for drag racing. It's one of those dual-quad Hemis that appears on the cover. That picture, and the photography accompanying the story, is shot by Chrysler.

Brock scolds the automaker for its "tongue-in-cheek" 400-horsepower rating for the single-carb Hemi, estimating its actual output at 550 horses. Of the drag motors, the 11:1 compression Hemi is rated at 415 horsepower, while the 12.5:1 version is rated at 425. "Probably their actual output, corrected to SAE standards, would be about 560 and 570, respectively," he writes.

Brock drafts his story as the Hemis make their debut at Daytona. "As we go to press, Plymouths and Dodges are smashing lap records at Daytona's 2-1/2 mile Speedway with fantastic speeds," he writes. "In an unofficial practice lap, Dick Petty registered 176-plus in a Plymouth. Last year, the 427 Chevrolets shook up everybody with speeds up to 166 mph and now this mark has been shattered."

What's missing from Brock's story is any talk of a street version of the Hemi. That is a round Chrysler will fire two years later as the muscle car wars go ballistic.

The other big story in this issue is the Winternationals. According to Dick Wells, the Big Go West has grown steadily in just a few years, "and presentation of the 1964 event proved beyond any doubt that the Winternationals is today the only race of its kind to ever approach the dramatic scope of the Nationals, and is one that must certainly be recognized for its importance in the world of auto racing."

The race results show Jack Williams beating Tommy Ivo for Top Fuel Eliminator, but the big newsmaker is Ford. A team of 427-powered Mercury Comets dominate A/FX competition, while Les Ritchey, Butch Leal, and Gas Ronda battle for Super Stock honors driving 427-fired Thunderbolts. Ronda is the S/S class winner on Saturday, though the Plymouths fight back for the Stock Eliminator title on Sunday, which is taken by Tom "Melrose Missile" Grove. Winner of Factory Stock Eliminator on Sunday is a 25-year-old Ronnie Sox in an A/FX Mercury Comet tuned by Buddy Martin. "I really like the Mercs," says Ronnie. That will change.

Chrysler Corporation photos and diagrams reveal details about the first new Hemi since the original generation was discontinued in 1958.

MUSTANG-FORD'S NEW SPORTS CAR

HOT ROD
EVERYBODY'S AUTOMOTIVE MAGAZINE

BAKERSFIELD FUEL SHOWDOWN

MAY 1964 50c IN CANADA 60c

COMET SAFARI CARS
African Rally Specials

'64 INDY PREVIEW
New Engines and Chassis

THE DAYTONA '500'
175 mph MoPar Stocks

151 MPH DRAG BIKE
The World's Quickest?

MANTARAY—OAKLAND ROADSTER SHOW TOURNAM...

May: Between the first road test of the Mustang and news of the new race Hemis dominating the Daytona 500, this is a historically important issue. But truly eye-catching is Dean Jeffries' asymmetrical, clear-canopied *Mantaray*, photographed by Eric Rickman.

September: The blown and injected Hemi in Big John Mazmanian's Willys produces a dyno-tested 824 horsepower, and Rickman's photography demonstrates the coupe is as beautiful as it is fast. Also in the issue, Dick Wells covers the Indy Nationals, while Ray Brock hits Pikes Peak.

PIKES PEAK HILLCLIMB

HOT ROD
EVERYBODY'S AUTOMOTIVE MAGAZINE

SEPTEMBER 1964 50c 60c IN CANADA

SPECIAL! IN FULL COLOR

HOT ONES READY FOR THE NATIONALS
ADJUSTABLE-VENTURI CARBURETOR
BIG JOHN'S 150-MPH RECORD COUPE

PLYMOUTH FASTBACK BARRACUDA

HOT ROD
EVERYBODY'S AUTOMOTIVE MAGAZINE

JULY 1964 50¢

Ford's 200 mph
Rear-Engine
Gran Turismo Coupe

Gearbox Swaps
Do's and Don'ts

Turbocharged
Chrysler
T-Bird

How to
Ram-Tune
Your Engine

July

STUDE'S 150 MPH LARK R-3

HOT ROD
EVERYBODY'S AUTOMOTIVE MAGAZINE

Riverside '400'
'Hemi' Chrysler Ford Swap
Dry Lakes Finale
Testing the 250cc Yamaha
World Boat Drags
Fluid Drive for Dragsters
Big Rail Review:
20-Page Dragster Feature

January

LIGHTWEIGHT 427 FAIRLANE

HOT ROD
EVERYBODY'S AUTOMOTIVE MAGAZINE

INSTANT ROADSTER
Build it in 8 hours!

HOT ROD BOLT-ON
SUPERCHARGER TIPS
How to set up a blower

February

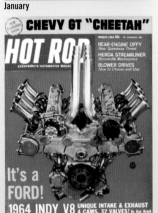

CHEVY GT "CHEETAH"

HOT ROD
EVERYBODY'S AUTOMOTIVE MAGAZINE

REAR-ENGINE OFFY
New Speedway Threat
HERDA STREAMLINER
Bonneville Masterpiece
BLOWER DRIVES
How to Choose and Use

It's a FORD!
1964 INDY V8
UNIQUE INTAKE & EXHAUST
4 CAMS, 32 VALVES! By Ray Brock

March

COMETS ON THE AFRICAN SAFARI

HOT ROD
EVERYBODY'S AUTOMOTIVE MAGAZINE

FIRST TEST! DRIVING THE HOTTEST MUSTANG
'HUSTLER' JET BOAT BUILT TO GO 300 MPH!
MORE PAGES • MORE COLOR • MORE FEATURES

WORLD'S FASTEST DRIVER CRAIG BREEDLOVE BUILDS A DRAGSTER

June

January: Tommy Ivo aims squarely at Rickman to get the "Big Rail Review" cover shot.

February: Plenty of speed secrets inside, but nothing about the big-inch Chevy.

March: Ford builds a four-cam, 400-plus-horsepower engine to take on the Offys at Indy.

June: Breedlove's back, this time in a four-wheeled, piston-powered dragster.

July: John Wingate's "wild Deuces" make the July cover, but their story is in August.

August: The *Wedge* is Tony Nancy's streamlined, rear-engine (and untested) dragster. He hopes for 185.

October: Another bait-and-switch: The story on Al Rogers' roadster doesn't appear until the November issue.

November: Garlits tears down *Swamp Rat VI* to share his secrets to reaching 200 miles per hour.

December: Steve LaBonge's A Touring "is what every rodder would like under his Christmas tree."

CHAMPIONSHIP DRAGS

HOT ROD
EVERYBODY'S AUTOMOTIVE MAGAZINE

Indy 500
IN FULL COLOR!

STREAMLINERS
NEW-LOOK RAIL
The Nancy 'WEDGE'

August

BONNEVILLE and NATIONAL DRAGS
COMPLETE STORY•PHOTOS•RESULTS

HOT ROD

SUPERCHARGING
THE MUSTANG

GARLITS JAMMER

EXCLUSIVE—Don Garlits tells all his speed secrets!

November

HRM LOOKS AT DISC BRAKES

HOT ROD

December

MODIFYING THE MUSTANG V8

HOT ROD
EVERYBODY'S AUTOMOTIVE MAGAZINE

OCTOBER 1964 50¢

Fastest 'Vette of All
World Record SK Dragster
V8 Power for Corvairs
Secrets for Strip Stockers

Hot Rod Looks
at the '65 Cars!

PERFORMANCE OPTIONS
SUSPENSION DESIGNS
DISC BRAKES
AUTOMATIC TRANSMISSIONS
STREAMLINED STYLING

October

1964

HOW FORD BROKE THE OFFY GRIP

HOT ROD

EVERYBODY'S AUTOMOTIVE MAGAZINE

AUGUST 1965 50c

MAKE YOUR VW A 13-SECOND STREET ELIMINATOR!

HOW-TO-BUILD TOP BRACKETS FOR ROADSTERS

STREAMLINING— TOO TOUCHY FOR 200-MPH RAILS?

CONNIE KALITTA'S DRAGSTER EXPLORES THE WIND TUNNEL

August

"Streamlining—Too Touchy for 200-mph Rails?" is the question. Seeking an answer, Connie Kalitta puts his Cammer-powered dragster in Ford's wind tunnel. The red trails of smoke flowing over the slicks are the exhaust stream from the engine's zoomie headers being blown back at 140 miles per hour. This was not an easy picture to get. Photographer Bob D'Olivo spent several hours in the wind tunnel taking long-exposure shots, while Kalitta ran a super-rich fuel mixture to get the visible exhaust plumes. "Nitro fumes made each photo session short as Connie and Bob took numerous fresh air breaks to shut off the flowing tears," the magazine reports.

Inside, the editors run another photo of Kalitta in the wind tunnel and several shots of streamlined dragsters, including Craig Breedlove's *Spirit of America II*, Tony Nancy's *Wedge*, the Mooneyham-Ferguson-Jackson-Faust dragster, Tommy Ivo's *Video-liner*, and a pioneer in dragster streamlining, Robert "Jocko" Johnson's rear-engine car from 1956. Writer Terry Cook explains the theory behind streamlining and presents a history of aerodynamic efforts on the drag strip. The pro-con argument, in a nutshell, is laid out in a photo caption: "Cutting the air like a knife one minute, getting knocked about like a kite the next—unpredictable!"

Hot Rod had been following the development of Ford's overhead-cam Indy motor—and the rear-engine cars it was going in—since one appeared on the cover of the March 1964 issue. A. J. Foyt managed one more Indy 500 win for Offy-powered roadsters in 1964, but the tide was turning.

1965

Eric Rickman writes Offy's obit in this issue with the story of how Jim Clark's Lotus-Ford won the 1965 Indy 500: 17 of the 33 cars on the starting grid were Ford-powered, and Clark jumped into the lead early and "coasted home with a 5-mile margin."

At the end of his report, Rickman writes, "The boy to watch will be Mario Andretti. He is without a doubt the smoothest and fastest young rookie to hit the Indy scene in many a year."

Also in this issue, Rickman test-drives a "Mustang with Fangs," the Shelby GT350. "The Cobra venom has given Ford's sporty little workhorse considerably more authority, enough to call it a race car," he says. Rickman's test mule is a street version; the differences between it and what would be the competition-ready R-model are detailed in the story.

And though the gas crisis is still years away, Eric Dahlquist writes an in-depth story about a bright orange 1956 VW Beetle and the modifications done by EMPI to turn it into a righteous, 13-second Gasser. It's interesting that this piece, and not the articles on Ford's win at Indy, dragster streamlining, or any of the other, more traditional *Hot Rod* subjects in the magazine, is the issue's lead story.

This outtake from the Kalitta cover shoot shows how much the exhaust smoke and glowing headers were enhanced for publication.

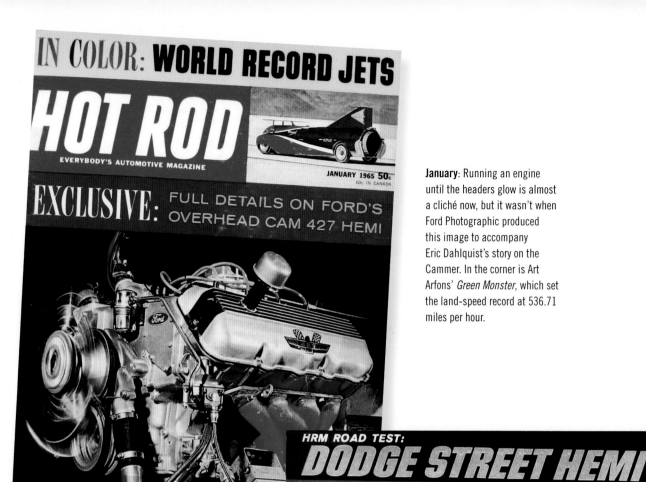

January: Running an engine until the headers glow is almost a cliché now, but it wasn't when Ford Photographic produced this image to accompany Eric Dahlquist's story on the Cammer. In the corner is Art Arfons' *Green Monster*, which set the land-speed record at 536.71 miles per hour.

December: A big issue for Dahlquist: He drives Chevy's *Mako Shark* concept car and predicts (hopes) it will see production, then goes crosstown to test one of the first Dodge Coronets equipped with a Street Hemi. He calls it "one of the fastest and most fantastic sedans ever."

1965

February: The Stellings and Hampshire dragster represents 200-mile-per-hour fuelers, though it's a tick under at 196.06.

March: Chevy PR produces the multiple-image cover of the new 396-inch big-block.

April: George Barris takes the Tom Daniel–designed *Surf Woody* to Waikiki Beach.

May: Fred Marasco's T roadster: "The finest car ever built," says Editor Bob Greene.

June: Bill Burke and his "slippery new Hemi" set their sights on 300 miles per hour.

July: Four Webers feed Mercury's "clean-breathin' hemi heads"; Don Nicholson's mill runs 9.8-second ETs.

September: John DeLorean wanted overhead cams for Pontiac, resulting in "Tempest's Tall Six."

October: GM Photographic shoots the 425-inch Super Rocket in Olds' front-wheel-drive Toronado.

November: The Haase-Smyser digger was Top Eliminator at the 1965 *Hot Rod* Magazine Championship Drags.

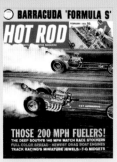

February

March

April

May

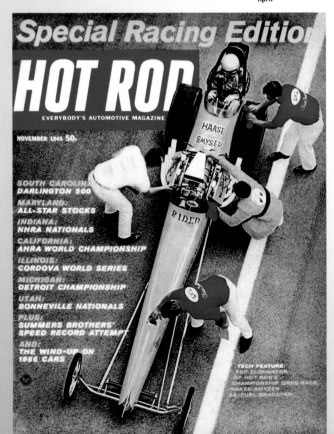

November

June

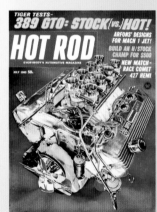

July

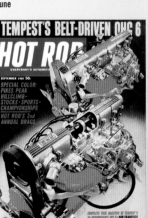

September

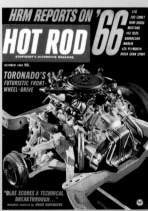

October

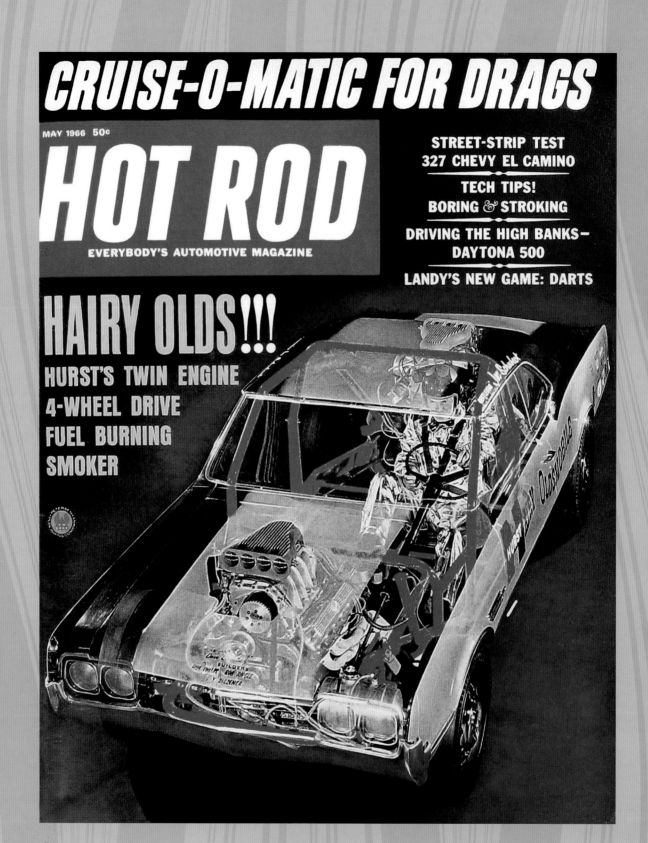

CRUISE-O-MATIC FOR DRAGS

MAY 1966 50¢

HOT ROD

EVERYBODY'S AUTOMOTIVE MAGAZINE

STREET-STRIP TEST
327 CHEVY EL CAMINO

TECH TIPS!
BORING & STROKING

DRIVING THE HIGH BANKS—
DAYTONA 500

LANDY'S NEW GAME: DARTS

HAIRY OLDS!!!
HURST'S TWIN ENGINE
4-WHEEL DRIVE
FUEL BURNING
SMOKER

May

1966

*I*n the days before digital photography and Photoshop, a see-through photo (or, as *Hot Rod* called it, a "phantom" shot) was a complex, painstaking, and time-intensive piece of work. Yet the editors felt that George Hurst's encore to the *Hemi Under Glass* was well worth putting Bob D'Olivo through the paces. "Almost Two Much" was the title of the story, and the four-wheel-drive *Hurst Hairy Oldsmobile* lived up to the billing.

At each end of the radically altered 4-4-2 is a blown and injected Toronado engine built with Mickey Thompson rods and pistons, Isky cams and valvetrain pieces, and Shiefer magnetos. Each engine is joined to its front-wheel-drive componentry and a Turbo Hydramatic transmission. Gentleman Joe Schubeck, the Olds' pilot, "is faced with a maze of gauges," the story says. "Two of each: tach, temp and oil pressure. And there are two shifters for Joe to control. Oh, yeah! Hurst shifters." The red tube frame that surrounds Schubeck doubles as a cooling system and is full of 33 quarts of water. The Cutlass body is lightened considerably with aluminum replacing the sheet metal in the floorpan, fender wells, deck lid, and bumpers. At each corner is a 9.50x15 M&H racing slick, all four of which generated a "smokescreen laid down by a thousand pounding horses," according to a photo caption showing the *Hairy Olds* leaving hard during its debut at the Bakersfield Fuel and Gas Meet.

Also in this issue is coverage of the 1966 Winternationals. It's a notable race for several reasons.

Much attention is paid to Don Prudhomme's new Top Fuel dragster and how it will stack up against his former, very successful ride, Roland Leong's *Hawaiian* (now driven by Mike Snively). As it turns out, Prudhomme goes out in the second round, while Snively and the *Hawaiian* win the Eliminator. In the Stock ranks, Shirley Shahan loses the Super Stock final on Saturday but goes on to win the Top Stock Eliminator on Sunday, becoming the first woman to win a major drag racing title. And NHRA is keeping close tabs on the new raft of "funny cars" showing up to race. Reports Feature Editor Dick Wells, these exhibition stockers are put into fuel dragster classes and so become "dragsters with fenders." Some criticize the NHRA for pitting sedans against rails; and in the class final on Saturday, Jack Christopher, driving a four-banger Tempest dragster, easily beats Jack Chrisman's 427 Comet. "Perhaps we'll soon see the fuel dragster classes broken into two divisions," Wells writes, "one for full-bodied cars, the other for dragsters. Whatever evolves, there's a great deal of interest in this 'new look,' and there is no doubt but what the sedan fuelers are here to stay."

Gentleman Joe Schubeck makes his tire-shredding debut in the *Hurst Hairy Oldsmobile* at the Smokers meet in Bakersfield, spring 1966.

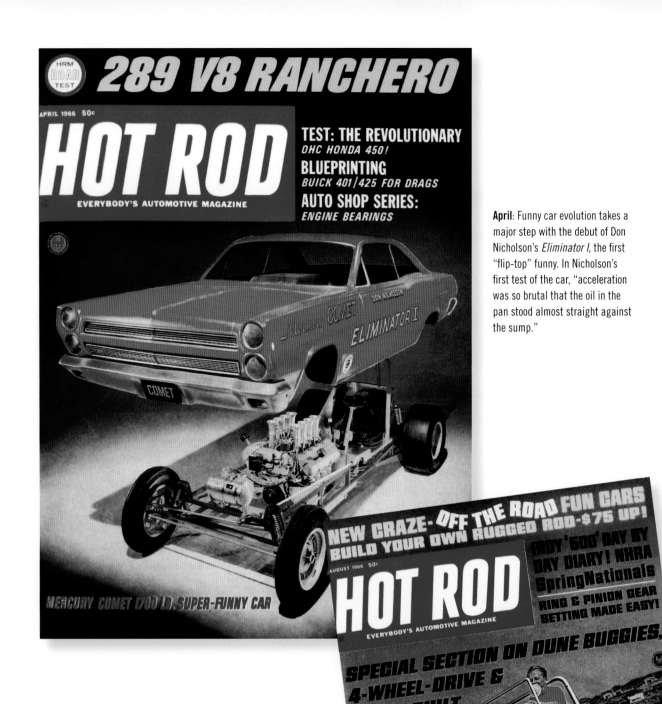

289 V8 RANCHERO

HRM ROAD TEST

APRIL 1966 50¢

HOT ROD

EVERYBODY'S AUTOMOTIVE MAGAZINE

TEST: THE REVOLUTIONARY
OHC HONDA 450!

BLUEPRINTING
BUICK 401/425 FOR DRAGS

AUTO SHOP SERIES:
ENGINE BEARINGS

MERCURY COMET 1700 LB. SUPER-FUNNY CAR

NEW CRAZE-OFF THE ROAD FUN CARS
BUILD YOUR OWN RUGGED ROD-$75 UP!

AUGUST 1966 50¢

HOT ROD
EVERYBODY'S AUTOMOTIVE MAGAZINE

INDY '500' DAY BY DAY DIARY! NHRA SpringNationals

RING & PINION GEAR SETTING MADE EASY!

SPECIAL SECTION ON DUNE BUGGIES, 4-WHEEL-DRIVE & HOME-BUILT CARS

April: Funny car evolution takes a major step with the debut of Don Nicholson's *Eliminator I*, the first "flip-top" funny. In Nicholson's first test of the car, "acceleration was so brutal that the oil in the pan stood almost straight against the sump."

August: Bruce Meyers catches air in his *Meyers Manx*—the quintessential dune buggy—to demonstrate "one of the thrills connected with 'off the road' vehicling." The "Terra Firma Funny Cars" featured inside include Jeeps, sand rails, and a Toyota Land Cruiser.

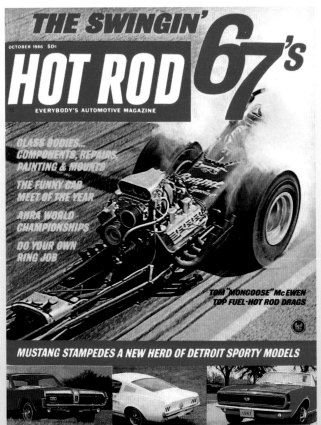

THE SWINGIN' 67's

HOT ROD
OCTOBER 1966 50¢
EVERYBODY'S AUTOMOTIVE MAGAZINE

GLASS BODIES...
COMPONENTS, REPAIRS,
PAINTING & MOUNTS

THE FUNNY CAR
MEET OF THE YEAR

AHRA WORLD
CHAMPIONSHIPS

DO YOUR OWN
RING JOB

TOM "MONGOOSE" McEWEN
TOP FUEL-HOT ROD DRAGS

MUSTANG STAMPEDES A NEW HERD OF DETROIT SPORTY MODELS

October

January

February

March

June

July

September

November

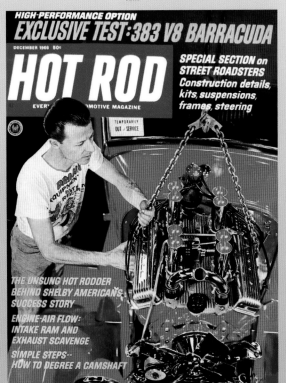

December

January: "Bonneville Giants" push up the speeds on the salt; Breedlove cracks the 600-mile-per-hour barrier.

February: Power mods for Mopar's 273 V-8; John Dallafior's 273-fired Barracuda is F/S champ.

March: Dale Drake builds a blown Offy to meet the Ford challenge at Indy.

June: George Bartell renders George Barris and some of his show-biz customs.

July: Eric Rickman catches Don Edmunds on the fly at Ascot for an oval track special.

September: Hot boats are a *Hot Rod* staple, but they didn't dominate the cover until now.

October: Hot Rod Drags' Top Fuel Eliminator Tom McEwen at work; the new pony cars debut.

November: Chevy's triple-carb 427 graces *Hot Rod*'s first fold-out cover; it makes 425 horsepower in a Corvette.

December: Dick Rundell lowers a 'Vette engine into a "modernistic 'old timer'" street roadster.

1966

INSIDE CHEVY'S SECRET ENGINES!

DECEMBER 1967 50¢   UK 3'6   Sweden KR. 3.95 Inkl. oms

HOT ROD
EVERYBODY'S AUTOMOTIVE MAGAZINE

NEW CLUTCH TRICKS
DON GARLITS REVISITED
LOW-BUDGET
CLEARANCE CHECKING
SHOP SERIES: IGNITIONS
THREAD RESTORATION

AMERICAN'S NEW YOUTH-CAR: 343-INCH JAVELIN

December

This cover shot would look familiar to *Hot Rod* readers in 1967. The same photo, but in black-and-white, had appeared in a profile of Zora Arkus-Duntov that Editor Jim McFarland wrote just a couple of months before in the September issue. *Hot Rod* uses the shot again on the December cover to illustrate McFarland's examination of some of the experimental engines in Chevy's skunkworks. In the story, called "Chevy's Moustache Curlers," Duntov explains that the engineering exercises "are a partial output of the Corvette engine group" and are "only a fraction of Chevrolet engineering efforts in this area."

The engines on the cover include a 16-plug overhead-valve V-8, a big-block with bolt-on hemi heads, and two single-overhead-cam hemis on experimental blocks. Much of the article inside concerns the development of a three-valve cylinder head intended as a bolt-on kit for a Corvette 283 block. "We felt the bolt-on approach was important because in that form it would become really a hot rodder's dream," Duntov tells McFarland, "and in serving the hot rodders' needs, attraction of their imagination to Chevrolet could not help but increase Chevrolet's appeal to the more youthful segment of the population." Youth market appeal is a common theme in Duntov's efforts; it was his "Thoughts Pertaining to Youth, Hot Rodders and Chevrolet" memo of 1953 that helped point Chevrolet toward the performance market and the younger buyers interested in hot cars.

McFarland's insider status with the top engineering minds of the day also puts him on the racetrack at Riverside when Smokey Yunick shows up with "the smoothest Camaro known to man." The Chevy proceeds to lap the track faster than Jerry Titus did to win the pole in the Mission Bell 250 Trans-Am race the year before. Typical for Smokey, all this is done on a day when Ford had reserved the track for its own test session. McFarland calls his story

"Is it or isn't it ... legal?"—always a good question when considering Smokey's race cars—and fills it with detail photos of the heavily massaged Camaro.

McFarland also spends some time with Don Garlits in the wake of his Top Fuel Eliminator win at the Nationals and his first sub-7-second ET. Garlits had said he wouldn't shave until he broke through the 7-second barrier, and the razor and soap came out on the track's starting line.

Also in this issue, Eric Dahlquist tests the all-new AMC Javelin SST. He has praise for the car's "jaunty lines" but finds the 343-inch, 280-horsepower V-8 lacking. It "isn't enough" when stacked up against the day's 327 Chevelles and Camaros. The coming 390 V-8 option should help, he reckons, and a station-wagon version "could be a sensation overnight if handled properly." Huh? There's no mention of the truly sporty AMX on the way.

"Chevy pries the lid off their experimental engine box and everybody gets a look" at overhead-cam-engineering studies.

TECH ANALYSIS OF THE 68's

OCTOBER 1967 50c

UK 3'6 Sweden KR 3.95

HOT ROD

EVERYBODY'S AUTOMOTIVE MAG

OVERDRIVES FOR 4-SPEEDS
DYNO-BUILDING A MoPar
VW TUNE-UP TIPS
Also: HOMEMADE ENGINE
MOUNTS, $9 TRACTION BARS

FULL DETAILS: THE RACE-STYLED '68 CORVETTE!

VW 1500 TEST: STOCK AND MODIFIED

JULY 1967 50c

HOT ROD

EVERYBODY'S AUTOMOTIVE MAGAZINE

HONDA CARBURETION
FOR MUSTANG 6

COMPLETE HEAD-
MILLING CHART

CHRYSLER MAGIC
FROM KEITH BLACK

FOLLOWING THE NASCAR TRAIL WITH A FACTORY TEAM
BY ERIC DAHLQUIST

TWIN PONTIAC V8 STREET ROADSTER

October: In December 1965, the editors put the Mako Shark on the cover and wondered if it was the 1967 Corvette. Nearly two years later, the Mako-influenced 1968 Corvette "sets the theme for the '68 super-cars" in a new-model-heavy issue.

July: Bob Reisner's *Invader* is as wild as they come, with two Pontiacs driving twin rear ends and futuristic aluminum bodywork stretched over a tube frame. "Bob built this car with two goals in mind: to win the National Roadster Show and to make the cover of *HRM*." Done and done.

1967

January

January: Dan Gurney hopes his new Weslake pushrod V-8 can win Indy. (It won't.)

February: Ford puts an Indy V-8 in a Mustang and goes hunting for 200 miles per hour.

March: Miss STP Paula Murphy sparks the question: Should women drive fuel cars?

April: Great (fake) wheelie shot of Jim Bishop's D/Gas 1955 Chevy.

May: Vince and Joe Granatelli and the STP turbine car they hope will "change Indy."

June: Mickey Thompson builds this three-valve, 565-horsepower Chevy for Indy.

August: Mike Snively drives Roland Leong's *Hawaiian* to Top Fuel Eliminator at the Hot Rod Drags.

September: Big John Mazmanian's chopped-top Austin fires an 8.92 salvo in the Gasser wars.

November: Gas Ronda's long-nose Mustang "is the livin' end in fueler funnies."

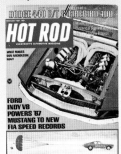

February

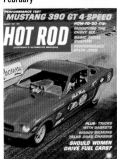

March

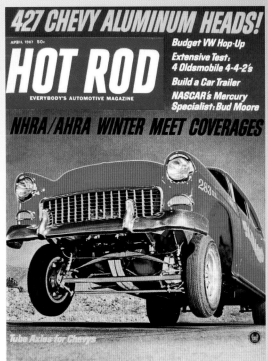

April

August

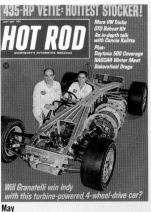

May

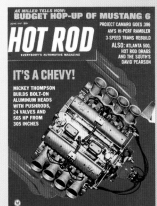

June

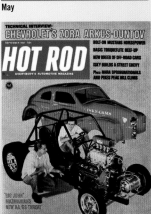

September

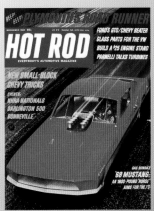

November

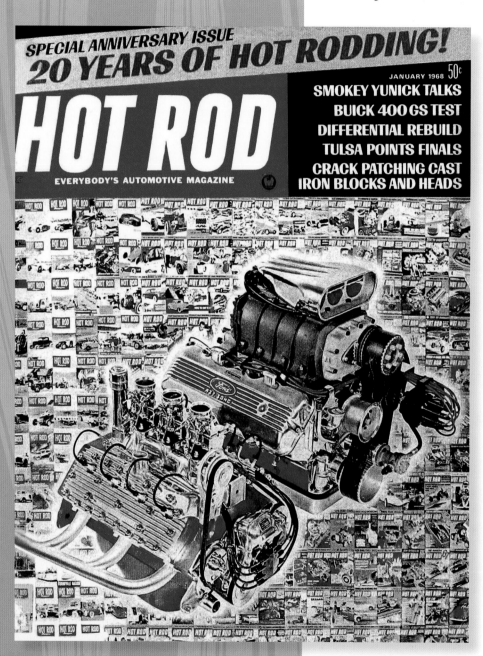

In celebration of the magazine's 20th anniversary, *Hot Rod*'s designers produce an eye-grabbing cover that imposes hot Ford engines old and new—a full-race flathead V-8 and a blown 427 Cammer—over every one of the magazine's 240 covers. Floating the engines over the magazines is done with graphic arts sleight of hand, but the collection of covers is shot the old-fashioned way. All 240 covers are laid out in the driveway of the new Petersen building at 8490 Sunset Boulevard, and Bob D'Olivo shoots them from the edge of the seventh floor. Then Bob Petersen steps in, kneels down, and looks up at D'Olivo as a sprinkle of rain starts to fall. D'Olivo gets his shot, and the magazines are hastily picked up before the rain begins in earnest.

The shot of Petersen and the magazines is used inside the issue as part of a 12-page anniversary scrapbook, compiled by Editor Jim McFarland, that is as much a history of hot rodding itself as it is the story of the magazine. A page away from the contemporary photo of Petersen is the iconic shot of him in the late 1940s working his camera at the dry lakes and another of him and then partner Bob Lindsay signing up new *Hot Rod* subscribers at a car show in 1950. Alongside those photos of the magazine's earliest days are images of hot rodding's genesis: pre-war land-speed racers, an early twin-engine dragster, the first meet at Bonneville, and speed-part pioneers Ed Iskenderian and Vic Edelbrock Sr. A handful of "old-timer" features throughout the magazine reprise favorite cars of the past, while the latest drag strip trend is represented by a story on Dick Landy's stock-bodied Hemi Charger and 440 Coronet R/T.

January

There are several other landmark stories in the issue as well. Tacked on to the end of Eric Dahlquist's road test of Buick's new 1968 GS 400 is a sidebar called "Buick's Staging Chart," which outlines the factory equipment available to build Buick's potent Stage 1 and Stage 2 performance engine packages. A few pages later, McFarland tells the tale of how Smokey Yunick crashed a Ford-sponsored testing session at Riverside International Raceway to do a few hot laps with his "Can-Am Camaro," an incredibly slippery Chevy pony car that he later took to Bonneville and "broke dozens of existing speed records."

This issue also includes coverage of the Mexican 1000 Rally, the very first Baja 1000 off-road race. Vic Wilson

1968

and Ted Mangles won the endurance contest in a Meyers Manx dune buggy. Among those who raced with them were Bill Stroppe in a Holman & Moody/Stroppe–prepped Bronco; Rod Hall, who has raced in every Baja 1000 since; and Malcolm Smith, who co-rode a 360cc Husqvarna to win the motorcycle class with J. N. Roberts.

Robert E. Petersen kneels on 20 years of magazines laid out on the driveway at 8490 Sunset Boulevard. Rain begins to fall minutes after the photo is taken.

HOT ROD 20th ANNIVERSARY

HOT ROD SCRAPBOOK
1948–1968

by Jim McFarland

It's 1948. It's also a steamy Sunday afternoon in Southern California, and in the distance, the moan of a flathead Ford is soaked up in the wastes of a dusty, cracked dry lake bed. Exhaust notes reach the ears of several dozen young men who stand and sit at a point soon to be passed by the fenderless '32 "high-boy." Scattered randomly near the group and farther on down the "course" where the now-nearing roadster began are a hundred or more similar expressions of mechanical experimentation. People were calling them "hot rods." They were also calling them unnecessary. Just before the lakes car whisks past, one of the young men in the group turns, pulls a camera to his face and permanently records the appearance of future automotive history as it strains by, leading a cloud of El Mirage dry lake dust. Letters on the back of the young man's shirt spell out his

R. E. Petersen, President, Petersen Publishing Company

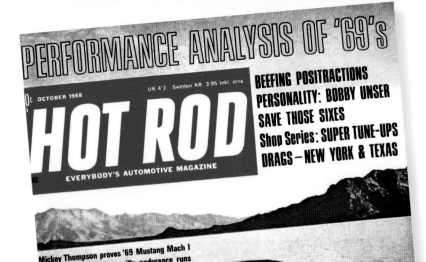

PERFORMANCE ANALYSIS OF '69's

UK 4'3 Sweden KR. 3.95 Inkl. oms

0c OCTOBER 1968

HOT ROD

EVERYBODY'S AUTOMOTIVE MAGAZINE

BEEFING POSITRACTIONS
PERSONALITY: BOBBY UNSER
SAVE THOSE SIXES
Shop Series: SUPER TUNE-UPS
DRAGS – NEW YORK & TEXAS

Mickey Thompson proves '69 Mustang Mach I performance with Bonneville endurance runs

October: There is so much in this issue—including a preview of the 1969 models from GM, Ford, Chrysler, and AMC—that the cover story is buried on page 92. Publisher Ray Brock writes about joining Mickey Thompson's team of 1969 Mustangs to go after endurance speed records at Bonneville.

December: Chevy's all-new, all-aluminum 427 V-8, the ZL1, receives a thorough dissection by McFarland. "Chevrolet wouldn't permit us to divulge exact power levels," he writes, "but 625 from a single 4-bbl gasoline 'consumer' is probably more than you'll see sprouting out of your neighbor's Rider-Mower."

A 625-HP LOOK AT:
CHEVY'S ALL-ALUMINUM 427

50c DECEMBER 1968

HOT ROD

EVERYBODY'S AUTOMOTIVE MAGAZINE

TEST: 4-SPEED "CUDA 340"
DICK SMOTHERS ON RACING
VW CHASSIS SNUBBER
$10 SOLVENT TANK
FORD 4-BBL REBUILD STEPS
THE INSTANT 'MINI-T'

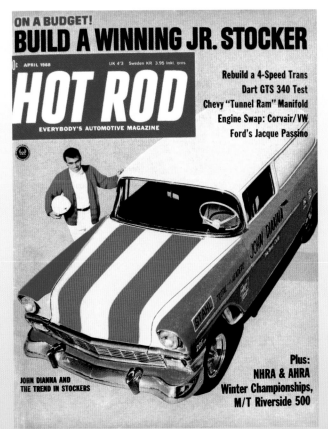

ON A BUDGET!
BUILD A WINNING JR. STOCKER

HOT ROD
EVERYBODY'S AUTOMOTIVE MAGAZINE

APRIL 1968

Rebuild a 4-Speed Trans
Dart GTS 340 Test
Chevy "Tunnel Ram" Manifold
Engine Swap: Corvair/VW
Ford's Jacque Passino

JOHN DIANNA AND
THE TREND IN STOCKERS

Plus:
NHRA & AHRA
Winter Championships,
M/T Riverside 500

April

A RAM-AIR PAIR OF 400 INCHERS!

HOT ROD

MoPar CLINIC TEAM OF SOX & MARTIN GEARS FOR '68

February

EXCLUSIVE:
PONTIAC'S OVERHEAD CAM V8's

HOT ROD

Mustang 428 Cobra-Jet
500 HP From 302 Chevy
How to CC Cylinder Heads
New Slant In Headers

March

LOTUS TURBINES FOR INDY 500

HOT ROD

May

CARB-RATING FORD'S 289/302

HOT ROD

July

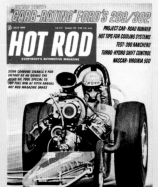

ART ARFONS' SUPERSONIC JET CAR

HOT ROD

DIRT TRACK RACING—MIDWESTERN STYLE

August

600-PLUS FROM CHEVY'S 427

HOT ROD

DON NICHOLSON'S COUGAR AIMS FOR LOW 7s

September

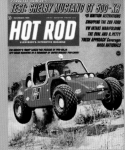

TEST: SHELBY MUSTANG GT 500-KR

HOT ROD

November

EXCLUSIVE:
FORD'S EXOTIC NEW V8's

HOT ROD
EVERYBODY'S AUTOMOTIVE MAGAZINE

JUNE 1968

VW CAMS AND HEADERS
INTERVIEW: DAVE ZEUSCHEL
$15 QUADRAJET HOP-UP
HOT ROD MAGAZINE DRAGS
PROJECT CAR: OLDS F-85

June

February: Ronnie Sox's launch leads to a story about Sox & Martin's Mopar Performance Clinics.

March: Engineer Malcolm McKellar and overhead-cam engines from "Pontiac's secret teepee."

April: John Dianna—prior to joining the mag—and his 1956 Sedan Delivery Jr. Stocker.

May: Andy Granatelli's STP car is among the turbines being readied for the Indy 500.

June: It's Ford's turn to reveal experimental engines, including a precursor to the Boss 429.

July: Steve Carbone, Top Fuel winner at the 1968 Hot Rod Drags, flashes V for victory.

August: "Wild and wooly" Super Modified dirt-track action in the Midwest.

September: "Dyno" Don Nicholson unveils his SOHC-powered 1968 Cougar funny car.

November: Vic Hickey's *Baja Boot* introduces a preview of the upcoming Mexican 1000.

1968

FIRST OF THE 1970 MUSCLE CARS

HOT ROD

EVERYBODY'S AUTOMOTIVE MAGAZINE

SEPTEMBER 1969 50¢ UK 4/3 Sweden KR. 3.95 Inkl. moms

"JR. STOCKING" 283 CHEVYS

BRAND-NEW 90-HP 1700 VW MILL

CARTER CARB POWER MODS

BORG-WARNER AUTOMATIC O.D.

ALL-OUT 340 MOPARS-Part II

FORD TORINO

PLYMOUTH 'CUDA

HOT 70s

DODGE CHALLENGER

MONTEGO SPOILER

September

1969

The 1970 model year would be the pinnacle for muscle car performance, and *Hot Rod* devotes the cover of its traditional new-car issue to four of the newest models. Two are Chrysler E-Bodies—the Challenger and 'Cuda—while the other two are full-sizes from FoMoCo—the Torino and Mercury Montego Cyclone.

Feature Editor Steve Kelly is complimentary about the styling of the new Mopars. "Total design of the new car is extremely smooth," he writes about the 'Cuda, "and there's virtually no controversial line or shape either on or in the car. It's just a good looking car, without qualification." The longer Challenger, he notes, lines up "in marketplace competition closer to the Cougar." Both cars are good handlers, he finds, though neither is a lightweight. He calls engine choices "diverse" and points out, "A 440 six-barrel 'Cuda feels better in stock form than the Hemi-engined coupe, which is to be expected."

The Torino moves up to the full-size class for 1970 and boasts totally changed sheet metal. "The slippery looking front-end and increased windshield angle will please the stock-car builders," he writes, noting that the "availability of the 429-cubic-inch engine in several performance models adds credibility to stock car racing with this powerplant. The true NASCAR-type hemispherical chamber engine is offered in limited quantity, with full emissions-control devices attached, for showroom customers."

The Torino's Mercury cousin, the Cyclone, doesn't have a fastback body style in 1970, "which may nullify the cars'

use in Grand National racing. We wouldn't bet on that right now," he adds. "The NASCAR-born 429 HO engine is very much alive in the Cyclone option list."

Demonstrating just how diverse *Hot Rod* is in these years, a page away from the four muscle cars is a story on Volkswagen's all-new 90-horsepower 411 engine. EMPI and other VW parts companies are developing speed equipment for the new flat-four, and Technical Editor John Thawley writes, "With adequate development time and some hop-up parts, a shaft horsepower of 165 doesn't sound out of place. Look for this one to 'grow' from the factory, since this will be the basic powerplant used in the mid-engine Porsche which is 'in the works.'"

Returning to more traditional ground, Thawley writes a profile of the "Old Master," Ed Pink. He's "an engine builder's engine builder. He asks no quarter and gives none in one of the most competitive aspects of the motoring sport."

Speaking of traditional ground, Publisher Ray Brock makes another trek to Pikes Peak to watch Mario Andretti win the Championship Division wheeling Al Unser's Chevy-powered USAC roadster. (Al is sidelined with a broken leg.) Bobby Unser wins the Stock Division in a 1969 Torino running a Boss 429 prepped by Smokey Yunick.

Dodge Challenger R/T convertible now: highly prized collectible. Same car then: fun to brodie in the dirt.

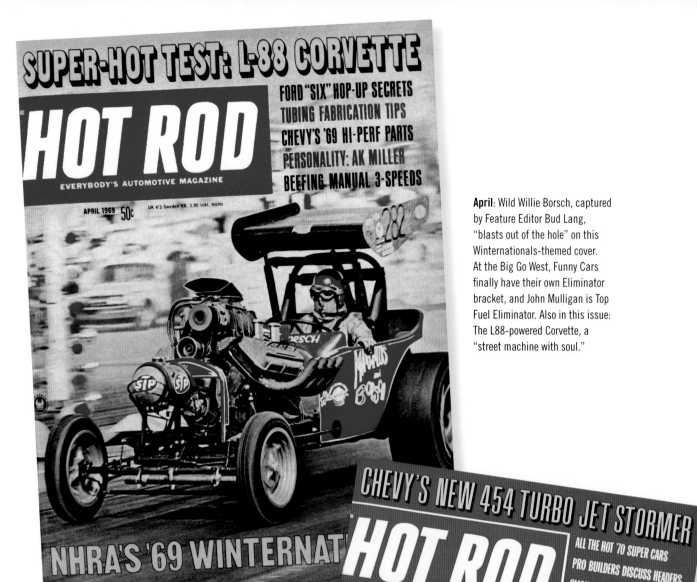

April: Wild Willie Borsch, captured by Feature Editor Bud Lang, "blasts out of the hole" on this Winternationals-themed cover. At the Big Go West, Funny Cars finally have their own Eliminator bracket, and John Mulligan is Top Fuel Eliminator. Also in this issue: The L88-powered Corvette, a "street machine with soul."

October: Another 1970 icon, Chevy's 454-inch "super Rat," gets an in-depth look by Steve Kelly. Peering into his crystal ball, Kelly writes, "This surely isn't the end of progress for the 454; it's fairly certain the Chevrolet Engineering Center is playing with digging out buried horsepower in this design." LS6, anyone?

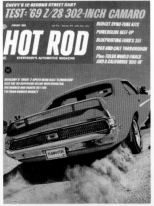

CHEVY'S 12-SECOND STREET GARY

TEST: '69 Z/28 302-INCH CAMARO

HOT ROD
EVERYBODY'S AUTOMOTIVE MAGAZINE

BUDGET DYNO-TUNE KITS
POWERGLIDE BEEF-UP
BLUEPRINTING FORD'S 351
1969 AND CALE YARBOROUGH

Plus—TULSA WORLD FINALS
AND A CALIFORNIA "BOG-IN"

January

CHRYSLER '69 HEMI CHARGER...
...PERFORMANCE WRING-OUT!

HOT ROD
EVERYBODY'S AUTOMOTIVE MAGAZINE

LOW-BUDGET 396 CHEVY TRICKS
MODIFYING FORD'S C-6 AUTOMATIC
JR. STOCK TIPS

Plus:
MEXICAN "GET DIRTY" 1000, REX MAYS 300, DIAL INDICATOR HOW-TO's, AND A TALK WITH RONNIE "SOX IT TO 'EM"

Exclusive Coverage: HUBERT PLATT'S '69 "Canted Valve" 429 MUSTANG Ford's answer to the Hemi MoPar Barracuda

February

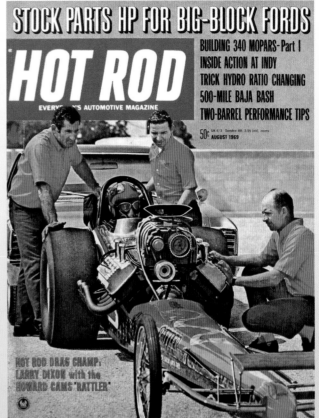

STOCK PARTS HP FOR BIG-BLOCK FORDS

HOT ROD
EVERYBODY'S AUTOMOTIVE MAGAZINE

BUILDING 340 MOPARS- Part I
INSIDE ACTION AT INDY
TRICK HYDRO RATIO CHANGING
500-MILE BAJA BASH
TWO-BARREL PERFORMANCE TIPS

50¢ UK 4/3 Sondea KR. 3.95 incl. oms AUGUST 1969

HOT ROD DRAG CHAMP: LARRY DIXON with the HOWARD CAMS "RATTLER"

August

FOR STREET OR OFF-ROAD:
VALUABLE BUGGY BUILDING TIPS

HOT ROD
EVERYBODY'S AUTOMOTIVE MAGAZINE

STRICKLER'S CHEVY TRICKS
ADJUSTABLE SHOCKS FOR DRAGS
Revolutionary Carburetor: CARTER'S NEW THERMO-QUAD
BIG VALVES FOR 351 FORDS
Interview: THE CONTROVERSIAL ANDY GRANATELLI

March

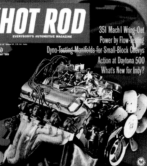

PONTIAC'S NEW TUNNEL PORT 400

HOT ROD
EVERYBODY'S AUTOMOTIVE MAGAZINE

351 Mach I Wring-Out
Power by Flow-Testing
Dyno-Testing Manifolds for Small-Block Chevys
Action at Daytona 500
What's New for Indy?

May

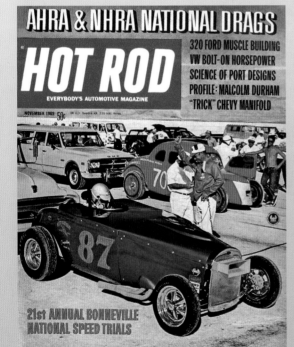

AHRA & NHRA NATIONAL DRAGS

HOT ROD
EVERYBODY'S AUTOMOTIVE MAGAZINE

NOVEMBER 1969 50¢

320 FORD MUSCLE BUILDING
VW BOLT-ON HORSEPOWER
SCIENCE OF PORT DESIGNS
PROFILE: MALCOLM DURHAM
"TRICK" CHEVY MANIFOLD

21st ANNUAL BONNEVILLE NATIONAL SPEED TRIALS

November

FORD'S BOSS 429's & KALITTA

HOT ROD

June

OLDS ALUMINUM CAN-AM 455

HOT ROD

July

NEW HOT PONY CAR:
DODGE CHALLENGER 440 TEST

HOT ROD

December

January: Cougar Eliminator peels out; does the *Z* in Z/28 stand for *Zora*?

February: Before it was "Boss," this was Ford's "twisted hemi," or "canted valve," engine.

March: *Hot Rod* stays abreast of the growing dune buggy craze.

May: Pontiac's new tunnel-port 400 V-8 is slated for the upcoming GTO Judge.

June: Now the 429 is Boss and in Connie Kalitta's rail and funny car.

July: Experimental Oldsmobile engines in the issue include this twin-turbo 455-inch Can-Am mill.

August: Howard Cams Rattler earns Top Fuel Eliminator at the Hot Rod Drags and a magazine cover.

November: "The Salt was Fine in '69," and records fell "like autumn leaves."

December: Bob Spar (in the window) and Don Spar demonstrate B&M's automatic transmission dyno.

1969

Chapter 4

1970–1979

The decade sure started out well. Muscle car performance was hotter than ever, Don Garlits revolutionized dragster design, and Don "The Snake" Prudhomme and Tom "The Mongoose" McEwen opened the door to big-time marketing dollars with their Mattel, Coca Cola, and Plymouth promotional deal.

But then ... stuff happened.

Emissions laws, insurance costs, and the decade's oil crises brought an end to Detroit's horsepower wars. Drag racing and other motorsports continued to be quicker and faster, but everyone felt the gas-crunch pinch.

So what's a high-performance magazine to do? Write about vans, apparently. The wheeled boxes first appeared on the cover in 1972 and showed up at least twice a year from 1974 through 1976. Why vans? The magazine's staff—and Detroit, no doubt—were looking for the next big thing to fill the muscle car vacuum. Vans offered a one-two punch as a new breed of custom vehicles built by companies eager to advertise them.

But vans were just some of the general nuttiness at *Hot Rod* during the disco years. Editor Terry Cook talked Pro Stock racing legend Bill "Grumpy" Jenkins into posing in his underwear on a bearskin rug. Staff members dressed up like German World War I pilots for an April Fool's test of the Goodyear blimp. And in what is sure to be the magazine's low point in graphic design, the October 1976 issue featured two modified Volkswagens (well, more like one and a half due to poor cropping) parked on giant Lifesavers candies.

This ugliness, though, doesn't represent the full picture of hot rodding and *Hot Rod* during the 1970s. Check out

the grin on Garlits' face as he flashes the V for victory with his rear-engine dragster in 1971. He has completely changed the way Top Fuel dragsters are built—then and to this day—and he already has the winning time slips to prove it. Want to banish the thought of da Grump naked? Gaze instead at Pam Hardy circa 1973 in hot pants and boots. Remember how hot funny cars got in the 1970s and how Jungle Jim Liberman could bring grandstands of people to their feet whenever he hit the track.

Sure, the 1970s editors did more van and V-6 tech than they probably wanted to. But those stories were a small part of the magazine compared to what was really important, like the growing street machine movement, for instance, or

Sure, the 1970s editors did more van and V-6 tech than they probably wanted to.

the comeback traditional hot rods were enjoying as street rods. Those cars were a product of their time, with blown motors sticking through the hood, wild paint jobs and jacked-up attitudes that looked a lot better then than they do now. But see through the tackiness and there's a vibrant performance market that wouldn't be beaten by OPEC, the Air Resources Board, or insurance companies. *Hot Rod*'s vital signs were strong, too, with thick editorial packages and growing sales numbers. See that look on Garlits' face? That's the 1970s to remember. Not the damn vans.

The flared and spoilered bodies of 1970s IMSA race cars would influence street car styling through much of the decade.

Don Garlits changes the face of Top Fuel drag racing with his rear-engine *Swamp Rat*.

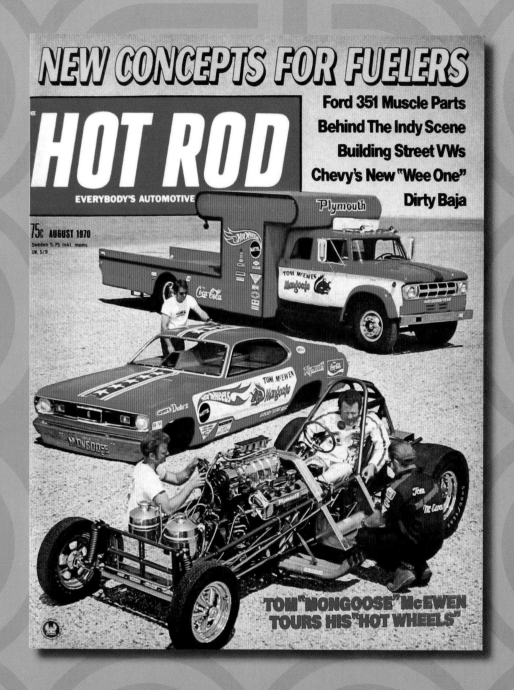

NEW CONCEPTS FOR FUELERS

Ford 351 Muscle Parts
Behind The Indy Scene
Building Street VWs
Chevy's New "Wee One"
Dirty Baja

HOT ROD
EVERYBODY'S AUTOMOTIVE

75¢ AUGUST 1970
Sweden 5.75 inkl. moms
UK 5/9

TOM "MONGOOSE" McEWEN
TOURS HIS "HOT WHEELS"

August

Tom McEwen has been a fierce competitor in drag racing for years and earned the nickname "Mongoose" for his quick reaction times. But a Mattel/Coca Cola/Plymouth sponsorship for a series of Snake/Mongoose national match races against Don Prudhomme really thrust him into the limelight. Well, that and about a zillion Hot Wheels cars getting pushed around the floors of homes all over America by kids dreaming of racing the real thing.

Eric Rickman's cover shot of McEwen's road-tour rig shows "just part of the equipment necessary to successfully tour a Funny Car on today's drag circuits." John Thawley's profile inside is of a thoughtful racer involved with tire development and concerned about driver safety. He credits "these smokeless tires" for making current dragsters easier to drive. "Of course the tires are not everything when it comes to control, but they help. My first digger was a 92-inch-wheelbase car. I never knew what it was like to drive a car straight down the quarter-mile. It was always cocked and changing positions. So as the cars got longer, they got safer."

McEwen's not convinced, though, that a mid-engine car would be safer. "They do have a lot going for them. In case of a fire, an explosion or an oil bath, you're looking pretty good with the motor in back of you. If you stuff it into the fence, then you've got the motor coming toward you. I don't like that."

He is, however, a big fan of the new onboard fire-suppression systems. McEwen admits that, after John Mulligan's fatal clutch explosion at Indy the previous year, he was scared to get back in a race car. "Now there is no reason for that type of accident to ever happen again. In the several months [fire bottles] have been out and in use, not one racer has even had a part of his fire suit turned brown with flames. Prudhomme had a fire in his Funny Car a couple of weeks ago. He triggered the fire bottle and he wasn't touched. Unbelievable!"

1970

The mid-engine cars McEwen refers to are a major topic in a story called "New Concepts for Fuelers," in which Don Prudhomme, Keith Black, Jack Chrisman, and other drag racing experts discuss "what more can be done to improve on something [AA/Fuel Dragsters] seemingly at its peak of development?" Aerodynamics, horsepower, tires, suspension, and engine placement are all on the table.

The breadth of *Hot Rod*'s reach—it is "Everybody's Automotive Magazine"—is demonstrated by racing coverage of two polar opposite 500s: Indy and Baja. Al Unser wins Indy leading 191 of the 200 laps in his *Johnny Lightning Special*; Parnelli Jones and Bill Stroppe cover 557 miles of Mexican desert in PJ's Stroppe-prepped Bronco in just under 12 hours.

With great backing and a brand-new Funny rig, Tom McEwen is more than ready to take on the rest of the country

MONGOOSE'S NEW "TOY"

"Happy as a kid with a new toy" is a very fitting description of Tom McEwen. Although his AA/FC is no toy, it's still apropos, because one of Tom's major sponsors is Mattel, Inc., and they're producing a new "Hot Wheels" race set featuring the funny car team of McEwen and Prudhomme. Tom and Don, better known as "Mongoose" and "Snake," are touring the country this summer with a pair of funnies (plus Tom's AA/FD just in case things get dull). Tom's "Wynn's Duster II" is a Fiberglass Trends replica of a '70 Plymouth Duster. With Wynn's sponsorship, the car uses every additive the Wynn Oil Company makes. If things get too hot, the third sponsor, Coca-Cola, provides the pause that refreshes. The 118-inch-long tube chassis was built by Ron Scrima of Exhibition Engineering. Ron hung the super-clean chassis on coil-over shocks all around. The aluminum paneling is the handiwork of Tom Hanna. Cerny's Custom Paint artfully covered the bod, then let Kelly do his

owner: Tom McEwen
Long Beach, California
car: '70 Duster AA/FC

mural and striping thing. The powerplant is a Plymouth hemi 426 assembled by John Hogan of Ramchargers Racing Engines. John used M/T pistons and rods, Federal-Mogul bearings and a Milodon oil system to help them live. A Hilborn fuel injector feeds a nitro/alky mix to the Engle-cammed engine. Cragar provided the blower manifold and drive system, as well as ignition, headers and wheels. The fuel and water tanks are by Moon Equipment Co. B&M modified the stock two-speed automatic TorqueFlite tranny to handle all the horses. The Plymouth rear end is equipped with Hurst/Airheart discs and Goodyear slicks. The latter get things going, while the former, aided by a Simpson chute, bring things to a screeching halt after those 200-plus-mph runs. When Tom makes a burnout with this car, the smoke cloud is unreal. In fact, if the competition is downwind, they've had it. Tom's best to date has been a scorching 7.21 e.t. in a match run against Don Prudhomme.

photography: Eric Rickman

Tom McEwen's new AA/FC Duster is no toy, but the title is apropos given his sponsorship with Mattel.

EXCLUSIVE FIRST REPORT:

JENKINS' NEW PRO CAMARO...

Clutch Blueprinting
MoPar Tuning Tips
Profile: Gas Ronda
VW Big-Bore Kits

HOT ROD

EVERYBODY'S AUTOMOTIVE MAGAZINE

75c JULY 1970

UK 5/9 Sweden 5:75 inkl. moms

GRUMPY'S TOY

July: Bill Jenkins' eighth *Grumpy's Toy*, a 1970-1/2 Camaro, pulls the wheels for Bud Lang's camera. Elsewhere in the issue is coverage of the *Super Stock* Nationals, where Plymouth sweeps all three Eliminators, and the season opener for the 1970 Trans-Am season at Laguna Seca, where Parnelli's Mustang dominates.

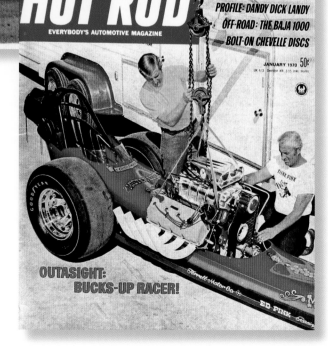

STREET/STRIP TEST:

HOT 1970 BOSS 302 MUSTANG

NHRA WORLD POINTS FINALS
DYNO-BUILDING THE VW
PROFILE: DANDY DICK LANDY
OFF-ROAD: THE BAJA 1000
BOLT-ON CHEVELLE DISCS

HOT ROD

EVERYBODY'S AUTOMOTIVE MAGAZINE

JANUARY 1970 50c
UK 4/3 Sweden XR. 3.05 inkl. moms

OUTASIGHT:
BUCKS-UP RACER!

January: Don Long and Ed Pink build a "Bucks-Up Racer" for Texan Ray Luckey. "About $35,000 will put you in this rig with a spare engine and super-deluxe trailer thrown in." Testing the Boss 302 Mustang, Steve Kelly writes, "Ford's Boss 302 is a real-life supercar in every sense."

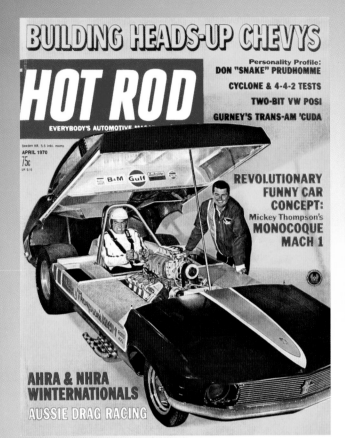

BUILDING HEADS-UP CHEVYS

HOT ROD
EVERYBODY'S AUTOMOTIVE MAGAZINE

Sweden KR. 5.5 inkl. moms
APRIL 1970
75c
UK 6/6

Personality Profile:
DON "SNAKE" PRUDHOMME

CYCLONE & 4-4-2 TESTS

TWO-BIT VW POSI

GURNEY'S TRANS-AM 'CUDA

REVOLUTIONARY
FUNNY CAR
CONCEPT:
Mickey Thompson's
MONOCOQUE
MACH 1

AHRA & NHRA
WINTERNATIONALS
AUSSIE DRAG RACING

April

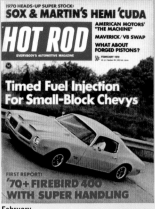

1970 HEADS-UP SUPER STOCK:
SOX & MARTIN'S HEMI 'CUDA

HOT ROD
EVERYBODY'S AUTOMOTIVE MAGAZINE

AMERICAN MOTORS'
"THE MACHINE"
MAVERICK/V8 SWAP
WHAT ABOUT
FORGED PISTONS?

**Timed Fuel Injection
For Small-Block Chevys**

FIRST REPORT!
'70+ FIREBIRD 400
WITH SUPER HANDLING

February

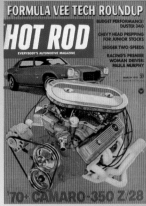

FORMULA VEE TECH ROUNDUP

HOT ROD
EVERYBODY'S AUTOMOTIVE MAGAZINE

BUDGET PERFORMANCE
DUSTER 340
CHEVY HEAD PREPPING
FOR JUNIOR STOCKS
DIGGER TWO-SPEEDS
RACING'S PREMIER
WOMAN DRIVER:
PAULA MURPHY

70+ CAMARO-350 Z/28

March

HOW TO-
572 HP FROM 327 CHEVY

HOT ROD
EVERYBODY'S AUTOMOTIVE MAGAZINE

"WILD WILLIE" BORSCH
DICK LANDY'S PRO-STOCK
1970 DODGE CHALLENGER
WHAT'S NEW FOR INDY?
RACING INJECTION
SYSTEM FOR VWs

EXCLUSIVE: Buick's
Experimental V8s

May

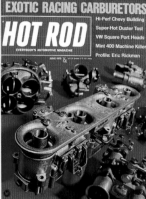

EXOTIC RACING CARBURETORS

HOT ROD
EVERYBODY'S AUTOMOTIVE MAGAZINE

Hi-Perf Chevy Building
Super-Hot Duster Test
VW Square Port Heads
Mint 400 Machine Killer
Profile: Eric Rickman

June

February: The 70-plus Firebird "is now what it should have been from the beginning."

March: Debuts of both the new Camaro and its 370-horsepower, 350-inch Z28 engine.

April: Borrowing ideas from F1 and Indy, Mickey Thompson builds a monocoque funny car.

May: Buick Chief Engineer Phil Bowser among "engineering exercises"; his hand's on a DOHC hemi.

June: The inline four-barrel Autolite is among the radical carburetors profiled.

September: Not a fad, dune buggies are the street roadsters for the 1970s.

October: An experimental Pontiac 427 with alloy block, hemi heads, port injection, and overhead cams.

November: Art Malone plants a Hemi—sideways—between his rail's slicks.

December: Bruce Crower pulls 720 horsepower from 203 inches of turbocharged Chevy.

ROADSTERS FOR THE '70s

HOT ROD

BUGGIES
New Generation
of Street
Roadsters

5-SPEED DRAG TRANS
HOW TO WIRE A CAR
E-J POTTER
HAVE CHEVY BIKE,
WILL TRAVEL!
INSIDE AN INDY FORD
USAC DOUBLEHEADER
CHAMPIONSHIPS & STOCKS

September

'71 CARS: WILL THEY PERFORM?

HOT ROD
EVERYBODY'S AUTOMOTIVE MAGAZINE

FRONT END SET-UP TIPS
WILD BILL SHREWSBERRY
VW TURBOCHARGING
SPRINGING FOR MORE RPM

PONTIAC'S
EXPERIMENTAL
ENGINE OF
THE FUTURE

October

COMPLETE MANUFACTURER INDEX
SPEED EQUIPMENT LISTING

HOT ROD

EXPERIMENTAL
203-INCH,
TURBOCHARGED,
PUSHROD
CHEVY-
720 HP

First Report
1971 HIGH
PERF. CHANGES
SOUTHERN-STYLE
MATCH RACING
WITH SOX & MARTIN
AMC 390 VS HORNET
BLOWER KIT FOR VEGA
PERSONALITY:
TENNESSEE BO-WEEVIL
NEW CARBURETOR FOR VW

December

CHEVY VEGA MUSCLE PARTS

HOT ROD
EVERYBODY'S AUTOMOTIVE MAGAZINE

Pro Stock Challenger
Blueprint: VW Cases
Racing Powerglides
Profile: Allison Bros.

75c NOVEMBER 1970
UK 5/9 Sweden 5.75 inkl. moms

EXCLUSIVE: ART MALONE'S
REVOLUTIONARY
SIDEWINDER

BONNEVILLE & NATIONAL DRAGS

November

1970

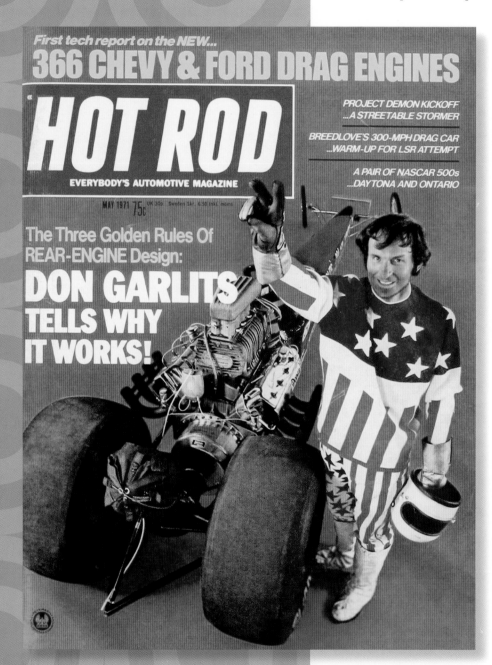

First tech report on the NEW...
366 CHEVY & FORD DRAG ENGINES

'HOT ROD
EVERYBODY'S AUTOMOTIVE MAGAZINE

PROJECT DEMON KICKOFF
...A STREETABLE STORMER

BREEDLOVE'S 300-MPH DRAG CAR
...WARM-UP FOR LSR ATTEMPT

A PAIR OF NASCAR 500s
...DAYTONA AND ONTARIO

MAY 1971 75¢ UK 30p Sweden 5kr, 6.50 inkl. moms

The Three Golden Rules Of
REAR-ENGINE Design:

DON GARLITS TELLS WHY IT WORKS!

May

Why is this man smiling? He has seen the future of Top Fuel drag racing, and the view is free of nitro fumes, tire smoke, and clutch dust.

A year before, the transmission in Big Daddy Don Garlits' *Swamp Rat XIII* exploded at the AHRA Winternationals, cutting the dragster—and Garlits' right foot—in half. While recuperating, Garlits "immersed himself in reading automotive theory," according to Ralph Guidahl Jr.'s cover story. He read about early experiments in rear-engine dragsters and, inspired, sketched a totally new *Swamp Rat*, placing his cockpit in front of the 1,500-horsepower Hemi.

Once back in Florida, Garlits and his crew used the sketches to build a tube-frame test mule that was completed "not quite three weeks from the pipe comin' down off the ceiling," says Connie Swingle, Garlits' engineering chief. Early test drives "read like a classic chapter out of Dr. Jekyll and Mr. Hyde's rear-engine-car book," Guidahl writes. "Things were looking fine up to an eighth-mile. Then the front end started carrying, the car began to dart, and the heavy tail section oscillated like a pendulum in an earthquake."

Garlits gets so frustrated with the car that he parks it and builds a conventional slingshot for the coming season. But his wife, Pat, insists he return to the rear-engine idea, and Garlits sorts out the handling, first by adding a wing over the front axle and later by slowing down the steering. "She's so much more sensitive and responsive than a slingshot," Garlits explains.

1971

Slow the steering is the second of Garlits' "Three Golden Rules of Rear-Engine Design" blurbed on the cover. The first: "Drop in a rearend that's completely open," Garlits says. "I beg 'em not to put spools or posis in these cars. Hit the least little funny thing (uneven surface, oil) on the track and ... zappo! You're into the next lane, or worse." And the third: the airfoil up front to keep the wheels from carrying.

Big Daddy loves the new car. His cockpit is roomier and "more relaxing," and he can ditch his old helmet, face mask, and goggles for a "Formula 1 racer-type Bell Star helmet and crystal-clear vision ahead," says Guidahl. How clear? Guidahl opens his story with this between-rounds exchange between Garlits and his main wrench, Tommy "T. C." Lemons. "Saw a big-ol' 3/8-inch bolt layin' down there in the lights," says Garlits. "Oh yeah?" T. C. replies. "Yeah," Garlits comes back, *"fine thread."*

The drag racing community is convinced Garlits' rear-engine rail won't work, but he proves them wrong at the 1971 Winternationals, where he qualifies ninth with a 6.8-second run and keeps getting quicker through the eliminations, eventually winning Top Fuel. Within two years, all Top Fuel dragsters will adopt the design.

"Last year, Don believed retirement was imminent," Guidahl writes. "The slingshot-configuration car exacted too much wear and tear on his psyche. 'But I'll say this: This new car will add at least three years to my driving career.'"

Photographer Pat Brollier experiments with many different poses and camera angles before coming up with the winning shot.

February: Jere Alhadeff captures Tom Sturm's Funny in one of the coolest chute shots in the magazine's history. Along with NHRA Supernationals and AHRA Points Finals coverage is a story explaining the new "instant green starting system" that NHRA unveiled at the Supernats—better known now as the Pro Tree.

July: In a year dominated by Funny Cars on the cover, finally a Fuel Altered—the Tocco, Harper, and Garten roadster—gets some love. A starburst blurb trumpets *Hot Rod*'s incorporating *Rod & Custom* and promises more pages, but the issue is actually 20 pages shorter than the previous month's.

1971

January: Ohio George can run his Maverick as either a Gasser or an Altered.

March: The Huff & Sanders Vega and Mickey Thompson Pinto are the first "Micro Funnies."

April: A super-patriotic graphic treatment for the Funny Car issue. Not sure why …

June: The year-old Pro Stock class is "where the action is." Stocks get 10 pages inside.

August: Dick Moser and Harvey Crane build DOHC heads for a Chevy small-block.

September: The new-car issue ditches the new-car photo, features the Barry Setzer/Kelly Brown 227-mile-per-hour Vega Funny.

October: Mallicoat Brothers' 172-mile-per-hour BB/A Barracuda shows turbocharging isn't just for Indy anymore.

November: Jack Chrisman's Sidewinder dragster gets the see-through photo treatment.

December: *Hot Rod*'s 340 Duster pulls the wheels. Too bad the photo's so small.

April

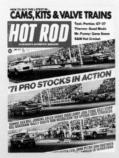
June

August

January

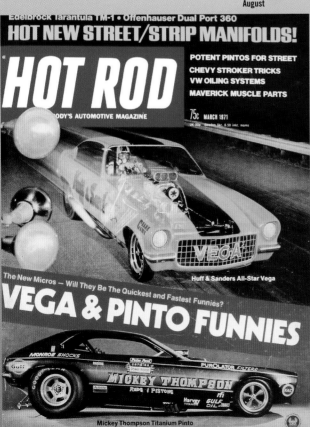
March

September

November

October

December

Photo Editor Mike Brenner poses (from left) John Wiebe, Don Prudhomme, Ed Donovan, and Don Garlits with Donovan's new, 417-cubic-inch aluminum Hemi, "drag racing's very own engine." Inside, Associate Editor John Fuchs notes the "select few" racing bodies that use engines developed for competition only—Indy 500, Can-Am, Formula 1—"and now, with the introduction of the all-aluminum, wet-sleeved Donovan 417 engine, drag racing joins that elite fraternity."

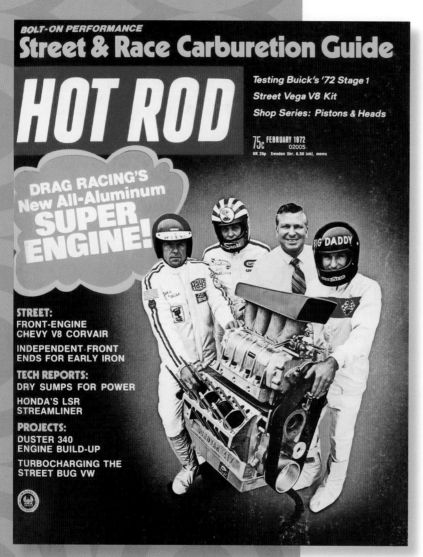

BOLT-ON PERFORMANCE
Street & Race Carburetion Guide

HOT ROD

Testing Buick's '72 Stage 1
Street Vega V8 Kit
Shop Series: Pistons & Heads

75c FEBRUARY 1972
02005
UK 29p Sweden Skr. 6.50 inkl. moms

DRAG RACING'S New All-Aluminum SUPER ENGINE!

STREET:
FRONT-ENGINE
CHEVY V8 CORVAIR

INDEPENDENT FRONT
ENDS FOR EARLY IRON

TECH REPORTS:
DRY SUMPS FOR POWER

HONDA'S LSR
STREAMLINER

PROJECTS:
DUSTER 340
ENGINE BUILD-UP

TURBOCHARGING THE
STREET BUG VW

February

Key to the engine's development: It should be able to use existing parts from an existing engine to keep costs down. But which existing engine? "To Ed Donovan, that was the easiest decision to make, for he is one of the many racers who are convinced that the hemi-head Chrysler 392 was the best engine ever made, bar none," writes Fuchs. The early Hemi is favored because it was "designed as a Hemi from the ground up, rather than being converted from a wedge-head engine," as was the case with the later 426 Hemi. Plus, "many racers also feel that the '92 is easier to 'tune for the strip' than the '26, and the 'good pieces' are more plentiful and less expensive than those for the later Hemi." The 392's weakness as a nitro-burner is its bottom-end strength.

Donovan's solution is to replace the 392 with an engine "that would retain all of its inherent advantages and cure its shortcomings." To be able to use the pieces available for the 392, the 417's deck height, bore spacing, cam-centerline-to-crank-centerline measure, and other dimensions mirror the older engine, "thus the Donovan 417 can accept the '92's crank, cam, pushrods, lifters, oil pump, heads, etc., so that the cost of this new engine to the racer has been greatly reduced," Fuchs writes. Strength issues are addressed with a block that has "received a significant amount of strengthening" yet still weighs just 125 pounds, a 32-pound one-piece aluminum girdle that attaches to the block via four studs per main bearing and nine studs per side rail, and the use of chrome-moly steel sleeves in the block. "These cast-steel wet liners are so strong," says Donovan, "that a racer should be able to 'lift' the heads off the block before he destroys the cylinders."

At the end of his article, Fuchs calls the Donovan 417 "a giant step forward ... sure to bring increased performance, along with increased safety" to drag racing. There's already evidence of the performance improvement: John Wiebe debuted the 417 at the NHRA Supernationals and set low ET of the meet at 6.53 seconds.

Also in this issue is a four-page buyer's guide of Carter and Holley carburetors, a review of a V-8-powered Chevy Vega, and a road test of Buick's 455 GS Stage 1. Buick, writes Steve Kelly, seems to be "the only automaker able to hang onto performance and deliver clean air at the same time."

1972

Unroll some seamless background paper in open shade and, voila! Instant photo studio. Wiebe, Prudhomme, and Garlits pose with Ed Donovan and his new drag race Hemi.

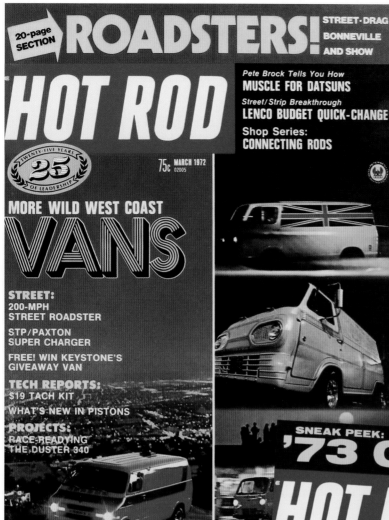

March: With 20 pages of roadsters in the issue you'd think the editors could shoot a nice Deuce for the cover. But no. Technical Editor Steve Green "captured the habitat and life style of Vannus Californius in all its colorful moods with Auto-Nikkor-equipped Nikon F and High Speed Ektachrome."

April: Fire burnouts were hot (sorry) in the 1970s, and Gerry Stiles captured Gene "The Snowman" Snow's fireball with his Hasselblad. Two illustrations provide the 1973 Chevelle sneak peek, for which Chevrolet "is still attempting to get the big-block engine clean enough to pass California emission standards."

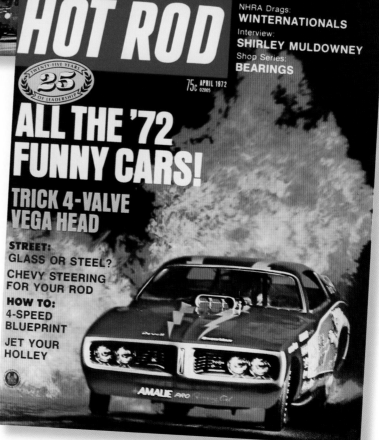

1972

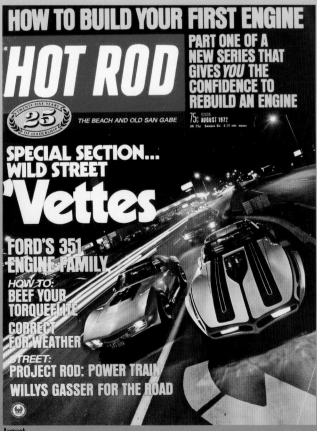

January

June

July

May

January: Chrysler's Tom Hoover, owner Ted Spehar, and driver Don Carlton with the new *Motown Missile*.

May: Dyno Don Nicholson's 351 Pinto Pro Stocker bursts out of the cover.

June: A tiny cover photo of Sam Gianino's team means it's tough to blurb over flames.

July: A sure sign of changing times: *Hot Rod* does a subcompact buyer's guide.

August: These "Wild Street Vettes" are tame compared to the wilder Vettes inside.

September: Barry Setzer's streamlined rail with John Buttera and Lou Baney in the suits.

October: The Colonnade-style Chevelle Laguna leads off *Hot Rod*'s review of 1973 models.

November: Despite the "Common Mistakes" cover line, Harold Buckley's Falcon is "dynamite."

December: "What Makes Grumpy Happy?" His 585-horsepower, 9-second Vega. The cover shoot, not so much.

August

September

October

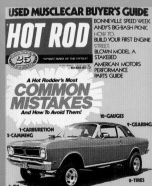

November

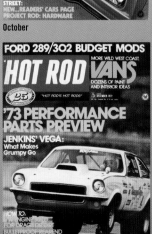

December

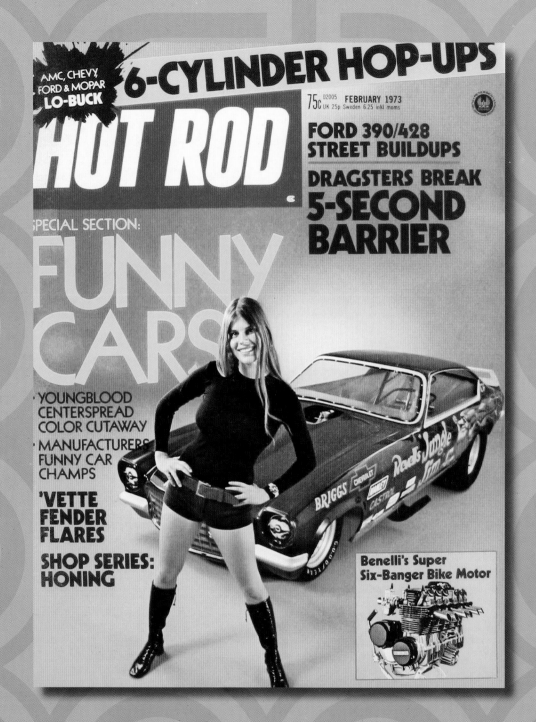

6-CYLINDER HOP-UPS

75c 02005 FEBRUARY 1973
UK 25p Sweden 6.25 inkl moms

HOT ROD

FORD 390/428 STREET BUILDUPS

DRAGSTERS BREAK **5-SECOND BARRIER**

SPECIAL SECTION:

FUNNY CARS

· YOUNGBLOOD CENTERSPREAD COLOR CUTAWAY
· MANUFACTURERS FUNNY CAR CHAMPS

'VETTE FENDER FLARES

SHOP SERIES: HONING

Benelli's Super Six-Banger Bike Motor

February

Pam Hardy made quite an impression on the *Hot Rod* editors—and everyone else—when she showed up at the 1972 NHRA Summernationals as part of Jungle Jim Liberman's crew. After running a photo of her in a miniskirt and white boots on the October 1972 table of contents page, the editors feature "Jungle Pam" on the magazine's cover with Liberman's Vega, quickening pulses all over America.

Liberman is one of drag racing's most popular drivers, not so much because of his low ETs, but because of the showmanship he brings to his appearances. Curvaceous Pam becomes a big part of that show, drawing even more attention to Jungle Jim's performances—and no doubt selling magazines during the winter of 1973.

Pam and Jungle's Vega promote a special Funny Car section inside (though neither appears in the section). It opens with an essay by Ben Brown, "Is the Funny Car Dead?" which is answered in the first line: "No way!" The Orange County International Raceway's Manufacturers Funny Car Championships, which pits brand teams against one another, is won by Ford, helped in large part by an 18-year-old Texan named Billy Meyer who "slipped in and blew everyone into the weeds" with the meet's low ET of 6.51. Closing the section is a feature on the *Wonder Wagon*, a Vega panel truck sponsored by telecommunications giant ITT and painted by Kenny Youngblood to look like a 6-second loaf of Wonder Bread. Youngblood also renders a nice cutaway illustration for the article.

The big news in this issue is the breaking of the 5-second barrier during the NHRA Supernationals at Ontario Motor Speedway. Mike Snively does the deed, driving Diamond Jim Annin's streamlined dragster to a 5.97 pass at 235.69 in the third round of Top Fuel. Turns out Snively was asleep at the lights and lost the round while making history. His isn't the quickest run, though;

1973

Top Fuel winner Don Moody runs 5.91 to beat Vic Brown in the final.

Everyone ran fast at OMS, making the editors wonder if there was an issue with the strip's length or the timing equipment. "But the track was the right length and NHRA was running the Chrondeks," writes Editor Terry Cook. "If you can't believe the times at an NHRA event, then the world is coming to an abrupt end last Wednesday." The reason for the "super times at the Supernats" was the track's surface. "They should really have called it the Flypaper Nationals," Cook notes. "On Monday morning after the event, paper and other trash which had blown out onto the starting line area during the night were stuck to the track!"

How rodding is changing in the early 1970s: A tech article about "Waking Up the Ford 390/428" is shorter than a story about "6-Cylinder Budget Hop-Ups."

Jungle Jim Liberman introduces Pam Hardy to the drag racing world at the NHRA Summernationals in 1972.

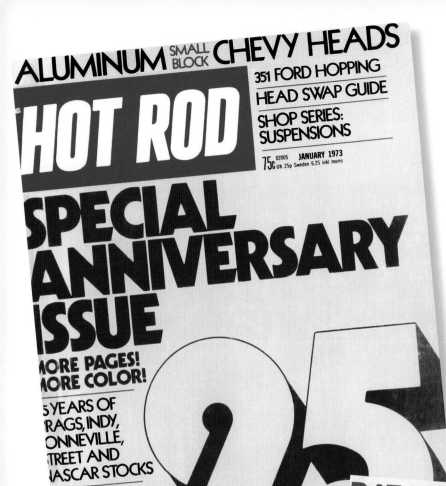

ALUMINUM SMALL BLOCK CHEVY HEADS

351 FORD HOPPING
HEAD SWAP GUIDE

SHOP SERIES:
SUSPENSIONS

HOT ROD

75¢ 02005 JANUARY 1973
UK 25p Sweden 6.25 inkl moms

SPECIAL ANNIVERSARY ISSUE

MORE PAGES!
MORE COLOR!

5 YEARS OF
DRAGS, INDY,
BONNEVILLE,
STREET AND
NASCAR STOCKS

PLUS THE
USUAL GOOD
STUFF!

January: The 25th Anniversary issue is the largest *Hot Rod* produced and undergoes a graphic redesign, which includes the return of "Roddin' at Random." About the cover: "...the decision was made to zonk you, the reader, with this all-blurb silver jobbie. Hope you're all zonked."

March: Dude, car, humble garage: a cover design template that will reappear often in the coming years. The image is shot in Hollywood by Larry Willett using the nicely detailed Noble & Norstedt 1955 Chevy Gasser. How-to's in the special section range from building a workbench to choosing street/strip gears.

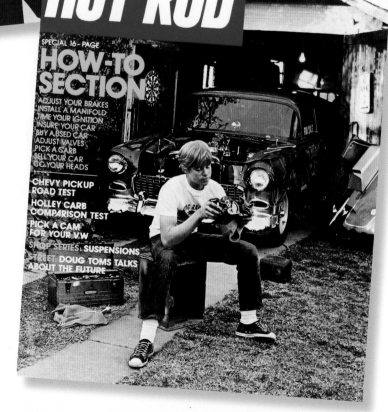

RAT MOTOR HEMI HEADS

MARCH 1973 75¢
Sweden 6.25 inkl moms
02005

HOT ROD

SPECIAL 16-PAGE
HOW-TO SECTION

ADJUST YOUR BRAKES
INSTALL A MANIFOLD
TIME YOUR IGNITION
INSURE YOUR CAR
BUY A USED CAR
ADJUST VALVES
PICK A CARB
SELL YOUR CAR
CC YOUR HEADS

CHEVY PICKUP
ROAD TEST

HOLLEY CARB
COMPARISON TEST

PICK A CAM
FOR YOUR V.W

SHOP SERIES: SUSPENSIONS
STREET: DOUG TOMS TALKS
ABOUT THE FUTURE

1973

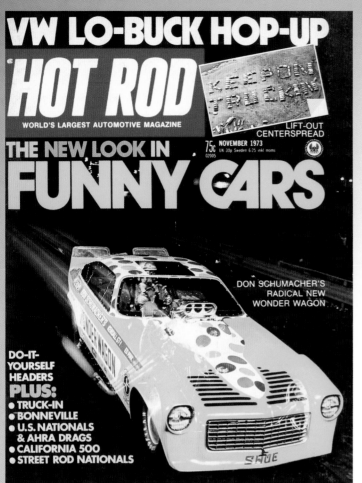

VW LO-BUCK HOP-UP

HOT ROD
WORLD'S LARGEST AUTOMOTIVE MAGAZINE

KEEP ON TRUCKIN'
LIFT-OUT CENTERSPREAD

75¢ NOVEMBER 1973
UK 30p Sweden 6.25 inkl moms
02005

THE NEW LOOK IN FUNNY CARS

DON SCHUMACHER'S RADICAL NEW WONDER WAGON

DO-IT-YOURSELF HEADERS
PLUS:
- TRUCK-IN
- BONNEVILLE
- U.S. NATIONALS & AHRA DRAGS
- CALIFORNIA 500
- STREET ROD NATIONALS

November

April: The Sien & Lankford Funny aflame; inside is *Hot Rod*'s first look at nitrous.

May: Turns out the Nickey Nova's L88 is (smog) legal and runs 12.03 on the strip.

June: Junior Johnson: "We're jus' pore ol' chicken farmers gone racin' I reckon."

July: Wash-off paint is used to write blurbs on Dan Bruno's custom Corvette.

August: As if the vans aren't wacky enough, there's also a flying Pinto inside.

September: Baja 500 action can't compete with the Grumpy Jenkins pinup.

October: Chevelle, 'Vette, and Road Runner represent "The high, low and in-between of street suspension."

November: No more bread loaf: The *Wonder Wagon* Vega represents Funny Car design evolution.

December: All the good stuff you'd want to find under your Christmas tree.

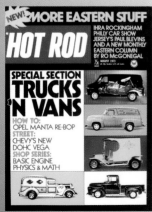

April

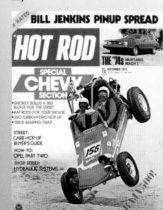

May

June

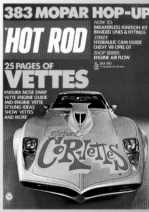

July

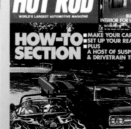

August

September

October

December

HOT ROD
WORLD'S LARGEST AUTOMOTIVE MAGAZINE
COMBINED WITH ROD & CUSTOM

SHOP SERIES: CARB TUNING TIPS
NASCAR: DONNIE ALLISON TEAM
BIKE TEST: OSSA 250 PHANTOM
DRAGS: INDY NATIONALS AND
PRO CHALLENGE RACE

$1.00 DECEMBER 1974
UK 50p Sweden Skr 7:50 inkl moms
22005   17.65% sales tax

IN TIME FOR XMAS

AUTO AUDIO
SPECIAL SECTION - INCLUDING RADIOS,
8-TRACK, CASSETTE, CB RADIO, PHONES,
SPEAKERS, INSTALLATION TIPS,
ANTENNAS & A GIANT BUYER'S GUIDE.

TRUCKIN: PITTSBURGH
VAN FAIR EAST • $100,000
BIKE HAULER VAN

RACING: TOWING &
TRAILERING TIPS

PROJECT CARS:
EIGHTY-HOUR MANTA
BUILDUP

RODDING: NORTHWEST
ROD RUN PARTY

TECH: TWO NEW VALVE-
TRAIN IDEAS

JOHN BUTTERA'S FABULOUS '26 T SEDAN SRN PRIZEWINNER

December

The finale of the California Street Rod Civil War is the cover feature on Lil' John Buttera's 1926 T, a marvel of modern componentry mated to vintage tin. The Civil War is Terry Cook's idea; he learned of a bragging match between Buttera and Andy Brizio at the Street Rod Nationals and turned it into a multiple-article series, starting in the January issue, pitting North (Brizio in San Francisco) versus South (Buttera in L.A.). Brizio's Mazda-powered fiberglass roadster is finished first and makes the June issue's cover, but Buttera's Tudor is an instant icon.

The car is a first for Buttera. Until now he's best known for the craftsmanship he puts into finely detailed dragsters, Funny Cars, and Pro Stocks. But all that is changing. Says Buttera, "I've seen drag racing go from a sport which has given me a great deal of personal satisfaction to a semi-organized state of insanity built around prostituted selfishness, self-destruct maintenance and snowballing lawsuits. Street rodders, on the other hand, appreciate the time and energy that goes into a finely finished chassis or component thereof and are willing to both pay for and maintain what I've built once it's finished."

Buttera's first completed street rod ("I've probably started 30 rods over the past 15 years but I could never finish one") sits on a double-tube frame with a scratch-built A-arm front suspension and a Jaguar-based IRS. Buttera's drag race buddies help out: Art Chrisman builds the car's 289 V-8, while Tony Nancy stitches the tan leather upholstery. Cook refers to the car as a "Cad-T" because Buttera wanted it to "appear as a '26 T on the outside, but circa '72 Caddy on the inside." In the T's tall cab go "a carload of Caddy components—complete with digital clocks, cruise 'n climate controls, gauges and idiot lights galore."

1974

After six months of 60-hour weeks, Buttera finishes the T just in time to drive it—yes, drive it—cross-country to St. Paul for the 1974 Street Rod Nationals, where it wins the award for Best Interior. Buttera opens shop in Cerritos and "wants to construct cars, chassis and components," Cook says.

The "Wild 26th Bonneville" story is the first on-the-salt reportage in *Hot Rod* by Gray Baskerville. He joined the staff in the July issue when Jim McCraw replaced Terry Cook as editor and *Rod & Custom* was, once again, combined with *Hot Rod*. Gray's light touch with the language is evident from the first sentence: "Bonneville—hot rodding's remembrances of things fast."

Lil' John Buttera turns a 1926 Model T Tudor into a 1972 Cadillac Eldorado—on the inside, anyway.

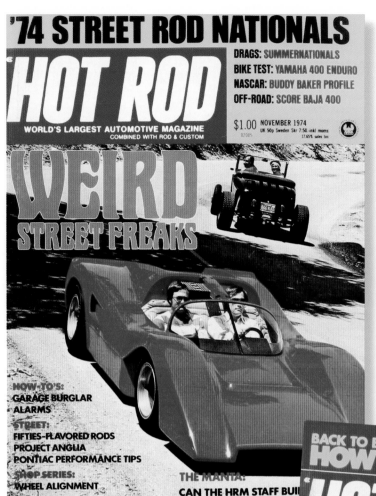

November: The 1970s would be weird enough that both *Hot Rod* and *Car Craft* would dip into the Street Freak well. In this issue, *Hot Rod*'s staff sets out to build a Manta Can-Am kit car in less than 80 hours and for less than $5,000. Spoiler alert: They won't make it.

May: The Weslake Chevy heads are cool, but we can't take our eyes off Ivo's fiery Winternationals crash. His only injury: He cuts his leg getting out of the car too fast. Shooter Paul Sadler was in the right place at the right time with his motor-driven Nikon.

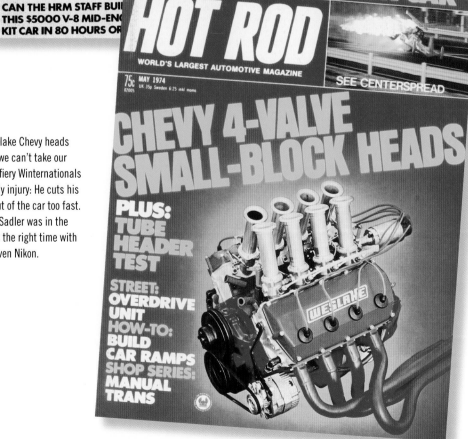

1974

January: Project Chevy II stars in a car-hop cruise-in scene from *Hot Rod Graffiti*.

February: Trucks, vans, and gas-saving tips: Hot rodding, 1970s style.

March: *Hot Rod* gets nostalgic with period photos of the 1955–1957 Chevys.

April: How do you sell fuel economy? Try the Charles Atlas route. It worked for him.

June: Andy Brizio's Street Rod Civil War Deuce sports twin Mazda rotaries.

July: Sam Foose did the 'glass and lacquer work on the Reif's 1969 ZR-1.

August: We would like to have seen more of Greg Sharp's chopped GMC.

September: Altereds at OCIR's first Altered Sweepstakes: Drag racing's "terrible-tempered troglodytes."

October: Monza, Astre, Skyhawk, Starfire, and Mustang II: "the strongest bets for minisupercars in 1975."

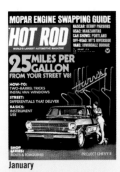

January

March

April

February

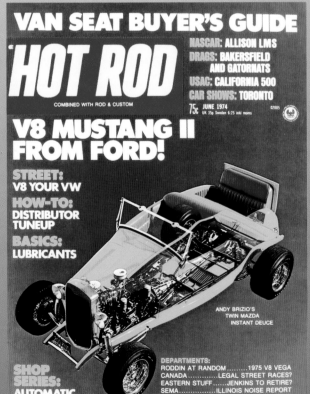

June

July

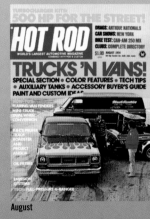

August

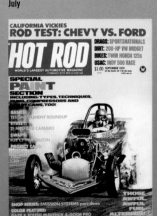

September

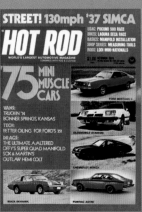

October

April

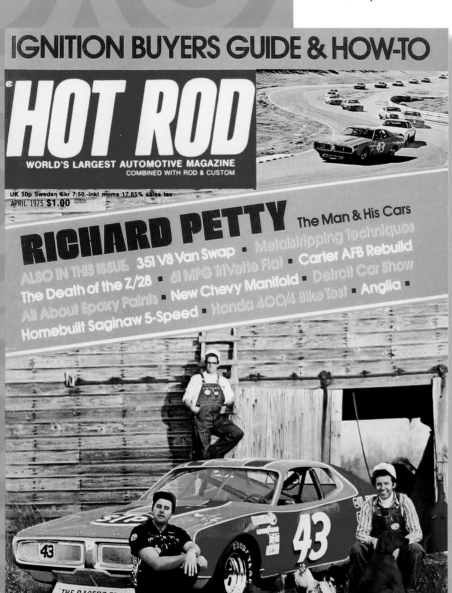

IGNITION BUYERS GUIDE & HOW-TO

HOT ROD

WORLD'S LARGEST AUTOMOTIVE MAGAZINE
COMBINED WITH ROD & CUSTOM

UK 50p Sweden 6kr 7:50.-inkl moms 17.65% sales tax
APRIL 1975 $1.00   02005

RICHARD PETTY   The Man & His Cars

ALSO IN THIS ISSUE: 351 V8 Van Swap ■ Metalstripping Techniques
The Death of the Z/28 ■ 61 MPG TriVette Fiat ■ Carter AFB Rebuild
All About Epoxy Paints ■ New Chevy Manifold ■ Detroit Car Show
Homebuilt Saginaw 5-Speed ■ Honda 400/4 Bike Test ■ Anglia ■

NASCAR has yet to reach the mainstream popularity it will achieve in the years to follow, but it has its share of stars and superstars. The biggest by far is Richard Petty. In 1975, at roughly the midpoint in his stock car racing career, Petty's records to date "stagger the imagination," writes Joe Whitlock in this issue's cover profile. "Through 1974 he had won 164 Grand National races during a career that started in 1958, when he was 21 years old. He won his fifth Daytona 500 in '74 and wound up with his fifth Winston Cup national championship. All are records for the sport, records he will surely perpetuate."

The cover photo, taken by Robert Andrews, plays stock car racing's redneck image for laughs, showing Petty down home in Level Cross, North Carolina, with his brother Maurice (left), who builds Petty's engines, and cousin Dale Inman (rear), who supervises the team. "He sorta runs the show," Petty says of his cousin.

The article touches on three generations of racing Pettys. Figuring prominently is Petty's father, Lee, with three Grand National championships of his own and his win at the first Daytona 500 in 1959. Lee gave his eldest son "immediate, although unenthusiastic permission" to enter his first race in 1958, where Petty "cruised to a ho-hum sixth-place finish." The family-oriented story later mentions "a lanky teenager hanging around the Petty pits. Slowly, the shadow of Kyle Petty, 15 and already a fraction over six feet, is growing."

Included in the story are a half-dozen photos of Petty's race cars, starting with his Wedge-powered Plymouth and ending with his current Dodge. A sidebar to the story shows the Dodge's inner workings, from its tube chassis to its small-block V-8.

Whitlock ends his essay with this prediction: "Richard Petty is favored to win his sixth Winston Cup Grand National championship in 1975. Don't bet against it!" Few would. In the months to follow, Petty would win a record 13 races and that sixth title.

Among the other stories in the issue is a requiem for the Z28 Camaro written by Eastern Editor Terry Cook. He tells the tale of the Z's birth in 1966, when Vince Piggins gave Chevy General Manager Pete Estes a fateful ride in "a high-compression 283 Camaro with four-speed transmission, front disc brakes, some exterior cosmetics and a host of other details to distinguish it from the standard Camaro." Estes was

1975

impressed, and Piggins explained it would be a slam-dunk to build a version that would fit in the new SCCA Trans-Am rules. "Estes said, 'Let's do it!' and the Z/28, not to mention the 302 V-8, was born," Cook relates.

Why did the Z28 have to die? Surprisingly, it wasn't emissions regulations that killed the car but its failure to meet new lower noise standards for the 1975 model year, writes Cook.

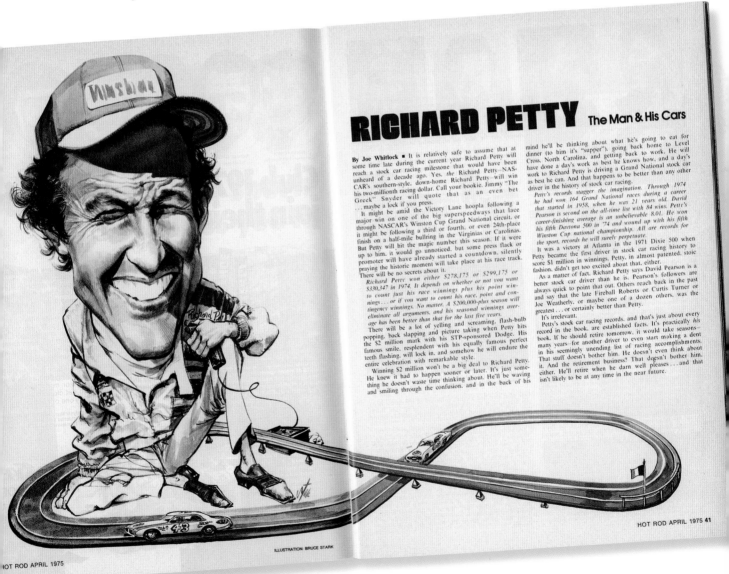

RICHARD PETTY The Man & His Cars

By Joe Whitlock ■ It is relatively safe to assume that at some time late during the current year Richard Petty will reach a stock car racing milestone that would have been unheard of a decade ago. Yes, *the* Richard Petty—will win his two-millionth racing dollar. Call your bookie. Jimmy "The Greek" Snyder will quote that as an even bet . . . maybe a lock if you press.

It might be amid the Victory Lane hoopla following a major win on one of the big superspeedways that lace through NASCAR's Winston Cup Grand National circuit, or it might be following a third or fourth, or even 24th-place finish on a half-mile bullring in the Virginias or Carolinas. But Petty will hit the magic number this season. If it were up to him, it would go unnoticed, but some press flack or promoter will have already started a countdown, silently praying the historic moment will take place at his race track. There will be no secrets about it.

Richard Petty won either $278,175 or $299,175 or $330,347 in 1974. It depends on whether or not you want to count just his race winnings plus his point winnings . . . or if you want to count his race, point and contingency winnings. No matter. A $200,000-plus season will eliminate all arguments, and his seasonal winnings average has been better than that for the last five years.

There will be a lot of yelling and screaming, flash-bulb popping, back slapping and picture taking when Petty hits the $2 million mark with his STP-sponsored Dodge. His famous smile, resplendent with his equally famous perfect teeth flashing, will lock in, and somehow he will endure the entire celebration with remarkable style.

Winning $2 million won't be a big deal to Richard Petty. He knew it had to happen sooner or later. It's just something he doesn't waste time thinking about. He'll be waving and smiling through the confusion, and in the back of his mind he'll be thinking about what he's going to eat for dinner (to him it's "supper"), going back home to Level Cross, North Carolina, and getting back to work. He will have done a day's work as best he knows how, and a day's work to Richard Petty is driving a Grand National stock car as best he can. And that happens to be better than any other driver in the history of stock car racing.

Petty's records stagger the imagination. Through 1974 he had won 164 Grand National races during a career that started in 1958, when he was 21 years old. David Pearson is second on the all-time list with 84 wins. Petty's career-finishing average is an unbelievable 8.01. He won his fifth Daytona 500 in '74 and wound up with his fifth Winston Cup national championship. All are records for the sport, records he will surely perpetuate.

It was a victory at Atlanta in the 1971 Dixie 500 when Petty became the first driver in stock car racing history to score $1 million in winnings. Petty, in almost patented, stoic fashion, didn't get too excited about that, either.

As a matter of fact, Richard Petty says David Pearson is a better stock car driver than he is. Pearson's followers are always quick to point that out. Others reach back in the past and say that the late Fireball Roberts or Curtis Turner or Joe Weatherly, or maybe one of a dozen others, was the greatest . . . or certainly better than Petty.

It's irrelevant.

Petty's stock car racing records, and that's just about every record in the book, are established facts. It's practically *his* book. If he should retire tomorrow, it would take seasons—many years—for another driver to even start making a dent in his seemingly unending list of racing accomplishments. That stuff doesn't bother him. He doesn't even think about it. And the retirement business? That doesn't bother him, either. He'll retire when he darn well pleases . . . and that isn't likely to be at any time in the near future.

ILLUSTRATION: BRUCE STARK

HOT ROD APRIL 1975 **41**

HOT ROD APRIL 1975

The hayseed cover photo was done for laughs, while the profile in the magazine is an earnest look at one of NASCAR's greatest drivers.

September: Dick Landy's 575-inch *Milodon Mastodon* proves size is everything. And check out the "Mongoose vs. F-14" top blurb. Two years in the making, the "Goose vs. the U.S. Navy" match race is the first—but not the last—showdown *Hot Rod* would stage between drag racers and fighter jets.

February: For the first time in 12 years, NHRA allows jet cars for exhibition runs. To celebrate, *Hot Rod* sends the *Daily C Untouchable* jet dragster out of this world. New Ford intake manifolds from Offenhauser and Weiand are for Capri and Pinto engines; Edelbrock sticks with the V-8s.

January

May

March

June

July

January: Carl Olson takes a last Top Fueler ride at the explosive 1974 Supernationals.

March: A "thoroughly modern" 1909 T contrasts with the previous month's jet car in space cover.

May: Tommy Ivo joins the successful Nationwise Rod Shop drag team for 1975.

June: The Sprinter belongs to Don Blair, owner of the famous pioneering speed shop.

July: The flamed SS396 Chevelle is a street/strip/show—and tow—car.

August: "Trucks and vans are the big growth segment of hot-rodding activity right now."

October: The C/Altered Anglia has "late-model thinking underneath early model tin."

November: Just in case you didn't get enough vans two months ago.

December: *Grumpy's Toy XII* puts a new Monza body on a proven Pro Stock chassis.

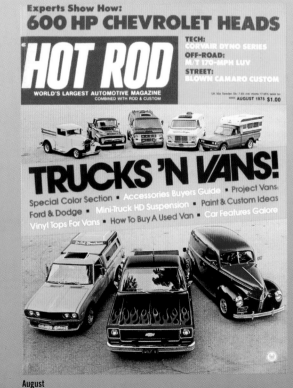

August

October

November

December

1975

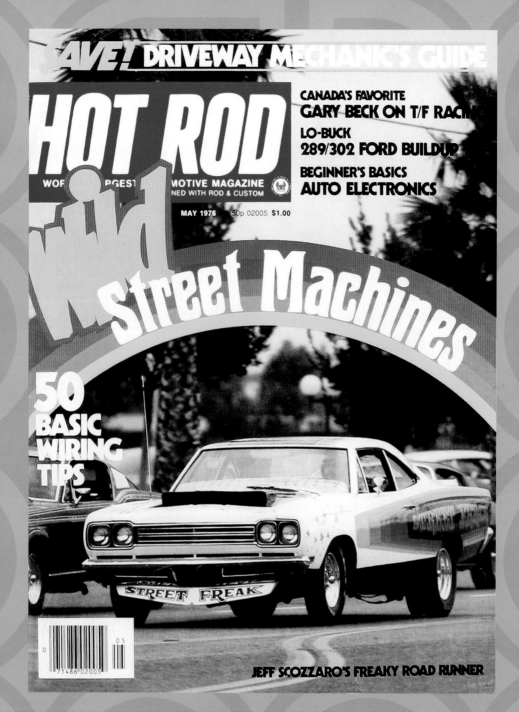

SAVE! DRIVEWAY MECHANIC'S GUIDE

HOT ROD

WOR   PGEST   MOTIVE MAGAZINE
NED WITH ROD & CUSTOM

MAY 1976   50p 02005 **$1.00**

CANADA'S FAVORITE
GARY BECK ON T/F RAC

LO-BUCK
289/302 FORD BUILDUP

BEGINNER'S BASICS
AUTO ELECTRONICS

Wild

Street Machines

50 BASIC WIRING TIPS

STREET FREAK

JEFF SCOZZARO'S FREAKY ROAD RUNNER

May

Hot rodding is getting really freaky by the mid-1970s, and the magazine is right there with it. Or is it the other way around? Is *Hot Rod* covering the Street Freak trend by featuring cars like Jeff Scozzaro's Road Runner, or is the magazine pushing readers to build ever wilder machines? Probably some of both.

Leading "The Wild Bunch" in this month's cover story, Scozzaro's Plymouth comes out of Jeff's Place, Scozzaro's custom paint shop in Anaheim, California, following a design by Kenny Youngblood. Under the hood is a 383 built by Performance Specialists with a Velasco crank, Isky cam, Speed Pro pistons, and Hedman headers, all working together to make the Runner an 11-second strip machine. On the outside, white pearl is accented with candy colors and gold-leaf lettering. The orange velour interior—the plush stuff covers the seats, console, dashpad, door panels, you name it—is produced by Joe Moreno.

The "Wild Bunch" story also includes more than a dozen other cars as freaky as Scozzaro's, from Gasser-style Tri-Five Chevys to a Pinto wagon. Scattered throughout the story are photos of cruise nights from all over the country. "Cleveland, Van Nuys, Omaha, Dallas, Dodge City, it makes no never mind. When the Street Freaks bring their mounts out for an evening cruise, everyone takes notice. Lotsa chrome, polished mags, wild paint jobs, capture everyone's attention."

The "Driveway Mechanics Guide" blurbed at the top of the magazine is a collection of basic maintenance tips—how to change your oil, rotate your tires, change points, and so on.

This issue includes coverage of the 16th Winternationals, which Executive Editor Jim McCraw dubs the "Rolling

1976

Thunder Review" and describes in very musical terms. The star of the meet is Don Prudhomme, who sets a national Funny Car record of 6.02 seconds in qualifying and beats Ed McCulloch in the final after a frantic engine rebuild between rounds. "Prudhomme tied all-timer Don Garlits with his 15th career major event victory in the quickest field of Funny Cars ever assembled by Parks," writes McCraw.

Hot Rod augments its Winternats coverage with profiles on two top drag racers, 1974 Top Fuel champ Gary Beck and Super Stock racer Judy Lilly. Beck, says Associate Publisher Holly Hedrich, has a five-part approach to staying on top in drag racing: finance, teamwork, dedication, ability, and pioneering. "Will he become World Champion again?" asks Hedrich. "At this point, his chances appear to be excellent." (Beck will win another championship, but not until 1983.)

McCraw, in "Sweet Judy Blue-Eyes & Her Mean Mother Mopar," describes Lilly as "not only one of the prettiest and brightest ladies in Littleton, Colorado— or anywhere else, for that matter—but she also happens to be the winningest lady drag racer of all time and one of the fiercest competitors in the sport."

Jeff Scozzaro's Road Runner is as freaky on the inside as it is on the outside.

September: Jeans are so hot in the 1970s that, at least for a while, they are used as upholstery. *Hot Rod* builds the *Denimachine*, an "in-jean-ious" giveaway van with Levi Strauss accents inside and out, including back-pocket stitching—with Levi's trademark red tab—painted on the double back doors.

April: The shopping cart prop would turn up many times in *Hot Rod* and other magazines after this, but here is the rolling basket's first cover appearance. The story inside offers tips on how to buy performance parts along with a roundup of some of the latest speed equipment.

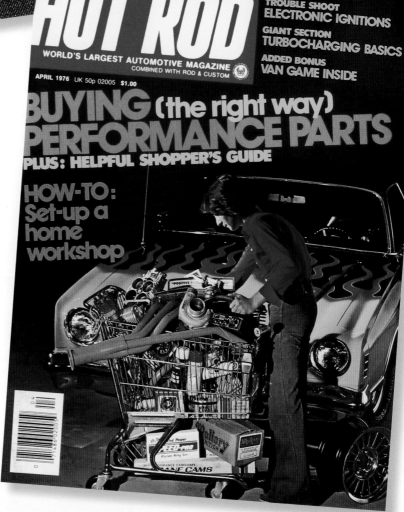

1976

January

February

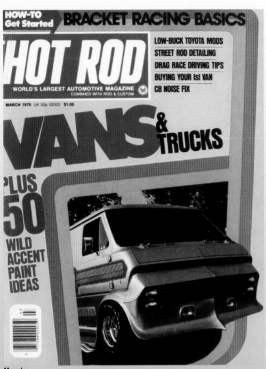

March

June

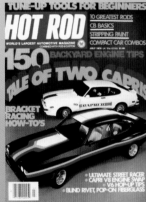

July

August

October

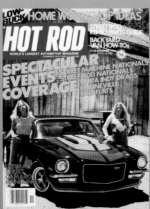

November

December

January: 'Vettes and vans, two of the hottest *Hot Rod* topics of the 1970s.

February: Three wild "Dy-No-Mite Datsuns" created for 1976 auto shows.

March: Graham Oates' "unusual Ford van" leads a "Carrier Carnival" of trucks and vans inside.

June: George Barris helped George Harrington build his IMSA-look-alike Monza.

July: The Bicentennial cover features Capris? At least the "10 Greatest Rods" are inside.

August: Lots of "Van-In Craziness" inside this special van issue.

October: Poorly cropped VWs on giant pieces of candy. Is this the worst cover ever?

November: Pretty girls and a wild Camaro—now that's more like it!

December: A special Chevy section combines weirdness with some solid tech info.

April

A hot rod that could "literally be sold to an enthusiast over the counter" is the idea behind Gratiot Auto Supply's Track-T. Gratiot's Angelo Giampetroni explains to Gray Baskerville that the car will be sold in four "phases," from bare frame to a complete runner. Gratiot will supply any of the necessary components—dropped-axle front suspension, 1972 Chevelle rear end, small-block Chevy (or Ford)—or the buyer can contribute his own. "And to make sure that the best-laid plans of rods and rodders don't turn to swill," Baskerville writes, Giampetroni has a turnkey prototype built called the Sprint-T.

Baskerville doesn't just write about the cars he features, he often drives them, too, to give the *Hot Rod* readers a "rod test" of the car. In this case, he's in Detroit in the winter, but that doesn't keep him out of the roadster. The cold prevents him from wringing out the car. "But you won't believe how many stares you get from the old folks or how many smiles you receive from the chicks."

To make sure this issue grabs attention on the newsstand, *Hot Rod*'s editors compose the cover with the T, Giampetroni, and Linda Vaughn who, in their words, "amply demonstrates the charms of the new Gratiot Sprint-T roadster."

The budget street V-8s in the top blurb include a 550-horse Ford 302 by Gapp & Rousch, a 501-horsepower Chevy 302 from Edelbrock, and a Kenne Bell Buick 350 that turns a Skylark into a 14-second flyer.

Detroit winter be damned, Baskerville is rod-testing the Gratiot Auto Supply Track-T.

Magazine cover text

$$ BUDGET-BUILDING STREET V8S

CHEVY: 501-HP, 302-IN. SCREAMER
FORD: GAPP & ROUSH BOSS 302
BUICK: 350-IN. BRACKET BUILDUP

'HOT ROD

WORLD'S LARGEST AUTOMOTIVE MAGAZINE
COMBINED WITH ROD & CUSTOM

$1.25 APRIL 1977 02005

BUILD-IT YOURSELF STREET ROD

GRATIOT'S ALL-NEW EASY-TO-ASSEMBLE TRACK-T KIT

PLUS:
• VAN CONSOLE HOW-TO
• HOW TO MAKE HORSEPOWER
• 50 VINYL TAPE TIPS

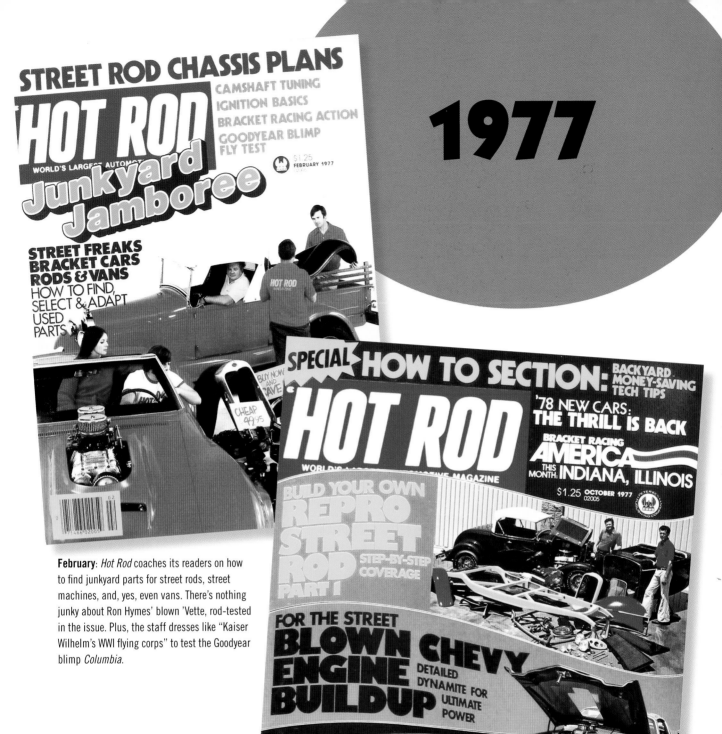

STREET ROD CHASSIS PLANS

CAMSHAFT TUNING
IGNITION BASICS
BRACKET RACING ACTION
GOODYEAR BLIMP
FLY TEST

$1.25
FEBRUARY 1977

HOT ROD
WORLD'S LARGEST AUTOMOTIVE

Junkyard Jamboree

**STREET FREAKS
BRACKET CARS
RODS & VANS**
HOW TO FIND,
SELECT & ADAPT
USED PARTS

1977

SPECIAL **HOW TO SECTION:** BACKYARD MONEY-SAVING TECH TIPS

HOT ROD
WORLD'S LARGEST AUTOMOTIVE MAGAZINE

'78 NEW CARS:
THE THRILL IS BACK

BRACKET RACING
AMERICA
THIS MONTH: **INDIANA, ILLINOIS**

$1.25 OCTOBER 1977
02005

**BUILD YOUR OWN
REPRO
STREET
ROD** STEP-BY-STEP COVERAGE
PART I

**FOR THE STREET
BLOWN CHEVY
ENGINE** DETAILED DYNAMITE FOR ULTIMATE POWER
BUILDUP

February: *Hot Rod* coaches its readers on how to find junkyard parts for street rods, street machines, and, yes, even vans. There's nothing junky about Ron Hymes' blown 'Vette, rod-tested in the issue. Plus, the staff dresses like "Kaiser Wilhelm's WWI flying corps" to test the Goodyear blimp *Columbia*.

October: Jerry Kugel's repro ragtop Deuce shares cover space with *Orange Juice*, a Z28 with a blown small-block bursting through the hood. New-for-1978 models with "the thrill" include the Mustang II King Cobra, 304-powered AMC Pacer, and diesel-burning Olds Delta 88.

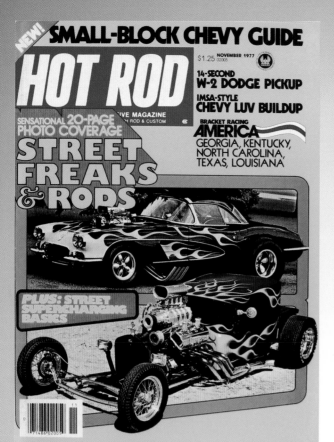

NEW! SMALL-BLOCK CHEVY GUIDE

HOT ROD
AUTOMOTIVE MAGAZINE
COMBINED WITH ROD & CUSTOM

$1.25 NOVEMBER 1977 02005

14-SECOND
W-2 DODGE PICKUP

IMSA-STYLE
CHEVY LUV BUILDUP

SENSATIONAL 20-PAGE
PHOTO COVERAGE

STREET FREAKS & RODS

BRACKET RACING
AMERICA
GEORGIA, KENTUCKY,
NORTH CAROLINA,
TEXAS, LOUISIANA

PLUS: STREET SUPERCHARGING BASICS

November

DRAG RACING CALENDAR
GIANT CAR FEATURE GALLERY
EASY 66-HP VAN BOLT-ON
NEW STREET ROD REPRO PARTS

HOT ROD
WORLD'S LARGEST AUTOMOTIVE MAGAZINE
COMBINED WITH ROD & CUSTOM

120 STREET & BRACKET PERFORMANCE TIPS
• BUILDING AN $1100, 11.6-E.T. CHEVY II
• INTAKE MANIFOLD FITTING • NITROUS OXIDE HOW-TO
• RACING TIRE BASICS • NHRA WORLD CHAMPIONS

January

BUILD A $50 VAN INTERIOR

HOT ROD
WORLD'S LARGEST AUTOMOTIVE MAGAZINE

VON DUTCH DISCUSSES PINSTRIPING BASICS
INSTALLING TURBOCHARGERS
BLUEPRINTING CLUTCHES
160-mph BLOWN KAWASAKI Z-1

BACKYARD Fiberglass Bolt-ons
• WILD IMSA-STYLE FLARES • GLASS BUILDING BASICS
• EARLY & LATE CAMARO FENDER LIPS • STEPSIDE PICKUP PARTS
• FIBERGLASS MOLD CONSTRUCTION

ALL-NEW
PACKER GT
& PONTIAC
CAN AM
FIRST ROAD TEST INSIDE

March

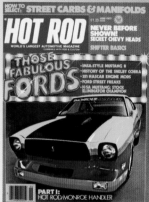

TECH REPORT & BUYER'S GUIDE
SHOCK ABSORBER BASICS

HOT ROD
WORLD'S LARGEST AUTOMOTIVE MAGAZINE
COMBINED WITH ROD & CUSTOM

11-SECOND, 120-MPH
BLOWN TWIN-ENGINE
HONDA DRAG BIKE

TRI-TEST
CHEVY, FORD, DODGE
4x4 PICKUPS

16 PAGES Money-Saving Backyard How-Tos

DAYTONA 500
RACE REPORT INSIDE

May

HOW TO SELECT: **STREET CARBS & MANIFOLDS**

HOT ROD
WORLD'S LARGEST AUTOMOTIVE MAGAZINE
COMBINED WITH ROD & CUSTOM

NEVER BEFORE SHOWN!
SECRET CHEVY HEADS
SHIFTER BASICS

THOSE FABULOUS FORDS
• IMSA-STYLE MUSTANG II
• HISTORY OF THE SHELBY COBRA
• 351 NASCAR ENGINE MODS
• FORD STREET FREAKS
• H.SA MUSTANG: STOCK ELIMINATOR CHAMPION

PART I:
HOT ROD/MONROE HANDLER

June

January: A Camaro holding off a 1955 Chevy leads an issue full of bracket-race tips and tech.

March: IMSA-style Camaro flares and the Can-Am, "a direct descendant of the famed GTO."

May: Another dude-working-on-car-in-small-garage setup. Greg Simons owns the 1970 Sundance Duster.

June: *Hot Rod*'s latest project: Turning a Cobra II into the IMSA-inspired *Monroe Handler*.

July: These 4x4s (called "Highriders") get into the truck and van act cruising Van Nuys Boulevard.

August: The much-talked-about "Triple Threat" Chevy II project lands a cover.

September: Mike Dale has L88 power in both his 1970 'Vette and his speed boat.

November: The Street Rod and Street Machine/Van Nationals brought out the freaks.

December: A Chevy section includes a Silver Anniversary 'Vette test and Vega V-8 swaps.

BRACKET RACING "SECRETS"
BACKYARD SUSPENSION SYSTEMS
BIG-BUCK BUDGET HOP-UPS

HOT ROD
WORLD'S LARGEST AUTOMOTIVE MAGAZINE
COMBINED WITH ROD & CUSTOM

Pickups Vans & 4x4 Highriders
MORE COLOR-CAR FEATURES
OVER-THE-COUNTER MOPAR BRACKET PACKAGES

PLUS:
NASCAR'S FINEST: PETTY'S DODGE
DCM PROFESSIONAL: KING OF THE FUNNYS
CB BUYER'S GUIDE

July

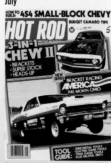

HOW-TO BUILD: **454 SMALL-BLOCK CHEVY**
BUDGET CAMARO TIPS

HOT ROD

3-IN-1 CHEVY II
• BRACKETS
• SUPER STOCK
• HEADS-UP

NEW SERIES
BRACKET RACING
AMERICA
THIS MONTH: OHIO

TOOL GUIDE:
SHEETMETAL TOOLS
ELECTRIC HAND TOOLS
TRICK RACER TOOLS
PLUS HELPFUL HINTS

August

SPECIAL! **CHEVY'S ALL-NEW ALUMINUM V8**
STREET GUIDE: TURBOS
BRACKET RACING
AMERICA
GROUP MICHIGAN

HOT ROD
WORLD'S LARGEST AUTOMOTIVE MAGAZINE

VETTES!

• GIANT VETTE COLOR SECTION
• VETTE HANDLING BASICS
• 25 VETTE TIPS

September

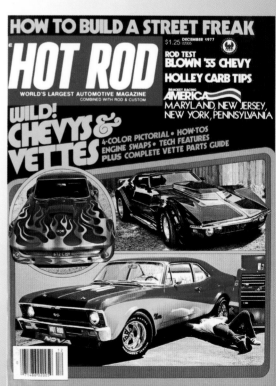

HOW TO BUILD A STREET FREAK

$1.25 DECEMBER 1977 02005

HOT ROD
WORLD'S LARGEST AUTOMOTIVE MAGAZINE
COMBINED WITH ROD & CUSTOM

ROD TEST
BLOWN '55 CHEVY
HOLLEY CARB TIPS

BRACKET RACING
AMERICA
MARYLAND, NEW JERSEY,
NEW YORK, PENNSYLVANIA

WILD! CHEVYS & VETTES
4-COLOR PICTORIAL • HOW-TOS
ENGINE SWAPS • TECH FEATURES
PLUS COMPLETE VETTE PARTS GUIDE

December

1977

AK PREVIEW!
'9 FORD TURBO COBRA

BUILD A CAMARO STREET FREAK

CUSTOM PAINT BASICS

SUPERCAR SUSPENSION TRICKS

JULY 1978

HOT ROD
WORLD'S LARGEST AUTOMOTIVE MAGAZINE

KIT CARS
STREET RODS & MEAN MACHINES

PHIL COOL'S '32 HIGHBOY

1978
July

In a year with covers dominated by trucks and Corvettes, Phil Cool's bright red Deuce is "a welcome throwback to the days of unlimited hot rodding hedonism," writes Feature Editor Gray Baskerville. Cool's hot rod, America's Most Beautiful Roadster, is "pure hot rod," Gray writes, "the epitome of a fenderless Ford roadster, a mother's worry, the personification of something that's bright, hungry-looking, loud, powerful and very, very fast."

Gray knows the fast part firsthand, as his story is a rod test, not a static feature. "You hunker down below the cut windshield and watch two things go around: the right front

Before it appeared on *Hot Rod*'s cover, Phil Cool's Deuce was America's Most Beautiful Roadster at Oakland.

tire and the three-inch blower belt. The serenade is strictly six-seventy-one counterpointed against an exhaust note that is as solid as a sheik's bank account. The ride is cushy, thanks to the soft slicks, yet you stick to the street like bubble gum to the underside of a tabletop."

Why pair an AMBR winner with a kit car blurb? "Kit cars were a hot button back then," Editor Lee Kelley explains 30 years later. "Many of the kit cars were better than what Detroit was building."

That would change with the "Ford Turbo Cobra," the all-new, Fox-platform Mustang. "Preliminary testing by Ford Division shows that the turbo four will run with the V-8 in the same Mustang from 0 to 60," writes Executive Editor Jim McCraw. "And the 125 pounds of weight saved on the front end makes the turbo four handle significantly better than the V-8 car."

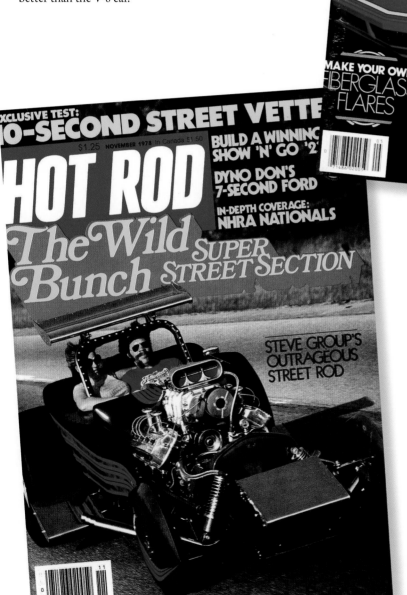

May: One of the better executed 'Vette covers in this decade features Al Kleiman's Can-Am-style wide-body Corvette. This issue also marks the first for new Editor Lee Kelley, who moves into the chair after John Dianna leaves for *Motor Trend*. And would you believe snow at the Winternationals?

November: Could this be the most outlandish car *Hot Rod* has ever put on a cover? Steve Group's Altered street rod, with its blown 392 Hemi, tube frame, and 1923 T body, "is what has had to happen—drag racing's influence on street rodding," writes Baskerville.

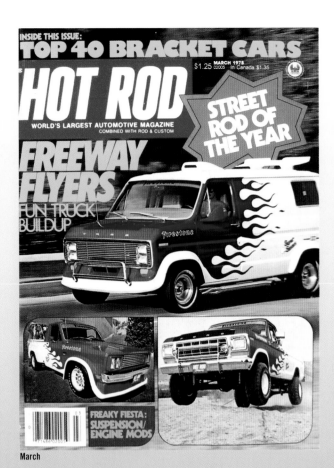

March

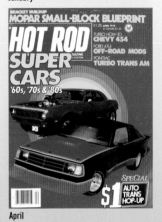

January

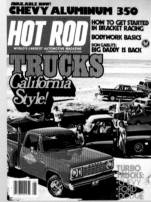

February

April

June

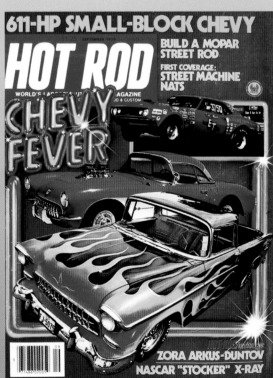

September

December

August

October

January: The 30th Anniversary issue puts the hot Buick V-6 front and center.

February: The "New Look" is emulating the wide-fendered IMSA racers of the 1970s.

March: Street Rod of the Year is Chapouris' *California Kid*, when traditional wasn't yet cool.

April: Project Roadmaster "may signal the shape of things to come in NASCAR racing."

June: "Trick trucks from the land of fruit and nuts."

August: Compared with the other freaks inside, Carl Popp's Z/28 is relatively sane.

September: A case of Chevy Fever plus a Duntov profile put Bowtie fans in heaven.

October: Bill Porterfield's wild mid-engine Olds is also an 11-second bracket racer.

December: The new Fox Mustang sparks interest in Ford ponies and sells a ton of magazines.

1978

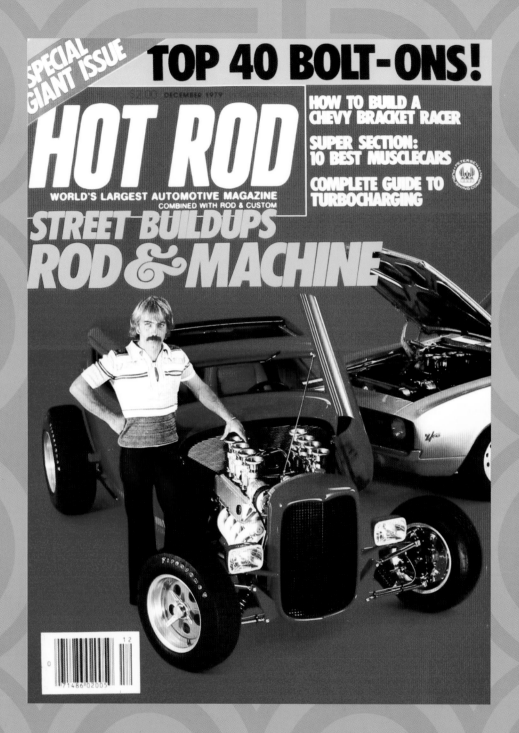

TOP 40 BOLT-ONS!

$2.00 DECEMBER 1979

HOT ROD

WORLD'S LARGEST AUTOMOTIVE MAGAZINE
COMBINED WITH ROD & CUSTOM

STREET BUILDUPS
ROD & MACHINE

HOW TO BUILD A CHEVY BRACKET RACER

SUPER SECTION: 10 BEST MUSCLECARS

COMPLETE GUIDE TO TURBOCHARGING

0 71486 02005

December

Five years after his Cad-T made the cover, Lil' John Buttera is back with what Gray Baskerville calls "the ultimate lowdown highboy coupe." The cover story is called "How to Build a Street Rod," but as the editors wisely point out, "We realize that John's capabilities far exceed those of most of our readers." However, the "ideas and concepts that John used to construct his ultimate '32 can be adapted to almost any street rod project."

Buttera's trademark craftsmanship is evident all over the rod project, from the Mopar 340 V-8's hand-built aluminum rocker covers to the wheel centers he machined and bolted to BBS rims with stainless-steel Allen cap screws. Buttera even smoothed the characteristic 1932 reveals out of the reproduction frame rails, seeing them as "one of those Deuce hiccups that I don't like." The front suspension is essentially the same double-A-arm setup he designed for the Cad-T; the rear hangs Jaguar half-shafts and fabricated uprights from a Halibrand center section.

The steel Deuce body is actually a combination of two, one a "hulk in a pile of '32 Ford parts I bought" that Buttera calls "one of the 'bleepingest' pieces of 'bleep' that I had ever seen." (We assume the "bleeps" were Baskerville's, not Buttera's.) To that he joined a second that had a completely crushed roof but sound metal from the beltline down. Steve Davis fabricated a belly pan, into which Eric Vaughn punched 592 louvers.

Baskerville ends his piece with this anecdote about how Buttera builds a rod: "A guy recently asked Lil' where he bought his rear-view mirror. 'I made it,' answered Buttera.

"'How?' came the reply.

"'Well, all you need is a piece of aluminum and cut away everything that doesn't look like a rear-view mirror.'"

The street machine side of the "How to Build" stories in the issue is also Buttera-centric, this time the tale of how John's son Chris built his 1969 Camaro. (The Z/28, with Chris and John's daughter Leigh, appears on the cover's fold-out half.) Rebuilt, actually, as Chris wrapped his car around a phone pole and then, "instead of taking a $3,500 bath, he learned how to take a car apart, clean up the various components, detail them, then put the entire package back together again," says his dad.

Since there was so much body damage to Chris' car, he stripped it of all the high-performance options he had installed and then bought a second Camaro to put them on. "Chris' Camaro is what we like to call the middle ground," Baskerville writes. "His Z/28 combines the best of the bolt-on world with some of the most eye-catching performance tricks—never forgetting, however, that he must not adversely affect the car's resale value."

The "Special Giant Issue" concept was the brainchild of Editor Lee Kelley and Circulation Director Nigel Heaton. It really was giant, too, with extra pages and a foldout cover. Newsstand buyers snapped it up, making it one of the year's best-sellers.

1979

Newsstand buyers see only half of this fold-out cover; here's the entire shot, with Lil' John Buttera's highboy and his son Chris' 1969 Camaro.

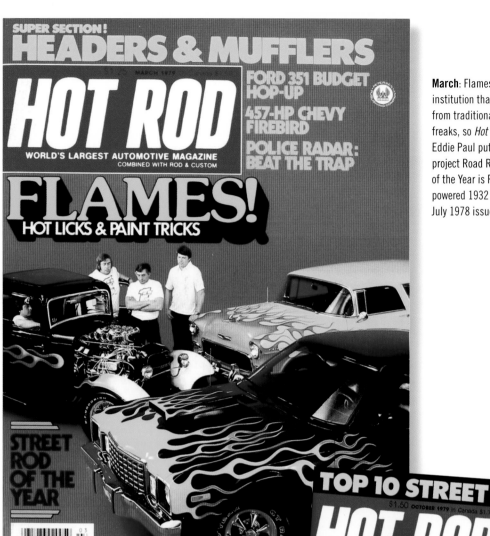

March: Flames are a rodding institution that cross boundaries from traditional rods to street freaks, so *Hot Rod* shows how Eddie Paul put hot licks on the project Road Runner. Street Rod of the Year is Phil Cool's L88-powered 1932 roadster from the July 1978 issue.

October: The Chevy small-block V-8's 25th birthday is celebrated with a profile of the landmark engine's development and this beauty shot of a Keith Black–built Mouse motor. Scott Sullivan's "blown and bad" 1967 Nova is Street Machine of the Year and a harbinger of the Pro Street trend to come.

1979

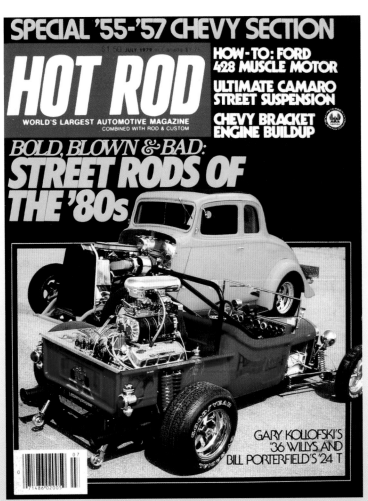

SPECIAL '55-'57 CHEVY SECTION

HOW-TO: FORD 428 MUSCLE MOTOR

ULTIMATE CAMARO STREET SUSPENSION

CHEVY BRACKET ENGINE BUILDUP

HOT ROD
WORLD'S LARGEST AUTOMOTIVE MAGAZINE
COMBINED WITH ROD & CUSTOM

$1.50 JULY 1979 In Canada $1.75

BOLD, BLOWN & BAD:
STREET RODS OF THE '80s

GARY KOLLOFSKI'S '36 WILLYS AND BILL PORTERFIELD'S '24 T

July

January: A hot 'Vette, 1957 post car, and Camaro lead off six Chevy Supercars pages.

February: A 10th Anniversary Trans Am—the end of the 400-inch V-8s—and a corner-carving 1969.

April: A roundup of 8-second bracket racers that "show just as well as they go."

May: Craig Dodd's blown 'Vette is no street poser; it's a 10-second strip terror.

June: The blurb placement is just wrong. Tom Hoover's Funny is no kit car.

July: *Hot Rod* predicts these rods will set the trend for the 1980s. Not quite.

August: This blown 1965 Mustang (foreground) was built in just two weeks. Behind it is a *Hot Rod* project car.

September: This blown and injected Ultra Z is a factory prototype; behind is the 1980 Z28.

November: Hey, that Shelby doesn't have a blower through the hood! How'd that happen?

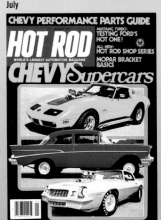

January

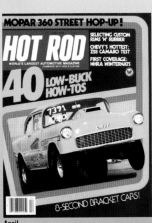

February

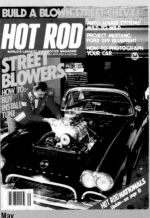

April

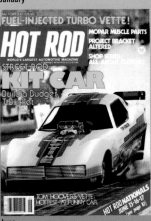

May

June

August

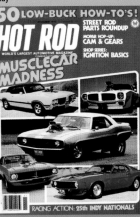

September

November

Chapter 5
1980–1989

When the Mustang II gave way to the all-new, Fox-platform Mustang in 1979, there was a glimmer of hope that exciting cars might be coming from Detroit again. Unfortunately, it would take a while for that to happen, so rodders and *Hot Rod* had to look elsewhere to fill that vacuum.

One of the hottest trends the magazine followed was Pro Street. The streetable Pro Stock style actually got its start in the mid-1970s but reached its outlandish zenith in the 1980s, when many of the cars had become trailer queens barely able to idle out of their own trailers. Editor Leonard Emanuelson remarked that "Pro Street is neither," and in 1985, *Hot Rod* examined the myth of the dual purpose Pro Streeter in "Who's Kidding Who?" A year later though, the magazine gave its Hot Rod of the Year award to Rick Dobbertin's Pontiac J2000, a study in Pro Street outrageousness. These cars may have frustrated hot rodding purists, but they were incredibly popular.

The 1980s also saw the rise of smooth, high-tech (and usually high-dollar) street rods. Lil' John Buttera originated the style, but it was Boyd Coddington who became synonymous with the look. Boyd's first cover car was Jamie Musselman's 1933 roadster, which appeared on the July 1982 issue and won that year's AMBR trophy. Boyd would bookend the 1980s with probably his most famous creation, *CadZZilla*, which ran on Editor Jeff Smith's July 1989 "Dare to be Different" cover.

In another 10 years these high-buck billet cars would generate a backlash, as traditionally minded rodders emulated the rough look of the earliest lakes roadsters and started the trad rod/greaser/rat rod movement. Foreshadowing the trend was the primered Pete Eastwood/Rick Barakat "rusto rod," as Gray Baskerville called it, which appeared on the cover just a few months after Musselman's roadster. As Emanuelson remembers, "I was more a fan of the basic, rippin' hot rod, so when Gray told me about the car, I jumped at the chance."

Detroit finally came to the party in 1982, with the 5.0L Mustang GT among the first of a new wave of muscle cars. New car excitement dimmed, though, as familiar carburetors gave way to fuel injection systems and computerized engine controls. Emissions laws went through another round of tightening, prompting *Hot Rod* to ask, "Can They Outlaw

In another 10 years these high-buck billet cars would generate a backlash, as traditionally minded rodders emulated the rough look of the earliest lakes roadsters and started the trad rod/greaser/rat rod movement.

Hot Rodding?" in the October 1984 issue. At the time, worries about the government "sealing our hoods closed" made it far more than a rhetorical question.

Yet despite the outrageousness of Dobbertin's Pontiac, the trend-setting style of Coddington's roadster, or the gravity of new smog laws, the most memorable 1980s cover was an April Fool's joke: Editor Pat Ganahl's spoof of the *Sports Illustrated* swimsuit issues. But what started as a joke turned out to be one of the best-selling issues of all time. For years after, Petersen's circulation directors wanted *Hot Rod*'s editors to repeat the special issue, much to the chagrin of school librarians—and many of those editors.

Graphics (and hairstyles) are huge in the 1980s, as illustrated by this fold-out cover Jim Brown shoots for the May 1986 issue.

The Pro Street phenomenon reaches its outrageous peak with Rick Dobbertin's Pontiac J2000, which Gray Baskerville photographs at dawn in front of the Lincoln Memorial.

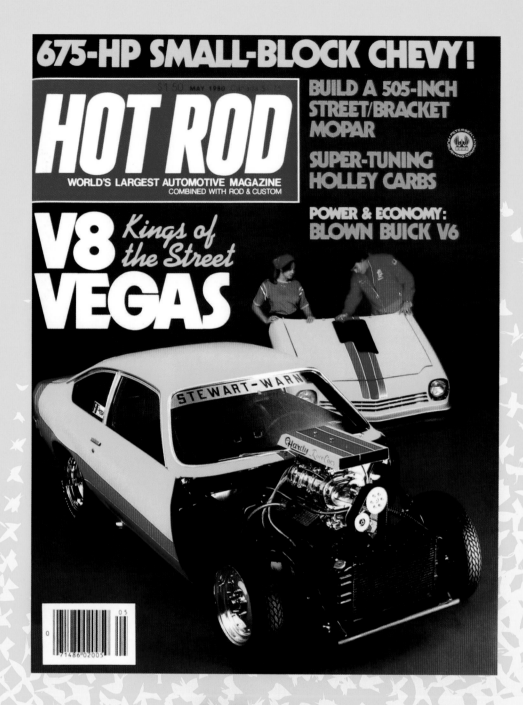

675-HP SMALL-BLOCK CHEVY!

$1.50 MAY 1980

HOT ROD
WORLD'S LARGEST AUTOMOTIVE MAGAZINE
COMBINED WITH ROD & CUSTOM

BUILD A 505-INCH
STREET/BRACKET
MOPAR

SUPER-TUNING
HOLLEY CARBS

POWER & ECONOMY:
BLOWN BUICK V6

V8 *Kings of the Street*
VEGAS

STEWART-WARN

0 71486 02005

May

Executive Editor C. J. Baker kicked off "The Ultimate Street Machine" V-8 Vega buildup in the March 1980 issue, and the third and final installment is the May cover story. When the project began, Baker's overview called it "a streetable Pro Stocker," and that's what builder Don Hardy would fashion, though there seems to be little "street" left in it. The foundation for the car is Hardy's Pro Stock Vega tube chassis, which uses motor plates to locate the 388-horsepower blown small-block V-8 and TCI Powerglide. A narrowed Dana 44—with wheelie bars!—sits between fat BFGoodrich Radial T/As in the rear, and a MacPherson strut suspension holds the skinny front runners. The body is a gutted 1974 Vega shell mated to a fiberglass nose (the grille is airbrushed), the wheel tubs and floor are aluminum panels, and the seats are thinly upholstered fiberglass buckets.

Baker's story describes climbing into the Vega ("careful not to put much weight on the thin aluminum floor panel"), firing the blown V-8 ("almost every aluminum panel in the car responds to the exhaust resonance from the side pipes"), and going for a drive ("squeeze into the throttle and the car moves instantly as it bounces lightly on every tar strip and ripple in the pavement"). An editor's note at the end of the story admits, "Our V-8 Vega project is in the twilight zone between a pure race car and a streetable vehicle" and goes on to describe the modifications necessary to truly drive a car like this in traffic—functioning grille openings and a softer suspension among them, but no mention of smog equipment. Baker does take the car to the strip, and with open pipes and 9-inch slicks, the car makes a "relatively easy" 11.45-second pass at 121.49 miles per hour.

Following the cover story is a resource guide to Vega V-8 conversions. "Thanks to the advances and advantages of the automotive aftermarket, mating the popular little Stovebolt car with the world's most popular powerplant has become almost entirely a standard backyard hot rodding affair," write Technical Editor Al Kirschenbaum and

1980

Associate Editor Marlan Davis. The inspiration for all the V-8 Vega madness is included in their story, too: Bill Jenkins' *Grumpy's Toy IX* Pro Stock drag car. "Legions of Chevy lovers followed with V-8 conversions of their own—for both street and strip—and the small-car/small-block motor combination soon became what we like to refer to as 'the '55 Chevy of the Seventies.'"

The 675-horsepower small-block Chevy featured at the top of the cover is a stock-block 355ci engine Smokey Yunick would build to test its potential in USAC Championship racing. Fitted with Hilborn injection, fueled by methanol, and breathing through an unusual eight-into-one header system with a big collector behind the motor, the engine looks promising, as that 675 power number was attained on the first dyno pull. USAC, however, decides not to return to the normally aspirated stock-block formula for Indy, and the project is stillborn.

Don Hardy's V-8 Vega project car, a "streetable Pro Stocker," turns mid-11s at Orange County Raceway.

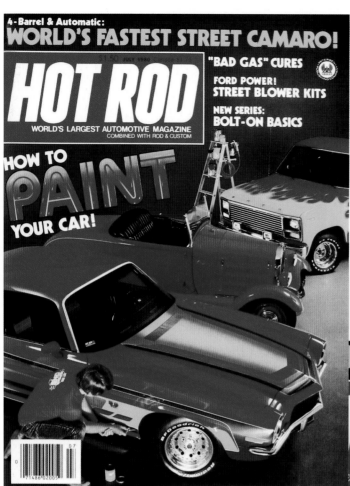

July: "Paint is definitely one of the most important ingredients in a sano rod," write the editors. Bill Carter paints Feature Editor Bruce Caldwell's 1970 Camaro in a multi-paneled scheme indicative of street machine trends to come, while Caldwell tries his hand at flaming *Hot Rod*'s shop truck.

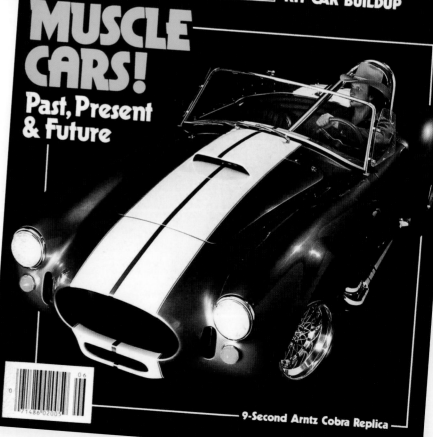

June: An Arntz replica kicks off a special section on Cobras old and new. "The Arntz Cobra delivers as much fun and excitement per dollar as any car in the world," writes Caldwell. The readers dig it, too, making this one of 1980's best-selling issues.

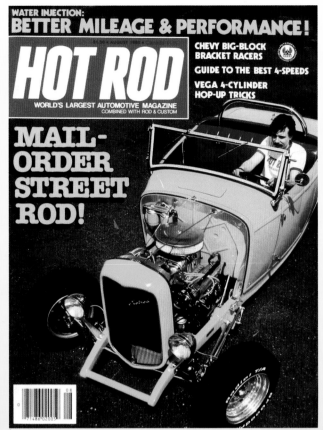

WATER INJECTION:
BETTER MILEAGE & PERFORMANCE!

HOT ROD
WORLD'S LARGEST AUTOMOTIVE MAGAZINE
COMBINED WITH ROD & CUSTOM

CHEVY BIG-BLOCK
BRACKET RACERS

GUIDE TO THE BEST 4-SPEEDS

VEGA 4-CYLINDER
HOP-UP TRICKS

MAIL-ORDER STREET ROD!

August

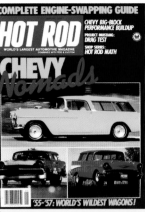

COMPLETE ENGINE-SWAPPING GUIDE

HOT ROD
WORLD'S LARGEST AUTOMOTIVE MAGAZINE
COMBINED WITH ROD & CUSTOM

CHEVY BIG-BLOCK
PERFORMANCE BUILDUP
PROJECT MUSTANG:
DRAG TEST
SHOP SERIES:
HOT ROD MATH

CHEVY Nomads

'55-'57: WORLD'S WILDEST WAGONS!

January

BEGINNER'S GUIDE TO DRAG RACING

HOT ROD
WORLD'S LARGEST AUTOMOTIVE MAGAZINE
COMBINED WITH ROD & CUSTOM

FORD 351 PERFORMANCE
BUILDUP
OLDS SMALL-BLOCK
HOP-UP
SHOP SERIES:
SUSPENSION BASICS

vette fever

February

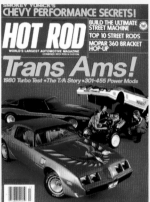

SMOKEY YUNICK'S
CHEVY PERFORMANCE SECRETS!

HOT ROD
WORLD'S LARGEST AUTOMOTIVE MAGAZINE
COMBINED WITH ROD & CUSTOM

BUILD THE ULTIMATE
STREET MACHINE
TOP 10 STREET RODS
MOPAR 360 BRACKET
HOP-UP

Trans Ams!
1980 Turbo Test •The T/A Story •301-455 Power Mods

March

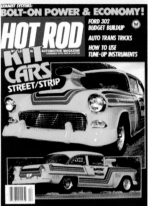

EXHAUST SYSTEMS:
BOLT-ON POWER & ECONOMY!

HOT ROD
AUTOMOTIVE MAGAZINE

FORD 302
BUDGET BUILDUP
AUTO TRANS TRICKS
HOW TO USE
TUNE-UP INSTRUMENTS

KIT CARS
STREET/STRIP

April

January: Chevy Nomads, the "World's Wildest Wagons," are featured throughout the issue.

February: Wild and way-out Corvettes return, bringing a case of "Vette Fever."

March: A trio of Trans Ams, including a road-test of the disappointing 1980 turbo.

April: In 1980, "kit" means Pro Stock parts under a stripped and tubbed body shell.

August: The mail-order Deuce roadster project ends. "Our Rodney is off and rolling!"

September: This Camaro Z28 special previews the 1981 model, a shadow of its former self.

October: Lil' John Buttera's T-bucket adds needed eye appeal to fuel economy tips.

November: Street Freaks return, including the Scott Sullivan–built Chevelle and a 427-powered Honda 600.

December: The Mustang Special includes GT350 history and Carroll Shelby's 12 new 1966 GT350 convertibles.

BETTER FUEL ECONOMY

HOT ROD
WORLD'S LARGEST AUTOMOTIVE MAGAZINE
COMBINED WITH ROD & CUSTOM

EXCLUSIVE COVERAGE:
STREET MACHINE &
HOT ROD NATIONALS
HOW TO INSTALL
HEADERS
GRANATELLI
STREET TURBO

Z28 CAMAROS!
'81 First Look • '69 Backyard Buildup • Inside Facts!

September

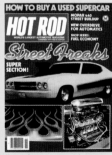

HOW TO BUY A USED SUPERCAR

HOT ROD
WORLD'S LARGEST AUTOMOTIVE MAGAZINE
COMBINED WITH ROD & CUSTOM

MOPAR 440
STREET BUILDUP
NEW OVERDRIVE
FOR AUTOMATICS
SHOP SERIES:
FUEL ECONOMY

Street Freaks
SUPER
SECTION!

November

75 LOW-BUCK TIPS

HOT ROD
WORLD'S LARGEST AUTOMOTIVE MAGAZINE
COMBINED WITH ROD & CUSTOM

HOW TO REBUILD
YOUR FIRST ENGINE
TOP 10 SMALL-BLOCK
SUPERCARS
STREET ROD BUILDUP
FOR THE '80s

Mustangs
GT350 HISTORY • RESTORATION • ROAD TEST

December

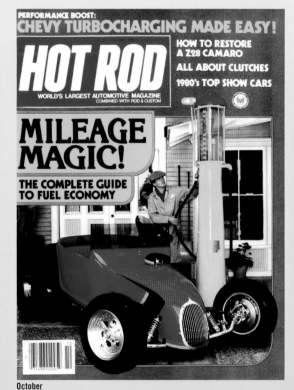

PERFORMANCE BOOST:
CHEVY TURBOCHARGING MADE EASY!

HOT ROD
WORLD'S LARGEST AUTOMOTIVE MAGAZINE
COMBINED WITH ROD & CUSTOM

HOW TO RESTORE
A Z28 CAMARO
ALL ABOUT CLUTCHES
1980's TOP SHOW CARS

MILEAGE MAGIC!
THE COMPLETE GUIDE
TO FUEL ECONOMY

October

1980

1982 Z28

The "Best Z28 Camaro Yet!" Huh? Either this cover line was written purely to sell magazines, or the editors had some very short memories. More accurately, this is the *newest* Z28. The 1982 model year marks the start of the third generation of GM's F-Bodies, and both the Camaro and Firebird are put through a downsizing program. Writes Technical Editor C. J. Baker, "The car is shorter, narrower, lower, and lighter—some 400 pounds lighter than a similarly equipped '81 model." Unfortunately, dimensions aren't the only thing on the chopping block. The 350-inch V-8 is gone, leaving the 305 V-8 as the largest engine available in a Camaro. When fitted with the optional Cross-Fire Induction throttle-body fuel injection, the 305 produces just 165 horsepower. The base, carbureted version of the 305 produces a mere 145 horses. Compare those numbers with the 360-horse output of the LT-1 V-8 in the 1970 Z28 and you'll understand our mockery of the cover blurb.

So why is Baker so enthusiastic about the new Z, other than to sell magazines? In part, he's putting on a brave face given the emasculation of a once-mighty muscle car. Fuel economy and emissions regulations are taking an ever bigger toll on enthusiast cars of all kinds in the early 1980s. This Camaro and its cross-town rival, the newly introduced 5.0L Mustang GT, are the best pony cars Detroit has to offer. And in fairness, the Z28 305's paltry 165 horsepower trumps the 157 produced by that first-year High-Output Ford 5.0.

December

But there's another aspect about the Z that Baker appreciates: its handling. In planning the new Camaro, GM's engineers "began by designing a Z28, reasoning that once they had the best possible handling vehicle, they could easily detune it for a milder ride in the regular Camaro and Berlinetta models," he writes. "As basic as that sounds, that's just the opposite of how it used to be done." This car delivers better ride and handling than previous models, "yet it won't murder your kidneys on a long trip, as earlier F-Bodies used to."

In a nutshell, Baker calls the new Z28 "precise." It "does just exactly what you direct it to do, without hesitation, and that goes for the steering, braking, and even the throttle."

The "50 Low-Buck Tips" bannered across the top of the cover are a collection of reader-submitted ideas for the

magazine's regular "It Worked for Me" department. "Since *Hot Rod* readers send in far more usable tips than we can fit each month, they pile up until we get enough of them to make a really special feature like this," write the editors. Among the more creative ideas are a "Po' Boy Caliper" made with a soda straw, a ruler, and a piece of cardboard; and the use of muffler clamps to mount gauges.

1981

By what yardstick is the 1982 Camaro Z28 "best"? Its precise handling, says Tech Editor C. J. Baker.

Eagerly Awaited, the 1982 Z28 Is Here, and It's Unquestionably...

THE BEST ONE YET !

By C.J. Baker

Here it is, the first detailed look at the new 1982 Camaro Z28! Yes, it's all new for '82. It's shorter, lower, sleeker, and a real eye-popper, but anyone can look at the photos and the spec chart and see that much. The real story is underneath, however—what went into completely redesigning the ever-popular Z28.

This is the year for downsizing the F-body (Camaro and Firebird); so when the task of redesigning the Camaro began, the Chevrolet engineers and designers were starting with a clean piece of paper.

The first and foremost consideration was handling. Essentially, the engineers began by designing a Z28, reasoning that once they had the best possible handling vehicle, they could easily detune it for a milder ride in the regular Camaro and Berlinetta models. As basic as that sounds, that's just the opposite of how it used to be done. Previously, Chevrolet designed a basic bread-and-butter Camaro and then did what they could to improve handling for the Z28 package. The result was always loaded with compromises and trade-offs. However, by designing for handling from the outset, both handling *and* ride are better than previous models. The new Z28 will pull in excess of .83G on the skid pad, yet it won't murder your kidneys on a long trip, as earlier F-bodies used to.

All of these improvements were no accident. The entire structure and geometry of the vehicle were redesigned to reduce or eliminate flex. Weight distribution was analyzed; definitions and perceptions of handling reevaluated; and acceptance of compromising components forbidden. Additionally, extra production steps, checks, and inspections were added to guarantee that cars leaving the end of the assembly line had been built as designed.

Upon sliding behind the wheel of the new Z28, you immediately get the feeling of being in a car with parts designed to work together. There's no feeling that one committee designed the front, another the interior, and yet another the rear. In other words, it's a thoroughbred, not some mixture of part horse, part cow, and part pig.

Yes, everything is downsized. The car is shorter, narrower, lower, and lighter—some 400 pounds lighter than a similarly equipped '81 model. The maximum engine size is also down from 350 to 305 cubic inches, the TH350 automatic has been replaced by the TH200, and even the gear ratios have been numerically lowered, but the horsepower per pound is up slightly, and that's good news. You'll also be happy to learn that interior room is nearly identical to that of previous years.

How's the new Z28 to drive? The best word to describe the '82 Z28 is "precise." The car does just *exactly* what you direct it to do, without hesitation, and that goes for the steering, braking, and even the throttle. Of course, purists never have enough power on tap to suit them, but we'll soon be showing you just how to bring that cross-fire-induced 305 V8 to life, along with a few backdoor tricks to make the '82 Z look and handle even better than it already does—and that'll take some doin'! HR

Very smooth, sleek, and slippery, the sloping hood, high tail, and flowing roof line let the Camaro slice through the air with minimal resistance. The Z28 models get the front air dam, side skirts, and the rear lower molding shown here. Note the 71-degree slope of the rear window.

(continued overleaf)

Photography: David & Ed Monaghan and C.J. Baker

els on the Z28 are 15x7
m versions that still retain the
4¾-inch, 5-lug bolt circle with
h 20 studs. Wheel offset is only
The tires are P215/65R-15
ar Eagle GTs with raised white
These steel-belted radials are to
ted at 35 psi both front and rear
Z28.

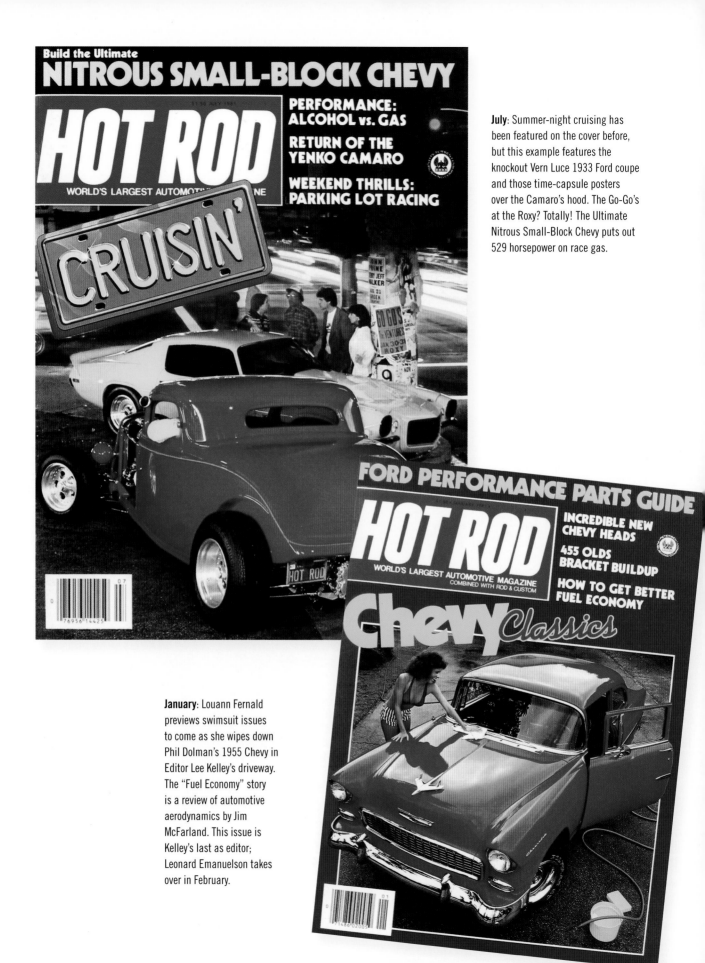

Build the Ultimate

NITROUS SMALL-BLOCK CHEVY

PERFORMANCE:
ALCOHOL vs. GAS

RETURN OF THE
YENKO CAMARO

WEEKEND THRILLS:
PARKING LOT RACING

HOT ROD

WORLD'S LARGEST AUTOMOTIVE MAGAZINE

CRUISIN'

July: Summer-night cruising has been featured on the cover before, but this example features the knockout Vern Luce 1933 Ford coupe and those time-capsule posters over the Camaro's hood. The Go-Go's at the Roxy? Totally! The Ultimate Nitrous Small-Block Chevy puts out 529 horsepower on race gas.

FORD PERFORMANCE PARTS GUIDE

HOT ROD

WORLD'S LARGEST AUTOMOTIVE MAGAZINE
COMBINED WITH ROD & CUSTOM

INCREDIBLE NEW
CHEVY HEADS

455 OLDS
BRACKET BUILDUP

HOW TO GET BETTER
FUEL ECONOMY

Chevy Classics

January: Louann Fernald previews swimsuit issues to come as she wipes down Phil Dolman's 1955 Chevy in Editor Lee Kelley's driveway. The "Fuel Economy" story is a review of automotive aerodynamics by Jim McFarland. This issue is Kelley's last as editor; Leonard Emanuelson takes over in February.

1981

February: Street Heroes are road-race-style cars, which "could be the visual wave of the future."

March: Ford's EXP and Mercury's LN7 are the "first all-new performance cars of the '80s."

April: The Radial Rod sedan delivery will be given away at the Hot Rod Nationals.

May: A Yamaha Seca 750, "today's speed king," shares cover space with a swoopy 'Vette.

June: Herb Adams' Cheverra—a 180-mile-per-hour race/street Camaro—heads for Daytona but crashes in practice.

August: PPG's Pace Car Program and four turbo four-bangers spur the "rebirth of Detroit Supercars."

September: "The Bow-Tie Brigade is on the march again down Main St. USA."

October: Art Director Charlie Hayward with future *Hot Rod* Editor Jeff Smith.

November: The all-new Mustang GT (tested in October) sparks some Mustang Magic.

February

March

June

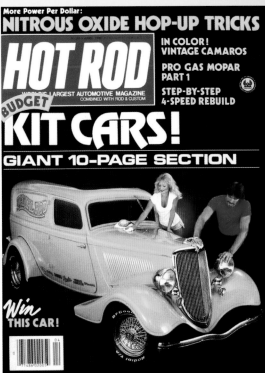

April

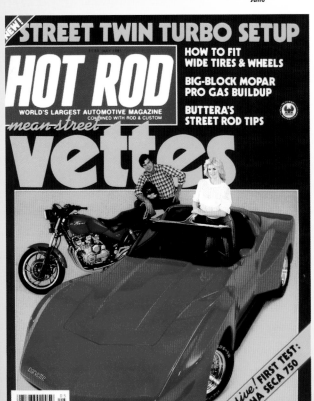

May

August

September

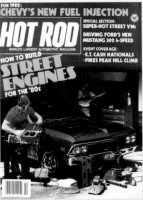

October

November

The "Graffiti Nights" cover blurb teases a feature story by Contributing Editor Dave Wallace about a 1950s-style cruise night in San Jose. The candy-colored 'Cuda in the foreground of Jim Brown's cover photo is featured inside with the apt title "Kaleido Kuda."

But it's the chopped 1932 Tudor that, in hindsight, makes this cover truly significant. Not only is this the first appearance of a primered car on the cover of *Hot Rod*, the Pete Eastwood/Rick Barakat Deuce foreshadows the rat rod movement that would come into its own in the late 1990s. While it's true that other magazines, notably Petersen stablemate *Rod & Custom*, had featured "vintage tin" and "beater" issues prior to this, the Eastwood & Barakat "rusto rod," as Senior Editor Gray Baskerville calls it, lays the groundwork for the less-is-more aesthetic of the retro rods to come.

"It's a pile," Baskerville writes. "It was built from a pile of parts scrounged from both P-Wood and Bearcat's garages. The body is, at best, a pile of rust. It's piles of fun to drive. And when you pile in the front seat, the cacophony generated from unfettered exhaust headers mixed with rattling tin and quivering quarter panels is strong enough to set off Cal Tech's seismograph. But it's bitchin'!"

And it's real. The body is a $300 1932 sedan that was in such bad shape that Eastwood and Barakat spent $400 stripping it in a hot tank, which ate most of the roof away. "So we had to ante up an additional $100 for a top." The chassis is an Eastwood highboy special, with boxed 1932 frame rails, a dropped 1934 I-beam axle and Pete & Jakes split wishbones up front and a 1957 Ford rear end out back. Barakat supplied the engine, a 355-inch Chevy small-block that's so mild Baskerville calls it "a less-than-mighty mouse motor."

But *Down 'n' Dirty* proves to be as fast as it is bucks-down. Without headlights or mufflers, and with slicks mounted, "the *rust*ults were mind-boggling," Baskerville says. "Ol' Bearcat proceeded to stop the clocks with an 11.59 e.t. while recording a top speed of 117.49 miles per hour."

The editors continue in econo-rod mode with the "Lo-Buck 'Hi-Energy' Engines" story, a profile of a new small-block V-8 available from Racing Head Service for just $1,295. The "Hi-Energy" moniker comes from RHS' sister division Competition Cams, which offers a line of High Energy street cams that offer good power without sacrificing drivability or economy. "Why not combine the High Energy concept

1982

with a blueprinted engine assembly?" ask the parts makers. The editors choose to test an engine with Comp's 268 cam (named after its duration spec) and find it produces 342 horsepower on the dyno while using less fuel at a steady 3,000 rpm than a 50,000-mile stock 350. Nearly 350 horsepower from an 8.5:1 engine that costs less than $1,500 to buy and is more fuel efficient than a stocker—"It almost seems too good to be true."

Rust never sleeps. In this case, the Eastwood/Barakat "rusto rod" goes 11.59/117.49 at the strip.

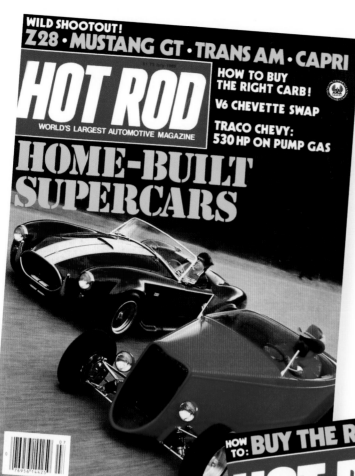

July: Another trend-setting rodder: Boyd Coddington makes his first *Hot Rod* cover appearance at the wheel of Jamie Musselman's 1933 roadster. The Thom Taylor–designed, Boyd-built smoothie captured the America's Most Beautiful Roadster trophy and really doesn't belong on a "Home-Built Supercars" cover. The Contemporary Classics' kit Cobra does, though.

April: Randy Lorentzen captures the action at Angelo's Drive-Thru for a Dave Wallace story about Orange County's popular cruising spot. Also inside is Don Garlits' *Sidewinder* dragster, which "Don is more excited about than he has been in quite some time" but doesn't live up to his expectations.

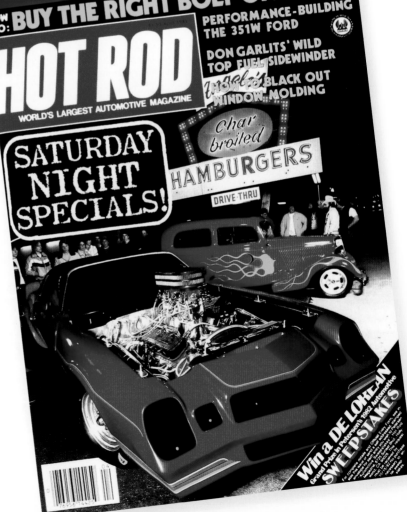

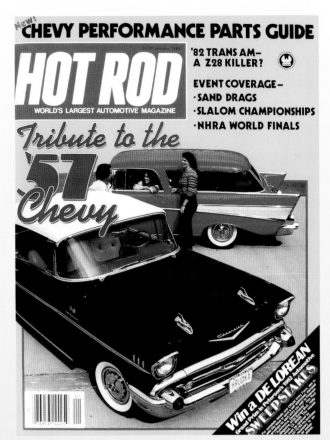

New! **CHEVY PERFORMANCE PARTS GUIDE**

HOT ROD
WORLD'S LARGEST AUTOMOTIVE MAGAZINE

'82 TRANS AM—
A Z28 KILLER?

EVENT COVERAGE—
- SAND DRAGS
- SLALOM CHAMPIONSHIPS
- NHRA WORLD FINALS

Tribute to the '57 Chevy

Win a DE LOREAN SWEEPSTAKES

January

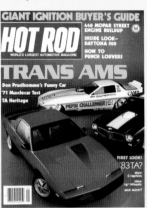

Win a DE LOREAN • SWEEPSTAKES

HOT ROD
Street Heroes!

HOLLEY CARB TIPS FOR BEGINNERS
HOW TO BLUEPRINT YOUR FIRST ENGINE
ALUMINUM FORD & CHEVY SMALL-BLOCKS!

February

'82 STREET ROD BUYER'S GUIDE

HOT ROD
NOVA
MORE MUSCLE PER DOLLAR

HOW-TO: HOOD SCOOPS AND RAM AIR PACKAGES
DISC BRAKE BOLT-ON FOR FORD REARENDS
FACTORY CHEVY V6 BUILDUP

Win a DE LOREAN SWEEPSTAKES

March

GIANT IGNITION BUYER'S GUIDE

HOT ROD
WORLD'S LARGEST AUTOMOTIVE MAGAZINE

TRANS AMS

440 MOPAR STREET ENGINE BUILDUP
INSIDE LOOK— DAYTONA 500
HOW TO PUNCH LOUVERS

Don Prudhomme's Funny Car
'71 Musclecar Test
TA Heritage

FIRST LOOK! '83 TA?

May

EXCLUSIVE! Z28 CAMARO INDY PACE CAR

HOT ROD
Little Guy Racers!

CLOSE-UP: 383 MOPAR SUPER STOCK CHAMPION
BRACKET RACE TIPS FROM THE PROS
GIANT INTAKE MANIFOLD BUYER'S GUIDE

June

January: Two rare 1957 Chevys, including an original fuelie convertible, from Mr. Gasket's Joe Hrudka.

February: Another Street Heroes issue, this time an "unusual Chevy high-performance parking lot."

March: Chevy Novas are "a low-cost way of building a super streeter."

May: *Hot Rod*'s Trans Am special includes a "what if" 1983 TA concept car.

June: "Little Guy Racers" are stars in the bracket racing wars.

August: Mike Kent's flamed roadster leads the 1932 Ford's golden anniversary.

September: More street heroes, but this time they're called Mean Machines.

October: The big-block swap into a Z28 is a bolt-in, says Marlan Davis.

December: Low-buck Christmas gifts, a slippery NASCAR T-Bird, and a super Camaro.

75HP CHEVY BOLT-ON!

HOT ROD
MEAN MACHINES

SPRINT CAR COLOR CUTAWAY
FIRST COVERAGE: STREET MACHINE & HOT ROD SUPER NATS
AV-GAS: OCTANE CURE!

September

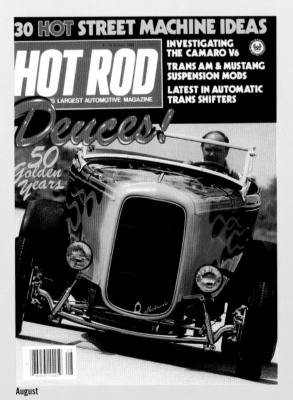

30 **HOT** STREET MACHINE IDEAS

HOT ROD
'S LARGEST AUTOMOTIVE MAGAZINE

INVESTIGATING THE CAMARO V6
TRANS AM & MUSTANG SUSPENSION MODS
LATEST IN AUTOMATIC TRANS SHIFTERS

Deuces!
50 Golden Years

August

NEW LIFE FOR OLD CARS!

HOT ROD
ENGINE SWAPS

TRACTION BAR ROUNDUP
BUDGET 10-SECOND BRACKET RACER
1983'S HOTTEST CARS

October

'83 FACTORY POWER PARTS

HOT ROD
Christmas Special
OVER 100 GIFTS UNDER $100

HOW TO: WHEEL & CHASSIS DETAILING
AUTO WIRING MADE SIMPLE
NEW NASCAR BULLET!

December

1982

The editors call Randy Lorentzen's cover shot "a classic *Beauty and the Beast*" pairing, putting the lovely Linda Vaughn with Warren Johnson's Hurst/Olds Pro Stock drag car. Inside, Executive Editor John Baechtel's article traces Johnson's development of a new Olds racing engine that has since come to be known as the Drag Race Competition Engine (DRCE).

At the time, Chevrolet's 500-inch big-block is dominating the Pro Stock ranks. But Dick Chrysler, owner of Cars & Concepts, had acquired Hurst the year before and "was determined to thrust the company back into the limelight," Baechtel writes. First out of the chute is a 1983 Hurst/Olds for the street, followed by the new Pro Stocker. "Since Warren Johnson was already running harder than just about anyone in Pro Stock with his Oldsmobile Starfire, he was the obvious choice to ramrod the program," says Baechtel.

The foundation for the new engine is a cylinder block and head designed around race-proven components. Johnson and Oldsmobile, writes Baechtel, "have, in effect, redesigned the rat motor and fixed all the mistakes that racers have had to live with for years. The bad features of the rat motor have been eliminated and a host of desirable improvements added to make it a truly bulletproof piece."

Though the engine has yet to run in anger, "prominent racers are already lining up for these high tech pieces—and that means just about everybody who runs a GM body," says Baechtel.

If you're trying to talk your way out of a ticket for not having a photo permit, let Linda Vaughn do the talking.

HOW TO:
BUILD A STREET ELIMINATOR

HOT ROD
WORLD'S LARGEST AUTO

GIANT SECTION:
SMALL-BLOCK MOPARS

TECH BASICS:
INSTALL HIGH-LIFT CAMS

"RAT" ALUMINUM HEADS
FOR THE CHEVY V6

KING-KONG
OF THE
BIG-BLOCKS
NEW 650-INCH OLDS

LOVELY LINDA
WITH WARREN
JOHNSON'S
HURST OLDS
PRO STOCK

Win the All-New Corvette
Sweepstakes

May

SINGLE 4-BARREL, 460-C.I.D.
NINE-SECOND MUSTANG!

HOT ROD
WORLD'S LARGEST AUTOMOTIVE MAGAZINE

FIRST STREET MACHINE NATIONALS COVERAGE

GREAT NEW TOOL & WORKSHOP SERIES

UNREAL TWIN TURBO 10-SECOND GTO!

SATURDAY NIGHT SPECIALS!

Rae's

1983

September: Yep, that's the ZZ Top Eliminator cruising Rae's in Santa Monica. Though the car would become iconic thanks to MTV, its popularity was just starting to rise in mid-1983, explaining its low-key presence on this cover. It's the first of several Billy Gibbons cars to make *Hot Rod*'s cover.

35th ANNIVERSARY ISSUE!

SPECIAL SECTIONS
- **EARLY RODS & CUSTOMS**
- **'55-'57 CHEVYS**
- **MUSCLECARS**
- **HI-TECH MACHINES**

GUIDE TO WELDING EQUIPMENT

HOT ROD
MAGAZINE

HOW TO BUILD A STREET BLOWER ENGINE

December: For the 35th Anniversary issue, shooter Lorentzen gathers Petersen Publishing staffers to pose with Lee Fabry's 1955 Chevy. Editor Leonard Emanuelson says the time has come "to reaffirm who and what we are as a group ... HOT RODDERS, and the cars we modify, build and drive are HOT RODS!"

76956 14425

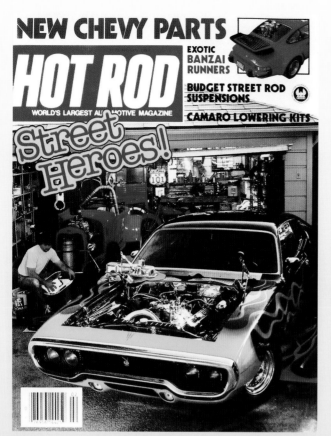

NEW CHEVY PARTS

EXOTIC BANZAI RUNNERS

BUDGET STREET ROD SUSPENSIONS

CAMARO LOWERING KITS

HOT ROD
WORLD'S LARGEST AUTOMOTIVE MAGAZINE

Street Heroes!

February

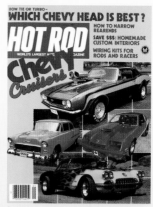

BOW TIE OR TURBO — WHICH CHEVY HEAD IS BEST?

HOT ROD Chevy Cruisers!

HOW TO NARROW REARENDS

SAVE $$$: HOMEMADE CUSTOM INTERIORS

WIRING KITS FOR RODS AND RACERS

January

Win the All-New Corvette Sweepstakes

HOT ROD 20 Race & Street Tips

MUSCLECAR FLASHBACK: ZL-1 CAMARO TEST

STREET Q-JET BUILDUP

NEW FORD RACE PARTS

THE NEW CORVETTE—IS IT FOR REAL?

March

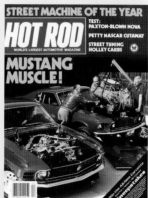

STREET MACHINE OF THE YEAR

HOT ROD MUSTANG MUSCLE!

TEST: PAXTON-BLOWN NOVA

PETTY NASCAR CUTAWAY

STREET TUNING HOLLEY CARBS

April

GIANT BOLT-ON PARTS ISSUE!

HOT ROD SUPER STREET

CHEVY 400 HP 305 SMOGGER

PRO GAS NORCAL STYLE

REAREND SNAPS: MUSTANG & CAMARO

PROJECT CHEVELLE BUILDUP

July

January: "We decided to bow tie one on with this fine collection of Chevy's best."

February: Did you spot the *Playboy* bunny in the Mopar's grille? Classy.

March: Wheels-up action heralds tips to go faster on the street and at the strip.

April: George Boskovich's "Shotgunned & Sock'ed 'Stangs" are "2 Bad," says Baskerville.

June: Some 1950s Flashbacks built by Chuck and Chuckie Lombardo, and Jim and JR McNamara.

July: *Hot Rod*'s alternative to Pro Street is Super Street—low buck and street drivable.

August: Dyno testing street blowers: They "*do* deliver what they promise."

October: Wild street cars include Rick Dyer's 9-second—and truly street-driven—Corvette.

November: Who will be King Rat, Lee Shepherd or Frank Iaconio? (Spoiler alert: It will be Shepherd.)

ALUMINUM ENGINES: PARTS & PIECES FOR ALL MAKES

HOT ROD STREET BLOWERS!

LEGAL STREET RACING!

HOW TO: BACKYARD BODYWORK

NOSTALGIA DRAGS RACE COVERAGE

DO THEY REALLY WORK? CONCLUSIVE DYNO RESULTS!

August

CHEVY'S PERFORMANCE FUTURE?

HOT ROD STREET SUPERCARS!

BUILDUP: 400-HP FORD 302 WINDSOR

400-C.I.D. CHEVY SMALL-BLOCK BRACKET SCREAMER

October

CHEVY BIG-BLOCK SECRETS

HOT ROD CHEVY KING

HOW-TO: HIGH-TORQUE STARTERS

CARTER CARB TUNING TIPS

BEGINNER'S GUIDE TO CAR STEREO EQUIPMENT

LEE SHEPHERD or FRANK IACONIO?

November

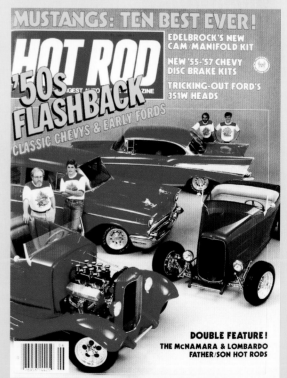

MUSTANGS: TEN BEST EVER!

HOT ROD '50s FLASHBACK
CLASSIC CHEVYS & EARLY FORDS

EDELBROCK'S NEW CAM/MANIFOLD KIT

NEW '55-'57 CHEVY DISC BRAKE KITS

TRICKING-OUT FORD'S 351W HEADS

DOUBLE FEATURE! THE McNAMARA & LOMBARDO FATHER/SON HOT RODS

June

1983

BUILD A $3500 **13-SEC STREET MACHINE**

$1.75 OCTOBER 1984 CANADA $2.25

HOT ROD

Can they
OUTLAW HOT RODDING?

WHAT'S HOT FOR '85!
- HOT NEW CARS
- 100 NEW PARTS

1984

1984

October

It's the year of Orwell and Big Brother, and the EPA is tackling air pollution by instituting vehicle Inspection and Maintenance (I/M) programs in much of the United States. The "dreaded I/M program is coming down on automobile owners like the Spanish Inquisition," writes Senior Editor Pat Ganahl, and with it comes the fear that hot rodding could be outlawed outright. Ganahl fills more than 10 exhaustively researched pages (pun intended) with data about air pollution; the fairness and cost-effectiveness of the I/M program; the tale of one hot rodder trying to pass I/M with a blown big-block Nova; and options available to rodders to keep their cars alive, from propane and alcohol conversions to swapping high performance chips into computer-controlled vehicles, "once we develop the technology to make such chips." Later he writes, "We seriously hope that our

Pat Ganahl follows this big-block Nova through a rigorous California smog test. It fails the visual inspection but runs clean. A referee later passes the car.

aftermarket industry will be awakened by this challenge, and will respond with high-performance, high-tech smog-control systems."

Former Editor Jim McFarland, working for Edelbrock as chief of development and design, is "one of the few members of the performance aftermarket industry to acknowledge the need for smog-control-compatible products," writes Ganahl. McFarland contributes a sidebar calling out "Some Inevitable Changes" that the performance enthusiast can expect, including extensive use of electronics, more fuel injection, coil-less ignition, even constantly variable transmissions (CVTs), which will be "available on selected U.S. models by 1986." Well, he was mostly right.

Note the first use of the redesigned "strobe-stripe" *Hot Rod* logo. It lasts about a year.

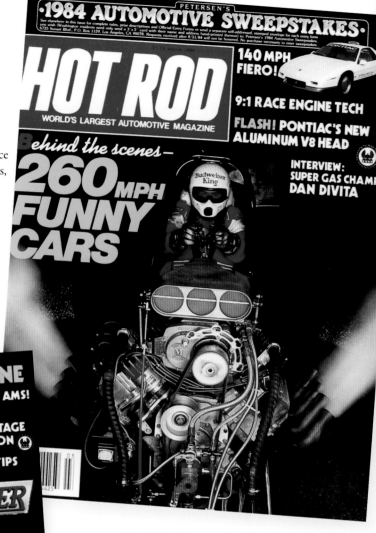

March: "What's one way to get lots of attention, wake up all the neighbors, and attract the police? On a peaceful evening, have Kenny Bernstein fire up the engine of his new Budweiser King Ford Tempo." That's what photographer Randy Lorentzen has Bernstein do; complaints come from literally miles away.

August: The cover description says Andy Granatelli's twin-turbo Z28 engine was glowing "like molten ore on the chassis dyno." Art Director Charlie Hayward created the effect with graphic arts trickery, but the Camaro did turn 219.53 miles per hour on a Nevada dry lake, then later tackled Ventura Freeway traffic.

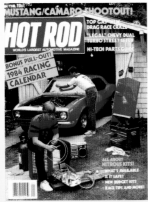
January

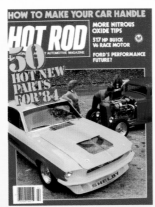
February

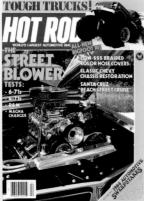
April

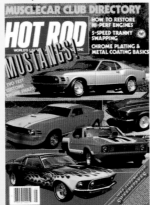
May

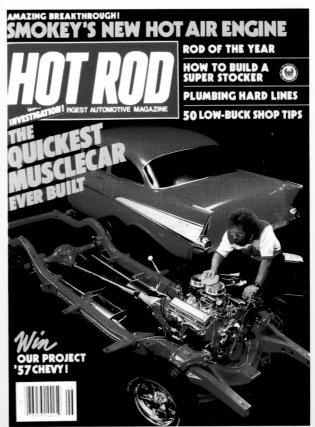
June

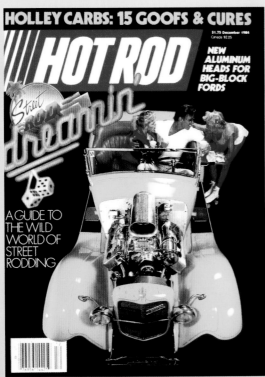
December

July

September

November

January: Dudes, car, detached garage: Remarkably similar to the March 1973 cover.

February: Two hot Fords from one family. What generation gap?

April: Trucks have been on the cover before, but this is a first for Bigfoot.

May: Hot Mustangs run the gamut from nearly resto to freaky and flamed.

June: The *Flashback '57* is immaculate, assembled, and ready for its sweepstakes.

July: Brad and Ron Berry's blown 1979 Camaro leads a cavalcade of Camaros inside.

September: The T-Bird is back as the new-wave supercar for just about anything.

November: The Mr. Gasket Aero Camaro street machine project hits the road.

December: Sitting in a hot roadster surrounded by pretty girls … what could be better?

1984

July

HOT CUSTOM WHEEL IDEAS

Canada $2.50 July 1985 $2.00

HOT ROD

HOT ROD MAGAZINE

SCOOP!
GLIDDEN & ELLIOTT'S
LATEST SPEED SECRET

BASIC BACKYARD
BODYWORK

*the new trend that's
spreading Fast & Wide
across America*

Hot Rod didn't discover fat-fendered rods, as Leonard Emanuelson writes in his editor's column this month. "Heck, fat-fendered hot rods have been around since '36. What we are touting here, however, are the new trends connected with these cars." Or, to put it in Baskerville-speak, "Fat is where it's at!"

Fueling the fat fire are rod builders Pete Chapouris, Jim Jacobs, and Fat Jack Robinson—"our three prophets of plump." Says Baskerville in the issue's cover story, the three "collectively had a brainstorm. They came up with the idea of pumping some interest into the one element of hot/ street rodding that has remained relatively stagnant since the great rod-related revival of the early '70s. 'Why not,' they said, 'build some performance-oriented fat-fendered hot rods?'" In doing so, they ignited a trend that continued to burn for years.

The pioneering fatties, photographed for the cover by Petersen's Jim Brown, take two different approaches to fat-fenderdom. Pete and Jake's *Portly Forty*—"actually a radically reworked '39 Gibbon 'glass replica ragtop bolted to a 'fixture-perfect' '40 Ford frame—represents the rod and custom part of the two-pronged Fat Attack," Baskerville writes. Emanuelson describes it this way: "It has the outward appearance of a custom, the performance of a drag racer, and hot rod hardware like Halibrand-style wheels, warmed-over small-block, and fenderwell headers." On the other hand, Fat Jack's '46 "is a smooth rod on the outside," but underneath "it's Pro Street all the way, the kind of thing that would make a Pro Street Camaro owner green with envy."

Unlike some Pro Streeters, though, these cars run. Both would make passes at the Nostalgia Nationals in Fremont, California. "Pete's '39 ran 12.20s at over 112 mph all weekend long, while Fat Jack's '46 laid down a 10.19 on only its second pass," Emanuelson writes. "And that's what

Opposite: The *Hot Rod* staff gets in on the Chapouris/Jacobs/Robinson Fat Attack.

these cars are all about—exploding the myth that early cars are for the geriatric generation."

In another trend-setting story, Baskerville offers his take on custom wheel ideas for mid-1985. The article opens with nine photos of how rodders can add color to the "visual wastelands" that mags or wires represent. Six pages later, after covering modular construction, backspacing, and other wheel tech, B'ville writes a sidebar on how Boyd "Hot Dogs by Floyd" Coddington is building "semi-custom modular wheels" from billet aluminum. It won't be long before Boyd's billet wheels—and all their emulators—will be *the* hot wheels for street machines of all kinds.

Glidden and Elliott's latest speed secret, revealed in a story by Senior Editor Pat Ganahl, is a "high-swirl,

1985

lean-burn cylinder head" built by Larry Widmer. These so-called "soft heads" (because the burn lasts longer, reducing cylinder head pressure) have until now been closely guarded. "To be sure," Ganahl writes, "neither the Elliotts nor the Gliddens are overjoyed about our discussing the subject; when you have an edge in racing—a 'secret weapon'—you don't tell the competition about it."

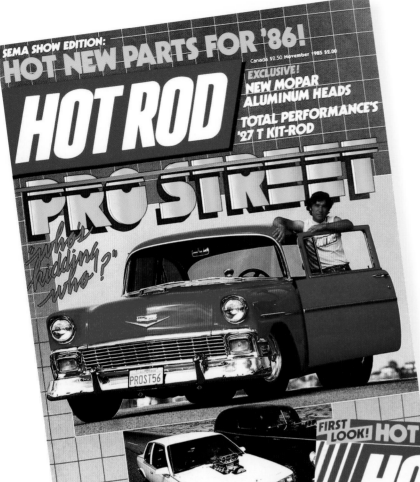

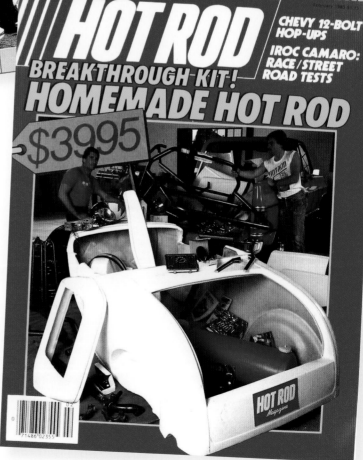

November: "To quote Editor Leonard Emanuelson: 'Pro Street is neither.'" So opens Ganahl's controversial "Who's Kidding Who?" story. It doesn't exactly condemn the Pro Street phenomenon but insists the dual-purpose car that can run 8.90s at the strip and cruise the fairgrounds all weekend long is a myth.

February: The antidote to mega-dollar dream machines is Speedway Motors' Lo-Boy, a fiberglass 1932 roadster kit available for less than $4,000. This car is built in a five-part series, then driven cross-country on the Victory Tour to the Hot Rod Supernationals in Indy.

1985

January: This special features hot trucks high and low, but none higher than *Bearfoot*.

March: Ganahl starts a how-to-paint series and a long-standing practice of spring paint issues.

April: A special see-through photo of Mr. Gasket Vette reveals the new tube chassis street car trend.

May: Engine swap special includes a small-block Chevy transplant into a Datsun 240Z.

June: Speedway Motors' Lo-Boy project is "finished, fast & fun"; Shelby flogs his four-wheel-drive Daytona.

August: Four of "L.A.'s baddest street machines" pose in front of the oldest McDonald's.

September: "Chevy came with no ammunition and Ford brought the big guns" to the 1986 shootout.

October: Inside is coverage of the Victory Tour, the granddaddy of today's Power Tour.

December: These are the 10 best (readers') cars featured in *Hot Rod* during 1985.

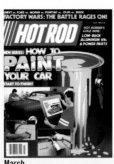

March

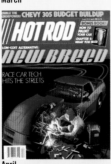

April

May

January

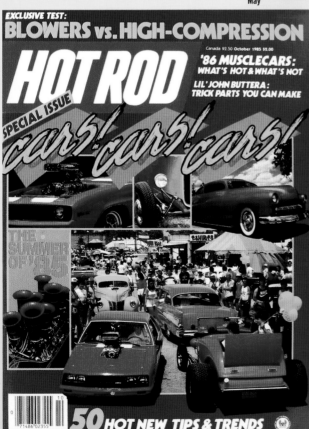

October

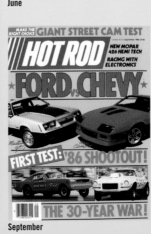

June

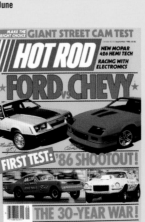

September

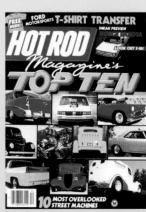

August

December

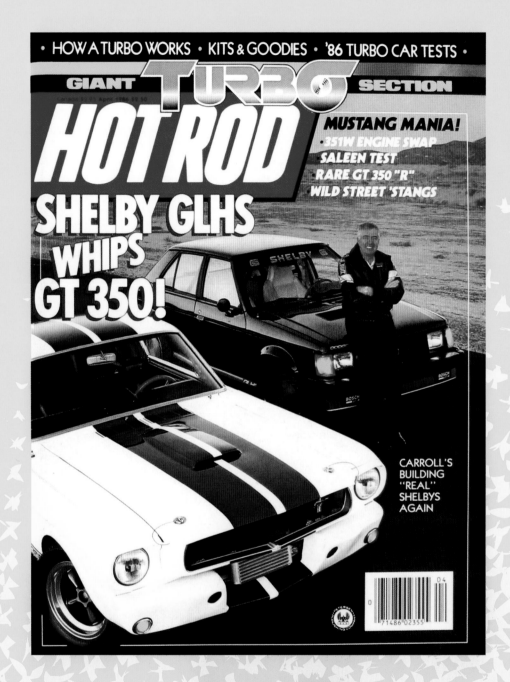

April

Die-hard muscle car purists weep, Shelby Club members are outraged, and *Hot Rod*'s newsstand buyers stay away in droves. But you can't argue with the clock: Carroll Shelby's front-wheel-drive, four-cylinder, turbocharged Omni GLHS really does get the better of a 1965 GT350 at Willow Springs Raceway. For its shock value alone, this is 1986's most fascinating cover topic.

Though he's still consulting for Dodge, Shelby sets up shop "to build the cars the bean counters won't let Iacocca make," writes Feature Editor Rick Titus. Says Shelby, "We'll be building today's cars ... you boys had better learn to deal with that fact." No more Cobras or Mustangs for ol' Shel. Instead, his aim is to build a "low-cost (about $11,000), front-wheel-drive (because that's what

Chrysler is manufacturing today), four-cylinder (mileage and economy still call the shots), turbocharged (because some folks still want to enjoy driving a car) little car (because today it's required to make better use of space and materials)," Titus writes.

Before the GT350 turns a wheel, Titus is impressed with what Shelby has done to the Omni GLH Turbo, including finding 30 more horsepower from the 2.2L four-banger. "Yes folks, this puppy is definitely quicker. Lots quicker. And it's quicker everywhere! On the straights, in the turns, everywhere." His only disappointment is with the car's brakes, which are overdriven to the point of catching fire.

The counterpoint to Shelby's new black 'banger is Phil Schmit's GT350, a well-restored track car with an "admittedly 'smiled on'" 289 V-8 producing some 350 horsepower. "Considered by his fellow [Shelby American Automobile Club] members to be a quick Shelby driver, Schmit was chosen to champion 'the good ol' days,'" Titus says.

"The two cars took to the track looking as mismatched as David and Goliath. It was a growling V-8 against a muffled straight four—a fat-rubbered, rear-drive, 3,000-pound muscle car versus a gumballed, front-drive, 2,300-pound shoebox." Yet the GLHS jumps out quickly and puts a 10-car-length lead on the GT350 that the older car just can't make up over three rapid laps. After letting the Mustang

1986

catch the Omni, "another three-lap ding-dong developed: this time the GLHS closed up. By mid-point of the second lap the GLHS was on the trunk of the GT350. To pass would serve no point. The cars returned to the pits together. Shelby beamed."

Objectively, the GLHS lapped Willow two seconds faster than the GT350, and its 14.7-second quarter-mile performance eclipsed period road tests of the Mustang by a full second. Does that make it a "real" Shelby, as the cover line promises? Time will tell.

The shootout inspires many related stories in the issue, including an eight-article special section on turbocharging and several Mustang features, including Titus' report on Steve Saleen's Signature Series Mustang. "If you don't know the name Steve Saleen, you will. He's an automotive designer who we're all going to be taking very seriously, very soon."

The GLHS may have surpassed the legendary GT350 on the track, but not in the hearts of muscle car purists.

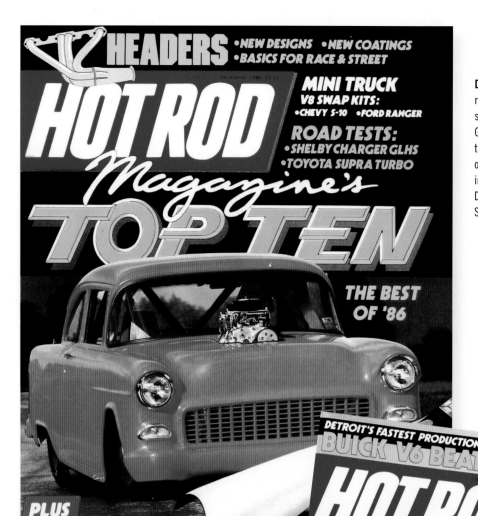

December: The Top Ten best hot rods are back, and this year one is selected as "Hot Rod of the Year." Given its cover placement, you'd think Dave Mordhorst's chubby orange Chevy was the top rod; instead, that nod goes to Rick Dobbertin's "beyond belief" Pro Street Pontiac J2000.

May: Also making a return is the custom paint theme, with young gun Ruben Huante airbrushing hot 1980s paint trends onto Frank Huante's Firebird. "Detroit's Fastest Production Car" is Buick's intercooled Turbo Regal, which turns 14.30 quarters "while you're surrounded by the plushest appointments this side of an airport limo."

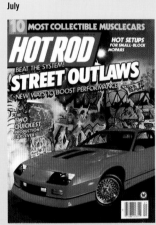

1986

July

January: *Hot Rod*'s 12-second IROC burns cleaner than stock but is a tampered-with "outlaw."

February: From monsters to minis, "Anything can happen when hot rodders go trucking!"

March: The fold-out cover makes the "Easy Modifications" line hard to understand.

June: Kit cars are upstaged by Garlits' 272-mile-per-hour run in streamlined *Swamp Rat XXX*.

July: Sign of the times: "Emissions equipment" makes the Power Tuning list.

August: Another sign of the times: hot rodded four-bangers from the Big Three.

September: Baskerville shoots "Atlanta's incredible Rat Pack"; Emanuelson leaves after 68 issues as editor.

October: Ganahl is the new editor; the Mustang, Firebird, and Daytona Shelby Z are hot for 1987.

November: Rocky Robertson's Pro Street Buick is way more powerful than the computers behind it.

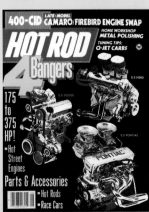

January

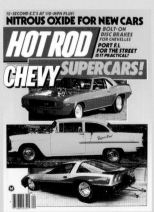

February

March

June

August

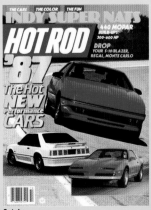

September

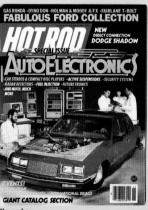

October

November

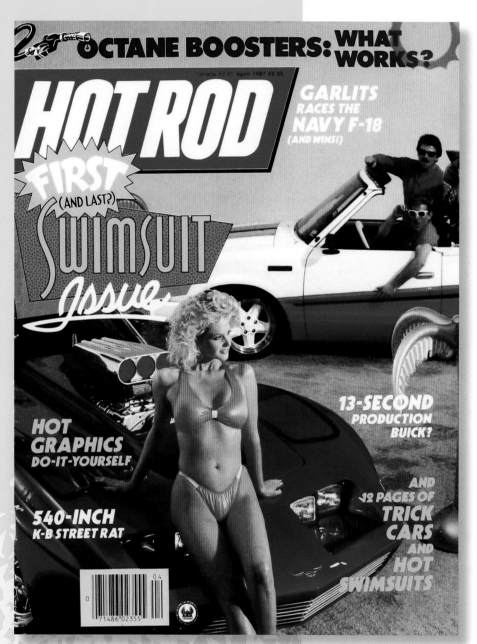

Do we have to explain the whole girl/car thing? Both are typically teenage obsessions, and they've been an auto mechanic's calendar staple since, well, since mechanics had tool boxes to put them in. *Hot Rod*, too, has a long-standing tradition of including pretty models on its pages; the "Parts with Appeal" pages, pairing Hollywood starlets with speed parts, began with the very first issue.

In 1987, only *Sports Illustrated* produces an annual swimsuit issue. Editor Pat Ganahl doesn't want to emulate *SI*'s format, he wants to spoof it, and all the other artificial, cheesy setups typical of girl-with-car photography. It's to be the issue's April Fool's joke.

Ganahl hires freelance photographer Randy Lorentzen to execute the section. Ganahl wants "real Southern California girls in real swimsuits," not biker babes in G-strings. And no matter where Lorentzen stages the photo—a garage, junkyard, or donut shop—Ganahl wants beachy props: umbrellas, folding chairs, a boom box. The only shot Ganahl supervises is the cover. He finds the cars he wants; buys props for the studio, including hundreds of pounds of sand for the floor and an inflatable palm tree; and also hires a second photographer, Robert Kittila, to make the shot.

As the photo is originally framed, there are a half-dozen guys in the bed of Randy Leach's Nissan convertible pickup, all whistling and hooting at model Stevie Sterling as she reclines on Allen Fossat's blown Corvette. The final version, though, crops most of those guys out, as their attitude was considered by management to be demeaning to women in general and Stevie in particular.

April

For reasons that had nothing to do with this section, this would be Ganahl's last issue as Editor. But he is still on the magazine's staff when the circulation results come in. The swimsuit issue increases newsstand sales by 100,000 copies, a phenomenal number. That kind of success turns Ganahl's spoof into a regular *Hot Rod* April issue feature for nearly a decade. Some joke.

Speaking of popular features, the "Which is faster, a jet or a dragster?" debate comes up again in this issue, as Big Daddy Don Garlits goes up against a Navy F/A-18 shot from a steam catapult. The shootout is staged at Lakehurst Naval Air Station, where a 300-foot "track"— the distance at which the jet leaves the ground—is set up. Art Hayward, the NHRA's chief timing technician, and Buster Couch, the NHRA's official starter, are there to set up the clocks and sanction the test. It's not a heads-up race; the jet leaves first and travels through the lights in 2.39 seconds (with Publisher Harry Hibler in the jet's back seat). Garlits can't hook up on the virgin concrete and settles for a 2.66-second pass. The following weekend, special 300-foot lights are set up at the Keystone Nationals drag race. With "excellent traction and a completely smooth surface," Garlits travels 300 feet in 2.29 seconds, beating the jet by a tenth.

What started as an April Fool's spoof becomes an annual feature in the magazine for nearly a decade.

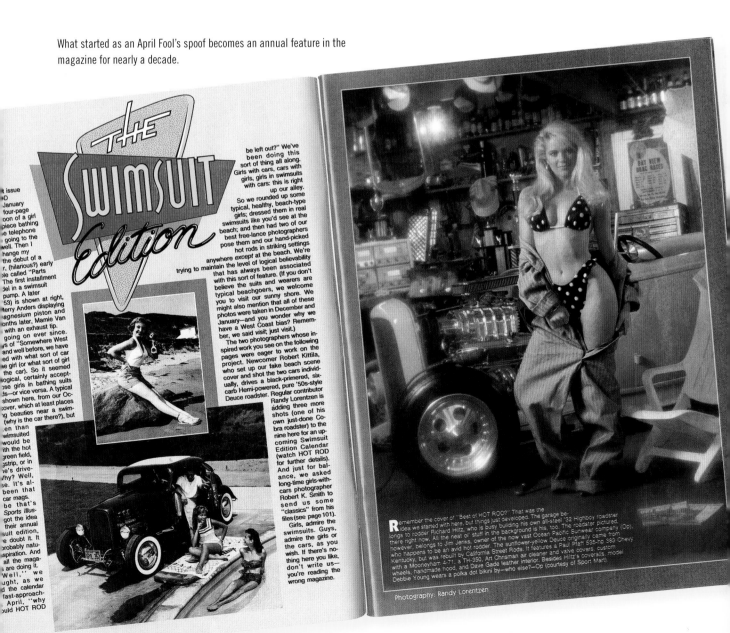

Photography: Randy Lorentzen

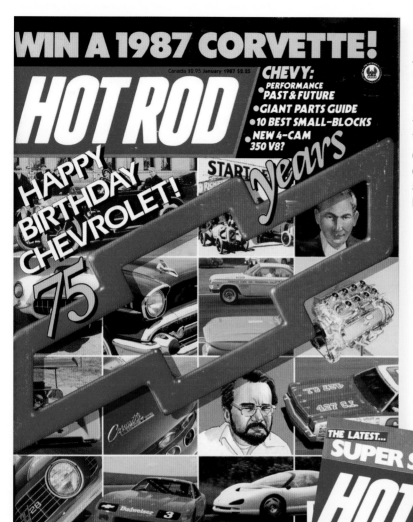

January: *Hot Rod* celebrates Chevrolet's milestone with a look back at the company's history (including a reprint of Duntov's famous "Thoughts Pertaining to Youth … " memo), a forecast of things to come (no, the mid-engine Corvette wouldn't happen), a cool 1956 Bel Air, and a 350 IROC Z road test.

December: Editor Jeff Smith kicks off a Mother Road tour in a 1962 Corvette, echoing the old *Route 66* TV series. The 'Vette comes from former editor Leonard Emanuelson, who got it from former editor Lee Kelley. "It was destined to stay in the family!" writes Smith.

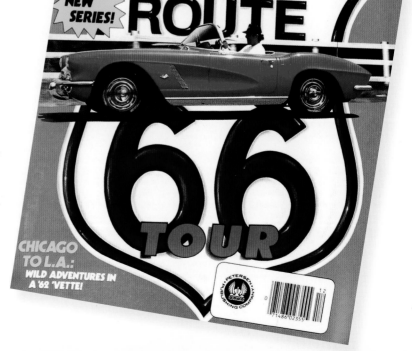

February: "Free Horsepower" refers to Ganahl's memorable "Caddy Hack" deVille massacre with a carbide saw.

March: How to make your street machine safely kick the leaded gas habit.

May: 'Vettes and trucks: "Two of the hottest vehicles in hot rodding today."

June: It's Z/28 versus Z28 in a 1960s versus 1980s muscle car confrontation.

July: How-to's with a basic plan: "Bolt-on, budget-conscious and brief," writes Baskerville.

August: Chevy, Ford, and Mopar parts combinations "that will make you a horsepower hero."

September: Editor Smith asks, "Why not build it wild and make it streetable, too?"

October: The secret Fiero on dyno rollers is topped by Pete Chapouris' *Limefire* centerfold inside.

November: Street Machine Nats, Monterey Historics, nostalgia drags, Pikes Peak … what a summer.

1987

March

May

June

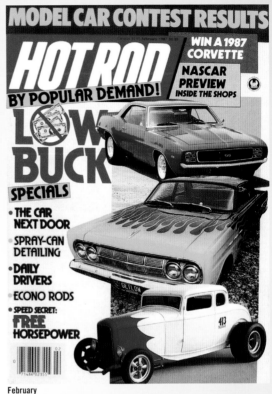

February

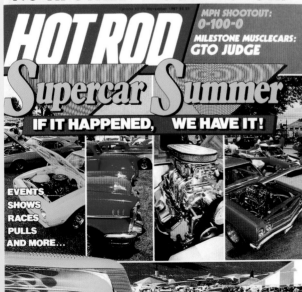

November

July

August

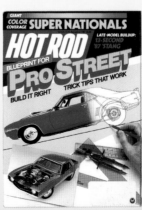

September

October

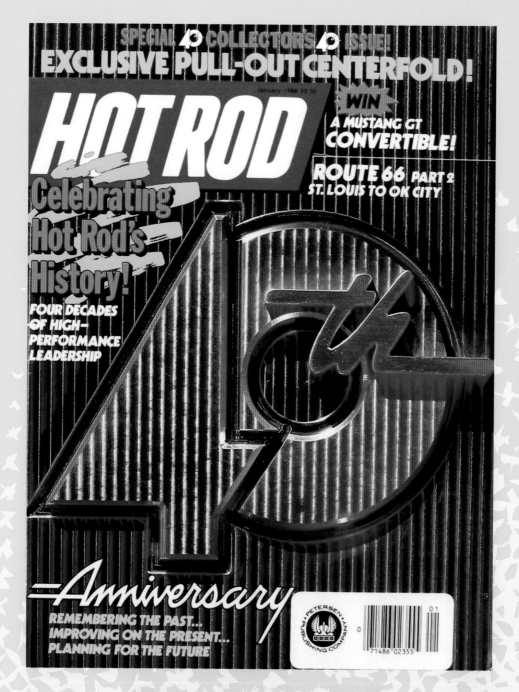

January

As *Hot Rod* ages, commemorating each milestone proves a new challenge to the editorial regime. This 40th anniversary cover is somewhat similar in concept to the 25th anniversary cover from January 1973—with the page dominated by large numerals and small blurbs—but the execution here is wholly different. Artist/designer Joe Goebel is commissioned to create a 40th anniversary logo, which is then turned over to hot rod fabricator Larry Ruth to be rendered in billet aluminum. Petersen staff shooter Lynne McCready-Coombes photographs the alloy sculpture under the direction of Art Director Craig Korn. How much the studio lighting contributes to the image's "pop" is illustrated by a photo of the sculpture—without the colored lights—on the table of contents. Ruth's alloy artistry falls somewhat flat when the aluminum is shown in its natural gray shade.

The anniversary content inside covers 32 pages and starts with a hand-tinted version of the famous photo of Bob Petersen photographing a lakes roadster at speed. Editor Jeff Smith writes about the founding of the magazine, and then each decade is covered with photos and captions. The chapters are a highlight reel of hot rodding's, and *Hot Rod*'s, most memorable moments, from lakes racing in the 1950s to the advent of Pro Street in the 1980s.

The section ends with a story predicting the future of rodding in the twenty-first century. Some of the guesses are remarkably spot-on. Feature Editor Philippe Danh writes, "Tomorrow's rodder [will be able to buy] a rear-wheel-drive automobile, possibly still V-8 powered, even at the turn of the century. No doubt this will be a sophisticated machine offering excellent overall performance and comfort, not just raw power and brutal acceleration." Danh also successfully predicts the reproduction of popular body styles of the past—Mustang fastbacks, 1955 Chevys and 1969 Camaros. What he doesn't foresee is the import tuner trend, instead guessing that "the affordable, high performance machines of the

1988

'80s (Z28/IROC Zs, Corvettes, Trans-Ams, Mustang GTs) will become the entry-level hot rods" by the year 2000.

Later in the issue, the historic theme is revisited with a twist. Senior Editors Pat Ganahl and Gray Baskerville compile the editorial content for a special Ford advertising section called "The Hot Rod Story." Far from the typical fluff found in most advertorial sections, this is a thoroughly researched and illustrated history of Ford performance, from Henry Ford racing Number 999 to the slippery NASCAR Thunderbirds.

The pull-out centerfold advertised at the top of the magazine offers a mix of old and new. The poster features Rick Worthington's 1969 Camaro, which was originally bought new by Rick's father. Rick got the car "with the promise that all I would do is put on a set of headers, rims, and tires," he says. But then he turned it, in stages, into a 1980s Pro Street machine. "Well, I guess I shot that promise all to hell. Anyway, he likes the car better now."

This anniversary issue includes a pull-out centerfold featuring Rick Worthington's Pro Street Camaro.

April: The first swimsuit issue may have been controversial, but it was a newsstand hit. So Smith is tasked with doing it again and hires Randy Lorentzen "to capture our heavenly hot rodders indulging in rod-related activities," writes the mysteriously named Rick Shaw. The issue—again—sells big.

March: Nothing says "1980s" like Day-Glo graphics, and the magazine features some of the latest licks, plus stories about how to apply them. And well before it is simple to do so in Photoshop, Art Director Korn has the printer change the cover Camaro's paint from white to yellow.

1988

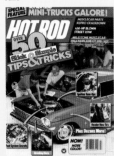
June

July

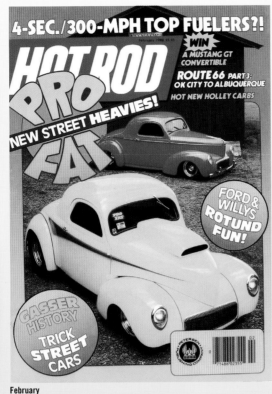
February

August

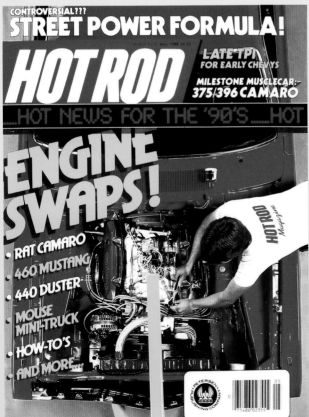
May

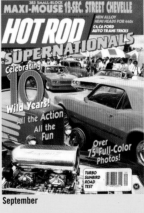
September

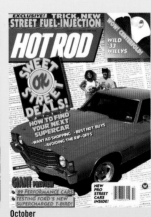
October

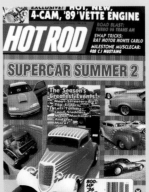
November

December

July

A good magazine does more than report trends, it leads them, and that's what happens when Editor Jeff Smith executes his first "Dare to be Different" cover theme. The germ of this idea goes back to a rendering by Thom Taylor of a blown and slammed bullet-nose Studebaker. While it looked weird at first, the more Smith studied the drawing, the more he wondered about the viability of non-mainstream car bodies as project-car potential. In his November 1988 editorial, he sent out a call to "shake things up in the street machine world." Just as street rodders have experimented with alternative body styles, "why not consider something completely different— such as a '53 Studebaker Commander or a '49 Ford—as a Pro Street candidate?" Taylor's Stude illustrates the column.

At about the same time, ZZ Top guitarist Billy Gibbons approaches Boyd Coddington with an idea for a radical car to follow up his popular Eliminator three-window coupe. Gibbons wants his next hot rod to blend the style of a 1950s custom with late 1980s technology,

and he shares his ideas with designer Larry Erickson. They come up with a starting point that is definitely different: a 1948 Cadillac Series 62 Sedanette, a fastback two-door that carried Cadillac's first tailfins. Erickson pens a long, low custom "with a Bonneville feel," and Boyd and his crew are tasked with turning Erickson's full-size 2D drawings into a rolling 3D masterpiece.

Boyd shares the idea with his friend (and *Hot Rod* publisher) Harry Hibler. They agree the car is a natural for the magazine, and Smith has the literal poster child—and cover subject—for his alternative body idea: *CadZZilla*.

As Gray Baskerville explains in his article, *CadZZilla*'s body remains all steel, though every panel is radically altered by "tin-bender" Craig Naff. Boyd mounts the body on a new space frame rather than modify the Cad's old chassis, and rodding pioneer Art Chrisman massages a 500-inch Caddy engine for the beast, what B'ville calls a "torque motor, the ones used to power all those armored presidential limos." The interior "is as awesome as the Cad'zz exterior," with its custom seats, restored original instrument panel and modern Sony sound system hidden behind the vintage glovebox door.

1989

Randy Lorentzen's cover shoot is one of the most complex in the magazine's history, with an intricately art directed backdrop and an appearance by all three members of ZZ Top for a double-gatefold poster inside the issue. The finished *CadZZilla* is so big it won't fit in the publishing company's photo studio, so another is rented, one with enough dressing rooms for each band member to have his own. As the car is photographed, Smith realizes its most dramatic angle is from the rear, and that's the angle he chooses for the cover, a decision that flies in the face of conventional cover composition wisdom.

CadZZilla's "Dare to be Different" issue goes on to be the best selling in *Hot Rod* history.

How to ensure a best-selling issue: Include this eight-page autographed poster featuring ZZ Top with *CadZZilla*.

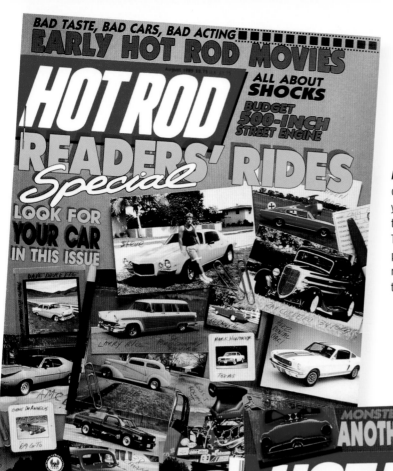

August: To answer the age-old question, "How do I get my car in your magazine?" Smith asks readers to send in photos of their projects. The response is huge, fills 22 pages of the issue, and kicks off a recurring cover theme that continues to sell well on the newsstand.

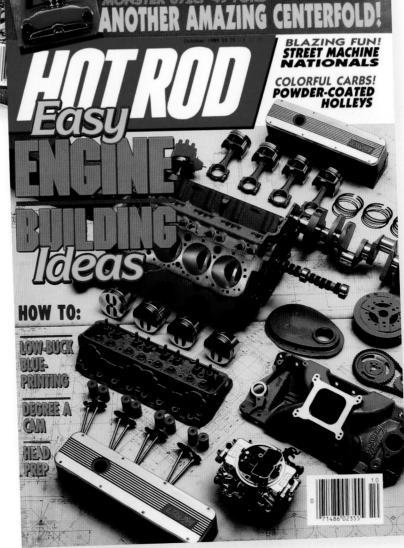

October: Thirty-three years earlier, a Chevy V-8's parts were laid out like this for a story on Vic Edelbrock's first small-block hop-up. Petersen Photographic's Jim Brown executes this late-1980s version, with parts donated by PAW, B&M, Ed Hamburger, Holley, and, yes, Edelbrock.

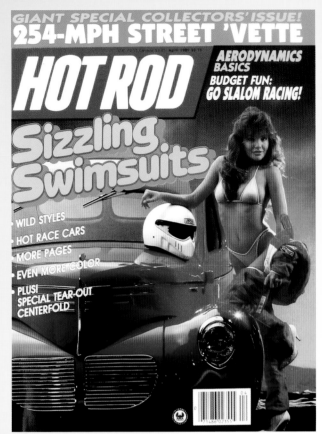

April

January

February

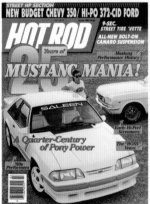

March

May

January: Turns out the Banshee isn't the next Firebird, but there's a preview of *CadZZilla* inside.

February: Scott Sullivan's "too hip" small-block, complete with raspberry-pink paint and dry-brush graphics.

March: New staffer Joe Pettitt looks cool surrounded by 25 years of Mustang performance.

April: School librarians be damned, here comes another swimsuit issue, rendered again by Randy Lorentzen.

May: Performance bolt-ons share space with another "Paint & Body" special.

June: The staff overdelivers with more than 125 "plans, schemes, ideas and dreams" inside.

September: The Supernationals remains a highlight of any car guy's summer.

November: The National Muscle Car Association's first showdown previews Fastest Street Cars to come.

December: How do you pick a "best" in a year full of such great cars?

June

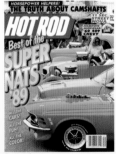

September

November

December

1989

Chapter 6

1990-1999

Cover designs were getting cluttered in the late 1980s, but by the 1990s they looked almost frantic. This was the peak of the "busy is better" period, when editors were told to essentially run their table of contents on the cover. Even the venerable *Hot Rod* logo, which had lived in the cover's upper left corner since 1948, was centered in mid-1991 to make room for more cover blurbs. (It moved back after about a year.)

The reason for this desperation? *Hot Rod*'s circulation peak in 1989 started to fall off within the first few months of 1990, and management was looking for ways to shore up the sagging numbers.

In some ways, *Hot Rod* and its parent publishing company were victims of the magazine's success. As far back as the late 1940s, Bob Petersen had spun off titles from his founding publication into areas not covered by *Hot Rod*'s editorial scope—*Motor Trend* was for new car buyers and *Cycle* for motorcycle enthusiasts. Some, like *Car Craft*, were awfully close to *Hot Rod*'s turf, but in the early years of car magazine publishing, there were enough readers to soak up the new magazines.

Starting in the 1970s, niche magazines began to populate the newsstands in greater numbers. By the 1990s, it seemed like every type of car love had its own publication, and they were stealing readers from the *Hot Rod* mother ship. The knee-jerk reaction at first was to throw a ton of stuff on the cover and hope something would attract buyers. But as the decade progressed, the magazine's editors found some worthy topics that generated plenty of reader interest, despite the crowded covers.

If there was a unifying theme to what sold magazines in the 1990s it was a return to cars that worked. *CadZZilla*, the ultimate Boyd Coddington custom creation, was a "reacher," as Gray Baskerville put it, a rod built for the long haul. Rob Kinnan and Steve Anderson proved the point by driving *CadZZilla* some 2,200 miles to the Hot Rod Supernats in 1990. The genesis of the Fastest Street Car Shootouts in the early 1990s was essentially to disprove Leonard Emanuelson's "Pro Street is neither" quip: You *could* build a drag strip terror that could also negotiate city traffic. (And they did, at least for a few years.) The Power Tour®, probably the most popular *Hot Rod* event ever, began in 1995 with the idea that people would want to join the magazine's editors as they drove project cars across the country. Seven did that year. Now Long Haulers number in the thousands.

> ## The Power Tour®, probably the most popular *Hot Rod* event ever, began in 1995 with the idea that people would want to join the magazine's editors as they drove project cars across the country.

Editor Ro McGonegal would close the decade with two issues devoted to a topic that combined this real car theme with the low-buck approach to engine building. The Junkyard Jewel engines featured in January and August 1999 were huge hits with the readers, so much so that the topic has been revisited almost every year since.

When Troy Trepanier debuts his 1960 Chevy Impala at the Hot Rod Supernats, suddenly wild graphics are just so 1980s.

Pete Walsh takes part in two of the hottest events in the 1990s by driving his Fastest Street Car Pro Street Nova on the first Power Tour® in 1995. He repeats the race/tour drill in 1996 with a Super Street Nova.

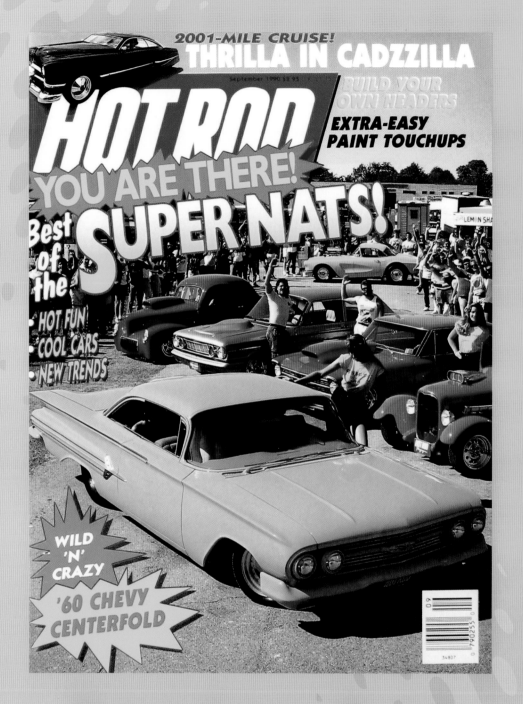

September

How super is the 1990 Hot Rod Supernationals? Ohio's Canfield Fairgrounds are packed with more than 2,300 vehicles and nearly 80,000 spectators. Among them are two clear standouts: Troy Trepanier's 1960 Impala and 1989's "Dare to be Different" cover model, *CadZZilla*.

The Imp isn't Troy's first car in *Hot Rod*, but it lands him his first cover and sets the wheels in motion for the young man from Manteno, Illinois, to eventually set up one of the country's premier custom shops, Rad Rides by Troy. In 1990, though, Troy is a 20-year-old who works on other people's cars by day and his own street machine projects at night. Gray Baskerville tells the tale of the car that Troy then called the *Greenhouse Effect* (but later renamed the *Pro Box*): It started life as a one-owner 40,000-mile cream puff that Troy bought in Texas. "It wasn't just the '60s body style I liked," he says. "You just don't see them around here. I knew when I slammed it down and tubbed it out, I would end up with a car that had the look."

"The look," though, goes further than your typical Pro Street stance. Troy is subtle with the body mods, staying away from the usual hole-through-the-hood treatment and simplifying the car's appearance by removing trim and the door handles and then coating the entire body—grille, bumpers, and all—in Winter Mint green. In his coverage of the Supernats, Feature Editor Joe Pettitt calls out Trepanier's monochrome paint as a new rodding trend. "Being wild for the sake of being wild doesn't strike a chord anymore; the color combinations work more with the vehicle's lines and styling, as opposed to being applied without regard to the shape of the car." Troy's mint Imp "simply stole the show," says Pettitt.

CadZZilla has farther to go to get to Canfield, but it does so in memorable style: It is driven there by *Hot Rod*'s two newest staffers, Feature Editor Steve Anderson and Editorial Assistant Rob Kinnan. Writes Anderson, "The

1990

idea of a road trip in CadZZilla started simply enough. ZZ Top's Billy Gibbons had a belief that CadZZilla was a true road car, not a useless garage queen." Gibbons, though, was busy in the studio with his band mates, so the magazine stepped up for the 2,200-mile road trip.

After leaving Boyd's shop, Anderson and Kinnan "drove cautiously the first few miles as we became attuned to CadZZilla's subtle ways, but soon, the road was ours." The radical custom drew crowds wherever it stopped, which was often, given its 10-mpg thirst. Along the way it was joined by other rods, including the original *California Kid*. And it ran flawlessly, through a desert sandstorm, over Colorado's Rockies and even in the rain. "CadZZilla is more than the ultimate hot rod," Anderson writes, "it's a profound statement about life, youth, adventure, and the simple joys of cruising the open road."

Just some of the cars that make the Hot Rod Supernationals so super.

SUPER NATS

Steve Haessly, from Marietta, Ohio, won Best Full Size Truck with his '56 Ford F-100 (top left). Dave Atwood, "the grandfather of cool," puts a new spin on kemps with his winged "Pro Sled" Merc (top right). Mark Tate's wild Gran Sport replica (above) made a splash, while subtle graphics accent this clean rod (above left). Meanwhile, "Kid" Kennedy acts up for the camera as Dave Shields' chopped red-on-red '56 Chevy is photographed.

Bob Morris' Pro Street '90 Poncho Grand Am (top left) with a TPI engine stirred things up at the Super Nats. Joe "Baby 'Bolt" McCormick's red Camaro (above right) is an ultraclean streeter that features Sullivan graphics and a high coefficient of cool. Back on the fat side of town, Colin Palmer of Dunville, Ontario, Canada, won the Fat Attack Award with his '41 Chevy Coupe. Bob Taddle won our appreciation for an inspired sport truck (above right). Bart Simpson says it all concerning Bob Maynard's '71 Camaro.

RADICAL CAR MAN!

January: Vaughn Barnes' Hot Rod Café (he's behind the counter) and Jonathan Nagel's 1958 "Pro Pink" Corvette set the stage for the entire *Hot Rod* staff to appear on the automobilia-themed cover, along with model Sheila Hamada (holding the tray) and car builder Scott Sullivan (way in the back).

July: In the November 1988 issue, Editor Jeff Smith challenged the rodding world to "Dare to be Different," using a Thom Taylor rendering of a Pro Street Studebaker by example. John Carter's Pro Stude brings Taylor's drawing to life and lands him on the second DTBD cover.

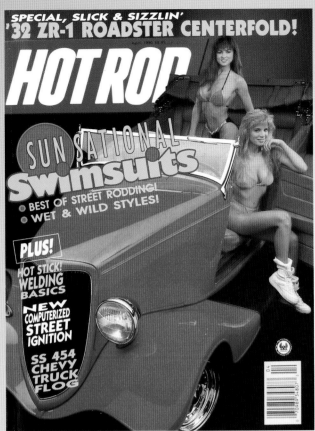

SPECIAL, SLICK & SIZZLIN'
'32 ZR-1 ROADSTER CENTERFOLD!

HOT ROD

SUNSATIONAL swimsuits

- BEST OF STREET RODDING!
- WET & WILD STYLES!

PLUS!
HOT STICK!
WELDING BASICS
NEW COMPUTERIZED STREET IGNITION
SS 454 CHEVY TRUCK FLOG

April

February

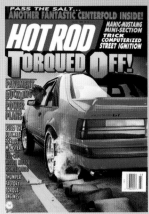

March

May

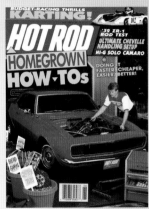

June

February: Low-buck supercars are topped by high-speed adventures on land and in the sky.

March: Kinnan ripples the pavement—OK, not really—in a 5.0L Mustang. Now that's torque.

April: Lensman Lorentzen trips the shutter again for the fourth annual swimsuit issue.

May: This month's cover section is the "wheel" deal, helping readers choose the right rollers.

June: The dude-car-garage cover setup is back, this time to illustrate readers' tech tips.

August: "Readers' Rides" is revisited, along with "Terror Trucks" in a special two-fer issue.

October: The theme is low-buck power, while the cover Camaro is, admittedly, fast, not cheap.

November: The second NMCA street-car Shootout dominates the Musclecar Action issue.

December: The "best" retrospective returns; a three-way tie for Rod of the Year goes to Troy.

August

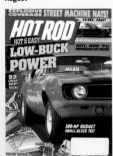

October

December

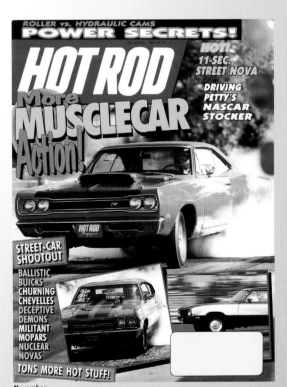

November

1990

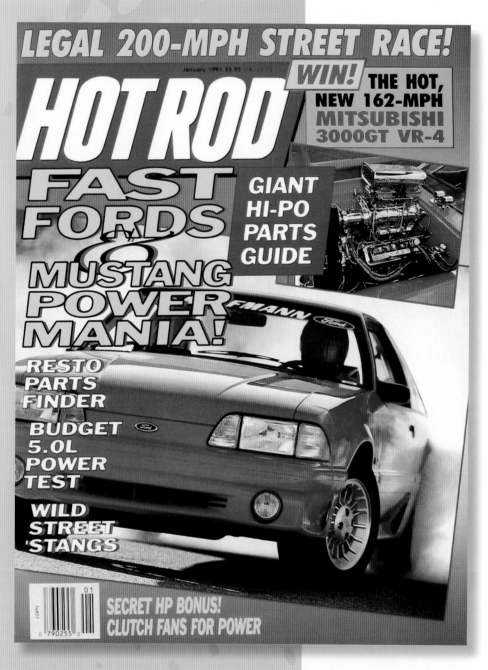

Few cars have had as much of an impact on the automotive performance marketplace as the 5.0L Mustang. While the first Fox-platform Mustang is introduced in 1979—bringing a merciful end to the Mustang II—the first glimmer of true performance appears when it's teamed with the 302-cubic-inch, 157-horsepower HO V-8 in the 1982 Mustang GT. From that hi-po starting point, Ford regularly refines its mass-market performance car. By the 1991 model year, the Mustang GT is fitted with a fuel-injected 5.0L that produces 225 horsepower.

Of course, FoMoCo isn't the only outfit improving the Mustang's performance. The 5.0L turns out to be as receptive to modification as the small-block Chevy V-8 was decades before, and the aftermarket responds with a growing array of products that range from simple bolt-ons to stroker kits and forced induction. Over time, the 5.0L Mustang will prove to be so popular, in fact, that it will develop a mini-industry of its own. Along with dedicated 5.0L parts and shops specializing in their manufacture and installation, there will be 5.0L race series and shootouts, and a number of Mustang-dedicated magazines. The performance and publishing industries will never be the same.

Hot Rod's January issue feeds into "Mustang Power Mania" as it's hitting its peak. There are pages of speed parts; a dyno test of Ford's remanufactured 5.0L engine outfitted with different power-making parts combinations (output climbs from 244 horsepower in stock configuration to 330 horsepower with Hedman headers, an Edelbrock intake manifold, and Dart II iron cylinder heads); and a roundup of "Power Ponies" from the street and the track. The "Fast Fords" side of the cover blurb encompasses Pro Street versions of a Cougar XR7 and a 1957 two-door, plus a comprehensive list of restoration resources for 1954–1973 Ford, Lincoln, and Mercury cars.

For those not into Fords, the issue is packed with other goodies, too. The "200-MPH Street Race" at the top of the cover is the Silver State Classic Challenge, a wide-open time trial held on (closed) public roads in Nevada. Editor Jeff Smith rides shotgun with John Lingenfelter in his 560-horsepower 1986 Corvette and sees the far side of 200 miles per hour, though transmission issues keep their 'Vette's average speed to "just" 156 miles per hour, good for a third-place finish. Joe Pettitt covers the event, which is won by Pratt Cole in a Ferrari

1991

Testarossa. Cole covers the 92-mile timed portion of the event in 31.43 minutes, averaging over 173 miles per hour.

Hot Rod again revisits the dragster-versus-Navy-fighter duel. This time Kenny Bernstein's Budweiser King Top Fuel dragster is hoisted aboard the USS *Saratoga* and posed next to an F/A-18 jet for a full-afterburner photo op. No race this time or discussion of which is faster. Just some way cool photos of two of the most powerful vehicles in existence.

As this outtake shows, there's a trick to photographing burnouts. Too little smoke is boring, but too much obscures the car. The shot on the cover hits the happy medium.

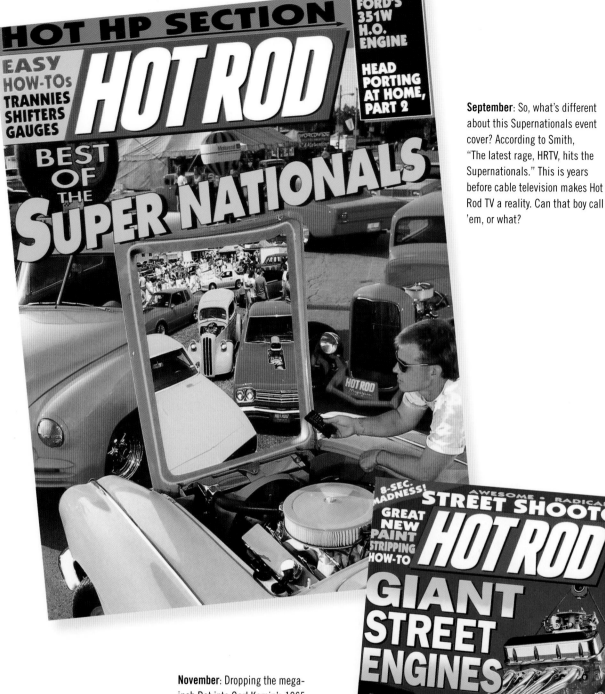

September: So, what's different about this Supernationals event cover? According to Smith, "The latest rage, HRTV, hits the Supernationals." This is years before cable television makes Hot Rod TV a reality. Can that boy call 'em, or what?

November: Dropping the mega-inch Rat into Carl Kamin's 1965 Nova was done for effect; the Deuce is small-block powered. The blurb at the top announces Bill Coogle's Top Gun Shootout in Atlanta, another step toward the Fastest Street Car racing that would become such an important part of the magazine.

1991

February

March

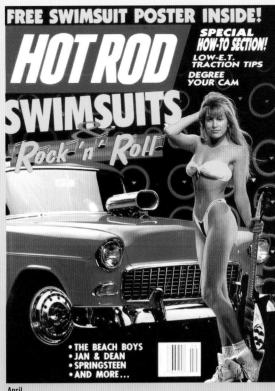

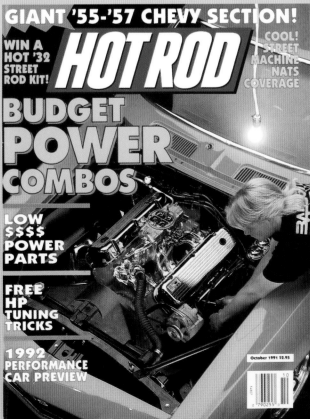

May

April

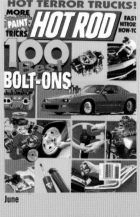

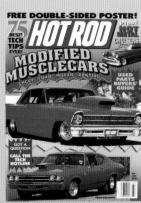

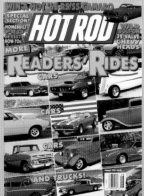

February: A Pro Street Geo Storm? Is there no end to the madness?

March: "Paint & Body" issues start to show up as regularly as swimsuits in April.

April: This one features rock 'n' roll lyrics with Lorentzen's shots of cars and beauty.

May: Inflation makes its mark. It used to be that 100 tips were good enough.

June: The *Hot Rod* flag is centered to fit more blurbs. That lasts a year.

July: "Hot Metal Cruisers" is another way to say "Dare to be Different."

August: Readers contribute the cover photos and 18 pages of rides inside.

October: Power on a budget is great; free horsepower is even better.

December: "Best" moves to the top to make room for the Mean Green Machine.

October

June

July

August

December

PAINT & BODY HOW-TO GUIDE TIPS & TRICKS

HOT ROD

Top Ten Hot Rods of 1992

SPECIAL 3-IN-1 ISSUE!

FASTEST STREET CARS IN AMERICA!

HOME-BUILT SUPERCARS!

8-SECOND SHOWDOWN!

COOL COLLECTIBLES!

December 1992 $2.95

HOW TO BUILD A SHOP

0 790255 0

December

Though it would become one of the magazine's hottest subjects, the whole Fastest Street Car Shootout idea was not a big hit with management. There was a lot of concern that it wouldn't be a strong newsstand draw, so the editors came up with this special "3-in-1" issue to add what are hopefully more popular subjects to the mighty muscle cars in Memphis.

Turns out they shouldn't have worried. The first Shootout, held in conjunction with the National Muscle Car Association's finals, blows everyone away with its intense competition and blazing quarter-mile times. After all the tire smoke has cleared, Max Carter walks away with the Number 1 Fastest Street Car jacket (yes, these guys do all this just to win jackets), driving his 1966 Nova past Rod Saboury's 1957 Corvette in the final and laying down an 8.383 ET at 160.85 miles per hour. "His Nova isn't as trick as you might expect," the editors write, "just a 557-inch Bow Tie with a Powerglide and a ladder-bar rear suspension. Your basic 'a whole lotta motor, but not a lotta car' combo."

C.A.R.S. Inc. team member Dan Scott turns in a performance that earns him a sidebar in the story called "The Consummate Racer." Dan collects "Best Sportsman" honors for his willingness to help keep other competitors racing that weekend—"he even made two late-night runs from the hotel to the dragstrip to give head gaskets and rings away to other racers"—while still running an impressive 8.490 in his all-steel 1967 Camaro. "And yes, we can vouch that this car sees plenty of street action."

Successful as the Shootout is, the whole notion of "What makes these street cars?" prompts Editor Jeff Smith to address the subject in his editorial column. "That's a question that will never be answered to everyone's satisfaction," he admits. "Our rules were intended to attract as many cars as possible, which means there was considerable difference of opinion as to the 'streetability' of tube-chassied, lightweight cars. The fact is however, that when a dozen or so of these cars show up every year at the Street Machine Nationals, it's difficult to dismiss them as not true street machines, regardless of the number of street miles they may (or may not) accumulate in a year." Smith goes on to suggest that the second Shootout, tentatively planned for the next NMCA Finals in Memphis, may have two classes, "one for the killer, tube-chassied, max-nitrous cars, and one for the more sedate,

1992

original-floorpan cars that may weigh more, but are closer to real street-driven cars."

The "Home-Built Supercars" section features four "blue-collar heroes of hot rodding": a Chevelle, Mustang, Mopar, and Deuce coupe. The "Collectibles" section includes stories on nostalgia drag racing, car collections, and automobilia. And Troy Trepanier wins his second Hot Rod of the Year award for the massive—and massively slammed—1950 Buick featured in the August issue.

Hot Rod's first Fastest Street Car Shootout draws street-car racing's heaviest hitters, all gunning for glory and a Top Ten jacket.

September: The Supernationals still packs in the fans and makes for a colorful assortment of rods for the cover. Smith uses his editorial column to announce the upcoming Fastest Street Car Shootout in Memphis, and the "Fastest Street Cars" roundup includes racers that will soon become very familiar.

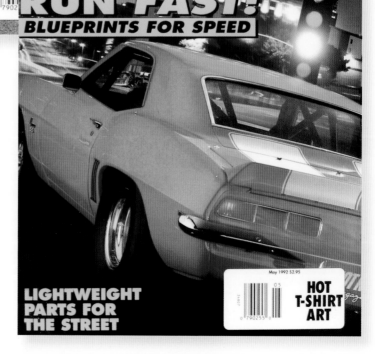

May: Petersen photographers Jim Brown and Mike Banks work hours to create this "street racing" scene in the photo studio, though Steve Flanders' "bad and blown" 1969 Camaro doesn't make it inside. Feature Editor Cole Quinnell's "Tools for Pennies" story is a big hit.

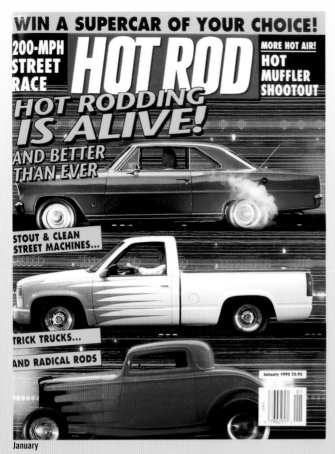

January

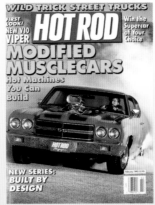

February

March

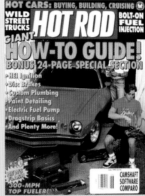

June

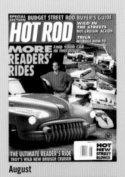

July

January: This is the glass-half-full approach to "Can Hot Rodding Be Outlawed?"

February: Despite the cool burnout, Gary Stifft's 1970 Chevelle doesn't rate a feature inside.

March: Two Summit V-8s go nose to nose in "Rodent Rivalry." Who wins? That depends.

April: No illustrations or song lyrics this time, just "hotties and honeys styling 'n' profiling."

June: Another dude(s)-car-garage setup. Do you think the guy hidden behind the words is upset?

July: The tricked-out chassis got the Boyd touch before sliding under a 1940 Ford.

August: Troy returns with his "mondo-wild and fully streetable '50 meaty, big & bouncy Buick."

October: Camaro versus Duster versus Mustang: a high-performance "three for all." Landy's Mopar takes it.

November: Tons of cars, plus Smith takes a ride with the Thunderbirds in an F-16.

August

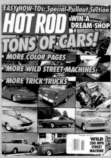

October

November

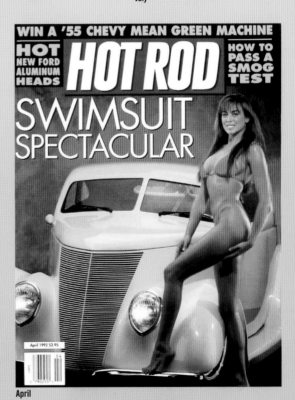

April

1992

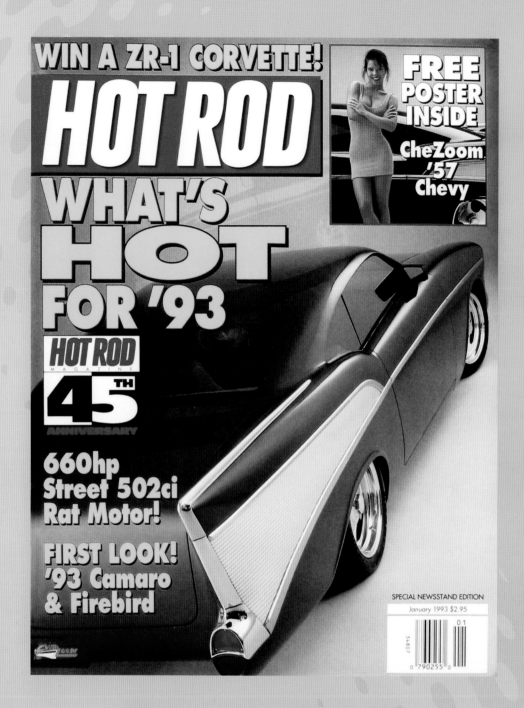

January

How do you follow an act like *CadZZilla*? For Boyd Coddington, *CheZoom* is the next step, a car that "would bridge the gap between a hot rod and a custom without losing its overall identity or its ability to function like a stocker in the real world," writes Gray Baskerville.

CheZoom is the brainchild of designer and illustrator Thom Taylor, who "pretended that I was commissioned to restyle a '57 Bel Air hardtop and give it a '90s look." Taylor wanted the car to be contemporary, "yet still retain the classic '57 flavor." Taylor's sketches found their way to Boyd's shop, where they would have remained in two dimensions had Boyd not found a customer for the car. That turned out to be Mr. Gasket's Joe Hrudka, who said "I'll take it!" after one look at the renderings.

As with Gibbons' Caddy, *CheZoom* was built from a donor car, though after the body was cut, reshaped, and welded back together, only about 10 percent of the original sheet metal remained. The radically low roof dictated a lowered seating position, which meant the original frame was set aside in favor of a mild-steel tube chassis. The front and rear suspension components came from a 1985 Corvette. In fact, as Baskerville explains, "*CheZoom* mechanically became the essence of conventional, while visually it is the essence of exotic." Beneath those swooping curves beats the heart of a stock 1992 Corvette LT1 V-8 backed by a 700-R4 automatic transmission. "The only non-OEM part of the chassis is its not-so-stock rollers. Billet Boyd just had to install a one-off set of 17-inch billet wheels (10x17 front and 11x17 rear)."

CheZoom's color "is another amalgam of past and present," Baskerville writes. "The dark PPG teal base, enhanced by a urethane clear, is a metallic/pearl version of the original '57 Chevy turquoise." What looks like stock 1957 side trim in the rear quarter-panels is actually a computer-generated appliqué applied by Dennis Ricklefs.

Baskerville spent weeks visiting Boyd's shop to document *CheZoom*'s buildup, and many of his photos

1993

appear on the backside of an eight-page, double-gatefold poster of *CheZoom* bound into newsstand editions of the January issue. Longtime Petersen photographer Bob D'Olivo photographed *CheZoom* for the poster as well as for the issue's cover.

Like *CadZZilla*, *CheZoom* is no trailer queen. B'ville plans a summertime tour throughout the Midwest, since illness prevented him from driving *CadZZilla* cross-country. "Hrudka has been apprised of the fact that his old/new streeter is ours. Fellow rodders, the year of the driver has just begun."

Baskerville reiterates that theme in his "What's Hot for '93" story. He has a name for long-distance haulers like *CadZZilla*: "reachers," a term he picked up from Lil' John Buttera. Baskerville calls reachers "the real hot rods" and says "what's hot for '93 can be summed up with one word ... real! Real cars do what they are supposed to do" and "'93 will be the year of the real stuff."

In an outtake from the *CheZoom* photo shoot, Linda Vaughn poses for photographer Bob D'Olivo.

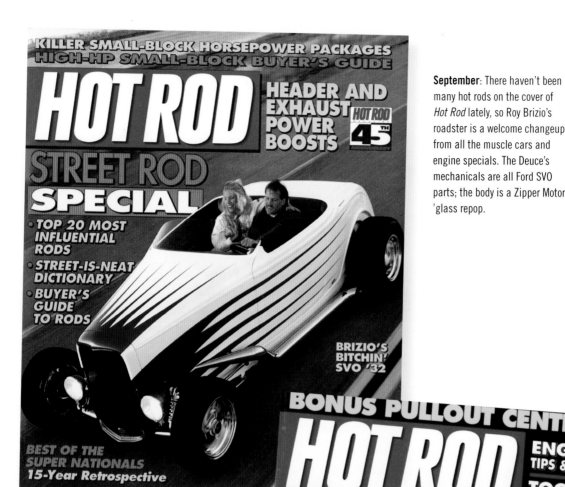

HOT ROD

September: There haven't been many hot rods on the cover of *Hot Rod* lately, so Roy Brizio's roadster is a welcome changeup from all the muscle cars and engine specials. The Deuce's mechanicals are all Ford SVO parts; the body is a Zipper Motors 'glass repop.

December: "What's Hot" worked well in January, so the magazine runs the theme again. C. K. Spurlock's *Merroder* is in the same vein as Boyd's latest reachers, except the modified 1949 Merc shell hides a 625-horse Rat motor, not like the stockers "that loafed under *CheZoom*'s and *CadZZilla*'s hoods."

February: Roger Conley's 540-motivated 1968 Camaro represents this month's tech-oriented content.

March: Quick, easy, low-buck tech—what every rodder with a smirk wants for his Mustang.

April: This time, the "hot rods and hot bods" are shot by Steve Coonan, not Lorentzen.

May: What's your favorite flavor of low-buck small-block—Ford, Chevy, or Mopar?

June: There is a lot going on in the Special Double Bonus Issue!

July: Will Handzel, not yet a *Hot Rod* staffer, poses with legendary Boyd "Curly" Coddington.

August: BDS supplied the full-dress big-block that leads the special supercharger section.

October: What's nastier, the hot 1971 Camaro or the "old ladies quake" cover line?

November: The headless guy under R. K. Smith's Deuce is editor-in-chief-to-be Freiburger.

1993

February

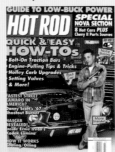

March

May

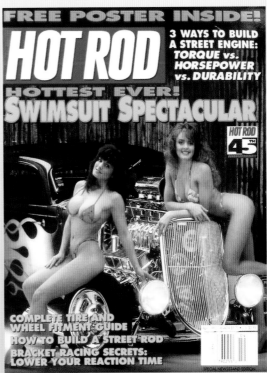

April

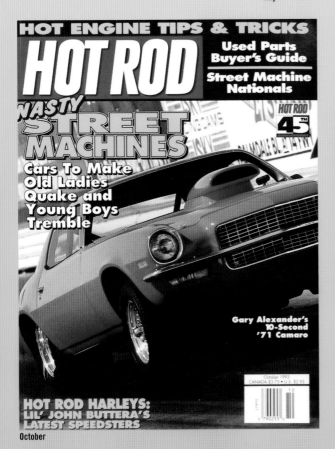

October

June

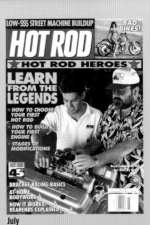

July

August

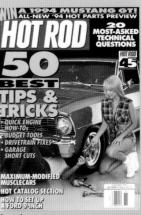

November

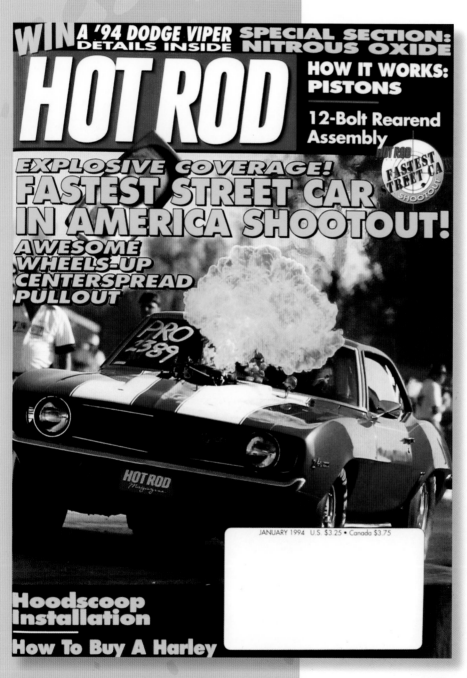

January

In just its second outing, *Hot Rod*'s Fastest Street Car in America Shootout cements its reputation as *the* event of the mid-1990s. There would be plenty more FSC racing in the years to come, but this particular chapter epitomizes the "flat-out, tire-frying, wheel-standing, flame-throwing, stand-packing" Memphis shootout. As Feature Editor David Freiburger puts it, "Elvis was there, but no one cared."

Part of what makes this event so memorable is pure accident: After burning four pistons during a qualifying round, Pro Street racer Joey Yatooma and Kurt Urban "threw an all-night wrench-a-thon" to get Yatooma's Camaro back into racing shape, only to have an air bubble in the fuel line cause a flaming nitrous explosion early in the day's eliminations. Technical Editor Cole Quinnell is in the right place at the right time with the right lens to catch the fireball at its peak, making for one of the most dramatic *Hot Rod* covers of all time. (Look closely and you can see Yatooma's hood scoop in the air behind the FSC cover lines.)

The top gun at this year's shootout is Mark Tate, who drives his 570 Rat-powered Pro Street 1967 Camaro to a 10th-of-a-second victory over the previous year's winner, John Carter's Nova with new driver Mike Moran at the wheel. Tate's 8.27/166.29 time slip earns him the event's quickest ET and fastest mile per hour. On the non-tubbed, Super Street side of the competition, Dave Henninger, in his 400-inch small-block Camaro, cuts an excellent light and squeezes by Randy Lambert's Impala for the win with a 9.51 ET.

The series is, and will continue to be, debated for its interpretation of what makes these "street" cars. The rules impose some limitations—all cars need a VIN, working lights, full interiors, and so on, but the true test of a car's streetability is the 25-mile drive each Pro Street competitor must successfully negotiate around the grounds of Memphis Motorsports Park. After the drive the cars are shut off and must be restarted within 30 seconds. This last requirement bounces some of the big-name drivers out of this year's race, including Monty Berney, Rick Dyer, and Dan Scott. Series sponsor Flowmaster quickly arranges a "consolation round" for these heavy hitters, where 7-second ETs are the rule, not the exception, and foreshadow FSC competition to come.

For those who want to take their cars to FSC power levels (hopefully without Yatooma's pyrotechnics), the editors put

1994

together a comprehensive special section on nitrous oxide injection, what Quinnell calls "the power-making tool of the '90s." The stories include tips on how to build an engine that will live on a nitrous diet, the basics of how nitrous systems work, how to modify the fuel system for nitrous injection, and the right way to plumb a nitrous system.

MEMPHIS BLEWS

THE FASTEST STREET CAR IN AMERICA SHOOTOUT!
By David Freiburger

s was there, but no one cared. That's how flat-out, tire-frying, wheel-standing, me-throwing, stand-packing wild the '93 HOT ROD Fastest Street Car In America Shootout was. In only its second year, the Shootout has become the event that e's talking about, and it has picked up such major sponsors as Flowmaster, The hop, Competition Cams, Global Television, Mickey Thompson, Musclecars Video ine, Nitrous Oxide Systems, Racer Components Inc., Racing Head Service

continued

THE FASTEST STREET CAR IN AMERICA

MARK TATE '67 CAMARO 8.27/166.29

year, Mark's Camaro struck fear into the hearts of Pro Street racers. This time their worries were jus- . Mark visited Roy Hill's Pro Stock driving school, while Mike Matheos redid the car to meet the '93 . The result was the Shootout's quickest e.t. and fastest mph. Mark met last year's winner in the ; he only had owner John Carter's Nova covered by about a 10th and would have to go against r Mike Moran's holeshot act. Mike Matheos threw some tune-up into the 570ci Rat, and Mark cut a bulb to Mike Moran's .494. All that was left was the chase. Mark scored the touchdown but slam ked a connecting rod in the lights. Was it worth it? You bet! As far as HOT ROD magazine is con- ned, Mark Tate and Mike Matheos have The Fastest Street Car In America. That is, until next year.

RUNNER-UP

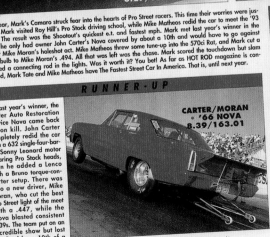

CARTER/MORAN '66 NOVA 8.39/163.01

last year's winner, the rter Auto Restoration rvice Nova came back on kill. John Carter mpletely redid the car th a 632 single-four-bar- l Sonny Leonard motor earing Pro Stock heads, en he added a Lenco ith a Bruno torque-con- erter setup. There was lso a new driver, Mike Moran, who cut the best ro Street light of the meet with a .447, while the Nova blasted consistent 8.39s. The team put on an ncredible show but lost the final by a 10th of a second.

Photography: The HOT ROD Staff & Scott Killeen/PPC Photographic

TOP TEN WINNER

ANNETTE SUMMER '68 CAMARO 8.64/157.50

We picked Annette as our own Queen of Memphis when her Pepto-pink Camaro ran solidly in the 8s with a Gene Fulton 615 Rat motor. She was a little soft on the Tree but was able to motor past Mike Thompson in the first round before she ran her squirrelly low e.t. on a bye run after Gene Deputy broke. She finally succumbed to a sticky shifter and Bruce Kimmen's holeshot, but she earned every bit of her Top Ten jacket.

TOP TEN WINNER

BRUCE KIMMEN '69 CAMARO 8.75/157.97

If there's a Top Ten car that exactly fits the intent of the rules, it's Bruce Kimm Camaro. The C.A.R.S., Inc.-sponsored streeter is a back-halved car with a stock int full glass and an all-steel body except for the hood. Bruce runs a single-four-barre with a Turbo 400 and has conservatively fed in the tune-up to run the number but the motor. He's also well-practiced on the reaction time, and he made it to the because he fed the Tree to the pink Camaro in the previous round. Bruce gets the cial HOT ROD "It's A Beautiful Thing" award.

Joey "Boom-Boom" Yatooma is so hot at the second Fastest Street Car Shootout he gets a cover and the main image on the story's opening spread.

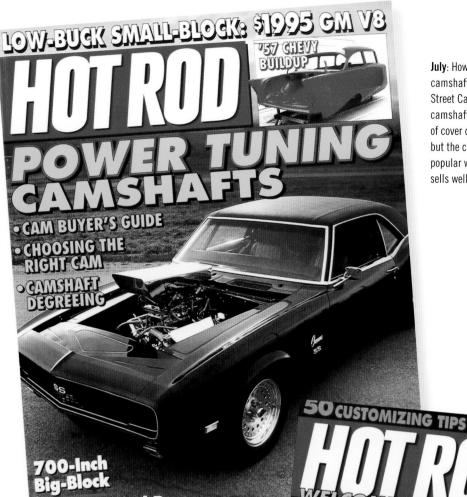

July: How do you tune a camshaft? And what does the Pro Street Camaro have to do with camshafts? Some very basic rules of cover design are broken here, but the cam topic proves to be so popular with the readers that it sells well despite itself.

September: In 1994 Petersen Publishing gets back into the events business and produces shows for several of its premier titles. *Hot Rod*'s inaugural Power Festival is held at Norwalk Raceway Park and attracts a small but high-quality turnout, with Troy Trepanier's Pro Street *Rumblur* wagon among the standout vehicles.

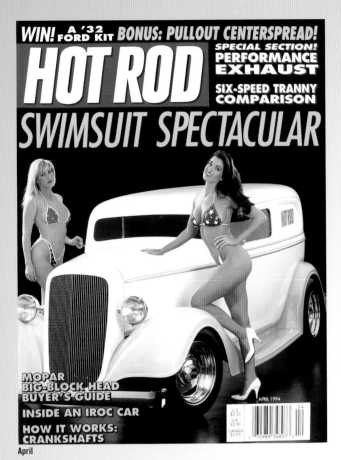
WIN! A '32 FORD KIT **BONUS: PULLOUT CENTERSPREAD!**

SPECIAL SECTION! **PERFORMANCE EXHAUST**

SIX-SPEED TRANNY COMPARISON

HOT ROD
SWIMSUIT SPECTACULAR

MOPAR BIG-BLOCK HEAD BUYER'S GUIDE

INSIDE AN IROC CAR

HOW IT WORKS: CRANKSHAFTS

April

February

March

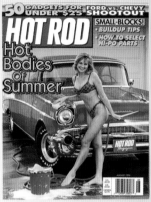
May

August

February: Danny Shaffer's 1955 Chevy; "Clunker Rescue" is the start of the Crusher Camaro project.

March: "Budget Buildup!" is Freiburger's *Cheap Thrills* Dart. "Can we run 12s for $2,000?"

April: Five different photographers shoot "beautiful bodies both mechanical and otherwise."

May: Kinnan's Fairlane goes from zero to hero for $150; *Cheap Thrills* hits its numbers.

June: The era's favorite buzzwords—*low-buck* and *Pro Street*—collide on one tire-shredding cover!

August: Newsstand buyers get the girl; subscribers get the car only. School librarians rejoice.

October: A Camaro Z/28 clone demonstrates the principles of building your first car.

November: *Son of Green Machine* makes its cover debut with Chuckie Lombardo and crate engines.

December: The Top Ten get shoved upstairs to make room for Mike Petralia's 12-second Camaro.

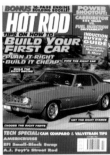
October

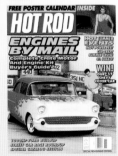
November

December

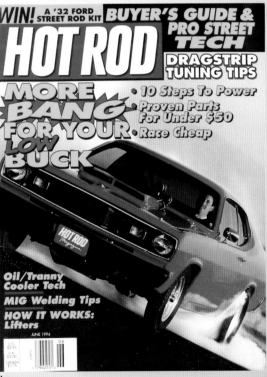
June

1994

Hot Rod's how-to-paint issue themes become so dependable as springtime newsstand sellers that editors are compelled to repeat them to keep their circulation numbers up. This year's section, though, is important for another reason: the cover car.

March

Regular readers recognize the *Crusher Camaro*, a sano 1967 that was saved from certain death at the hands of Chevron's "accelerated retirement" car-crush program a year prior. Incensed at the idea that potential collectibles were doomed simply because they were old cars, Feature Editors David Freiburger and Rob Kinnan stepped up and saved this Camaro by offering its owner—the car's original owner—the same $700 Chevron would have paid him to destroy it. They drove it some 100 miles home, then had it smog checked at a Chevron station, where the original six-cylinder passed with no modification whatsoever.

From there, the Chevy is transformed "into a to-die-for street beast," wrote Kinnan in December 1994. "It'll run a highly respectable quarter-mile, get decent gas mileage, look completely bitchin' and, finally, show the smog cops that a fast hot rod can be environmentally conscious and isn't the deadly, scum-belching behemoth they seem to think all old cars are." At this stage in the buildup, Bernt Karlsson of Classics by Bernt has fixed some of the car's sheetmetal issues and sprayed it with "the brightest, most violent Chrome Yellow on the planet," writes Kinnan. That's Karlsson buffing the paint outside his spray booth in Scott Killeen's cover photo.

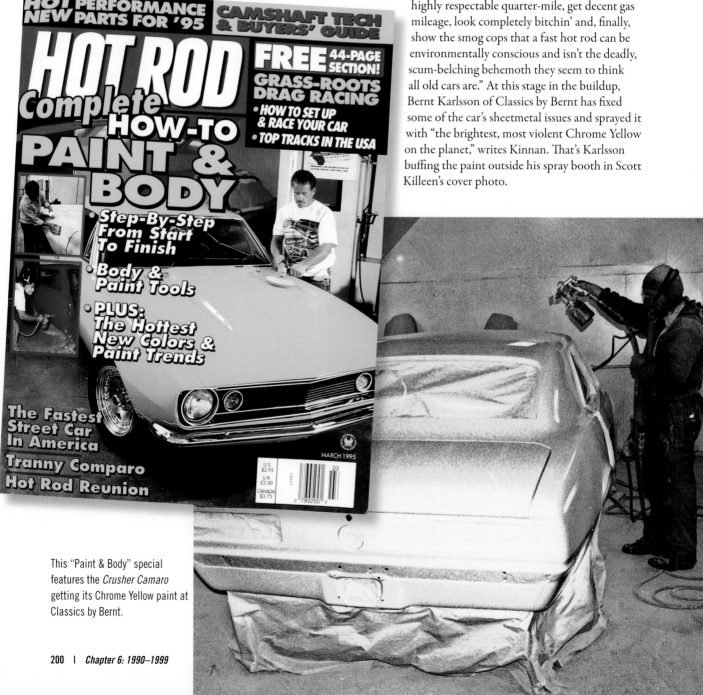

This "Paint & Body" special features the *Crusher Camaro* getting its Chrome Yellow paint at Classics by Bernt.

1995

September: *Hot Rod* is back at the Power Festival in Ohio, getting there by way of the inaugural Power Tour®. Just seven reader cars, plus an assortment of magazine project and staff-owned vehicles, make the Long Haul® from LA to Norwalk, covering 2,858 miles in a week.

July: Not just another shootout, this big-block battle pits big-name engine builders—Jon Kaase, Dick Gazan, Herb McCandless—in a pump-gas track war. Another big name, Dyno Don Nicholson, is among the drivers. The McCandless-powered Super Bee wins with a 10.00 ET at 133.72 miles per hour.

1995

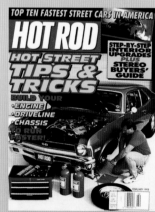

January

January: The *Smoothster* is "*the* hottest street rod for '95," when Chip Foose works for Boyd.

February: A wheelstand took out Speedy Petey in Memphis, but he still made the cover.

April: Peter Linney shoots swimsuits in natural light; the Greer-Black-Prudhomme digger is back.

May: Mark Stielow and the *QuadraDeuce*, "one of the coolest street rods of all time."

June: The Smiths—Greg in blue, Jeff in black—planning some low-buck hop-ups.

August: A three-ring circus of a cover, when "busy is better" ruled cover design.

October: Old cars, new cars, hardcore hands-on tech: This cover has it all.

November: Bruce Kimmen's Camaro: "What a back-halved street/strip car should look like."

December: The on-again/off-again Top Ten is on again; Danny Scott's Chevelle is top rod.

February

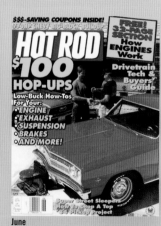

April

May

June

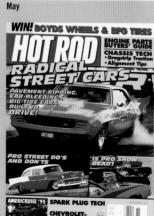

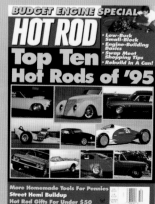

August

October

November

December

DECEMBER 1996

1996

December

Look at all the other covers in this chapter—and many of the chapters preceding it—and you'll see just how bold this cover design was. In the "busy is better" era, putting a single vehicle on the cover, and a *truck*, no less, without a single word of copy was ballsy, to say the least. The effect was muted on the newsstand, though, by placing this issue in a plastic bag with cover blurbs on it.

The truck is the Sidewinder, a Dodge Dakota concept vehicle that Feature Editor Rob Kinnan likens to other groundbreaking Chrysler design studies, like the Viper and the Prowler, that went on to production after their time on the show stand. It began as a sketch by Mark Allen, fresh from the Center for Creative Studies in Detroit. He "envisioned a radical Dakota utilizing the basic lines of the new truck but heavily flavored with

The Sidewinder Dakota concept truck was hand fabricated from steel at Metal Crafters.

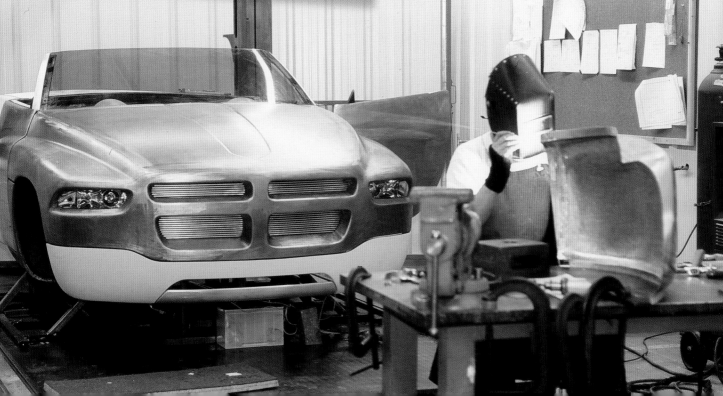

hot rod tradition," Kinnan says. The all-steel body is hand fabricated by Metal Crafters and sits on a square-tube frame with Viper suspension components. A standard Viper mill would have been powerful enough, but the Sidewinder's V-10 has been modified for endurance racing and puts out 600 horsepower and 600 lbs-ft. of torque. Among the concept's most striking features are its 21- and 22-inch wheels, huge for the time.

Kinnan realizes "you'd have a better chance of stuffing Courtney Love in a convent than you would of finding this creature on a showroom floor" because it's so radical, but he and other Dodge fans hope the truck inspires the maker to produce some sort of limited-edition Dakota with V-10 power.

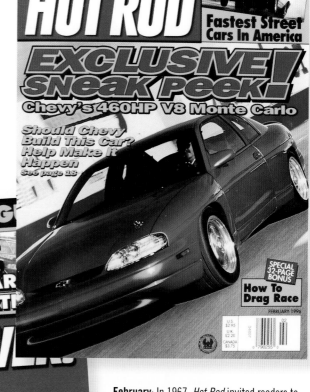

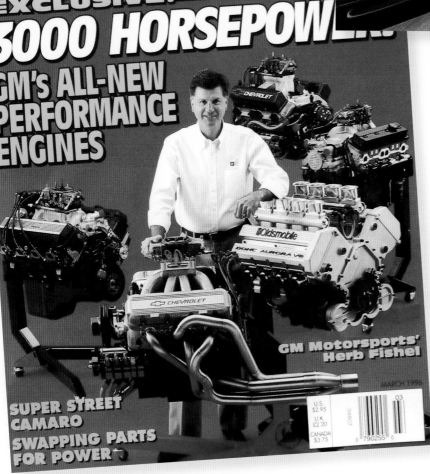

February: In 1967, *Hot Rod* invited readers to write Ford and ask it to make Bob Tasca's KR-8 Mustang. The response was overwhelming, and the Cobra Jet was born. Can *Hot Rod* pull off the same trick with this rear-wheel-drive V-8 Monte Carlo? Did *you* see an RWD Monte in 1997?

March: Another cover inspired by the past. In December 1967 Zora Arkus-Duntov posed surrounded by experimental Chevrolet engines. Now it's Herb Fishel's turn, surrounded by hot GM big- and small-blocks. Front and center is the SB2, which is designed specifically for NASCAR racing.

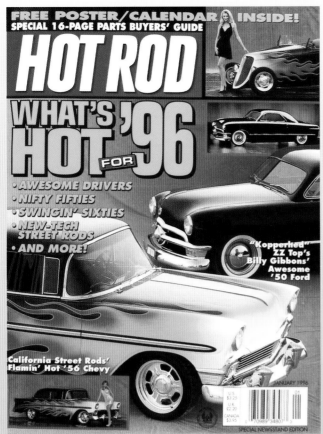

January

April

June

July

August

January: California Street Rods' flaming 1956 is hot; Billy Gibbons' *Kopperhed* is so hot it's cool.

April: Shocking! An April issue without bikini models. School librarians rejoice.

May: Boyd, Chip, and America's Most Beautiful Boydster. Inside: *Hot Rod*'s big rig.

June: Will Handzel and his dog, Cooper, stage the cover at Mothers Wax headquarters.

July: The red Camaro is the 1967 *Hot Rod* project car, still boiling the hides.

August: Mark Stielow's Camaro is a work in progress, but it still earns "ultimate" honors.

September: The second Power Tour® achieves equal cover billing with the Power Festival.

October: Two Camaros—the top one's Kinnan's—illustrate the easy tips and tricks.

November: Lunati's *Street Heat* project Chevelle strikes a (faked) wheels-up stance.

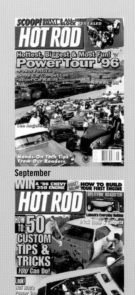

September

October

November

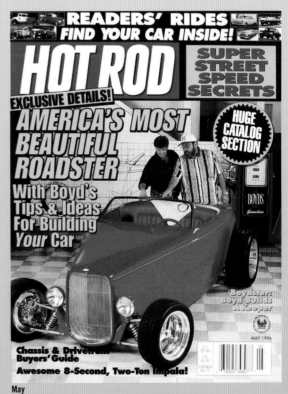

May

1996

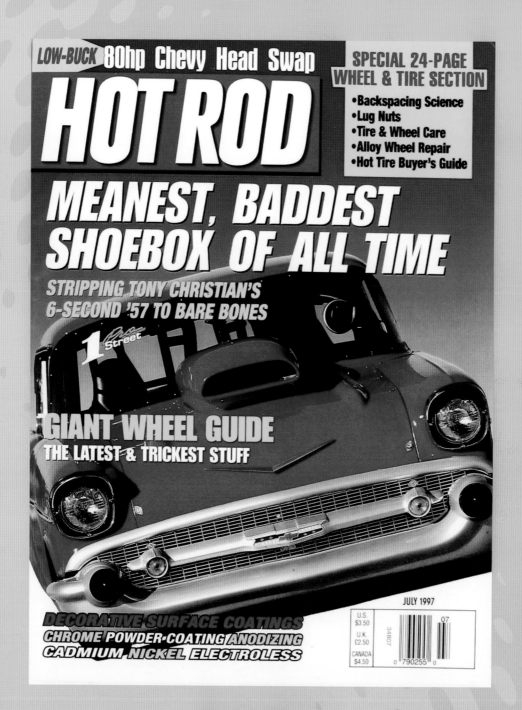

LOW-BUCK 80hp Chevy Head Swap

HOT ROD

SPECIAL 24-PAGE WHEEL & TIRE SECTION
•Backspacing Science
•Lug Nuts
•Tire & Wheel Care
•Alloy Wheel Repair
•Hot Tire Buyer's Guide

MEANEST, BADDEST SHOEBOX OF ALL TIME

STRIPPING TONY CHRISTIAN'S 6-SECOND '57 TO BARE BONES

GIANT WHEEL GUIDE
THE LATEST & TRICKEST STUFF

DECORATIVE SURFACE COATINGS
CHROME POWDER-COATING ANODIZING
CADMIUM NICKEL ELECTROLESS

JULY 1997

U.S. $3.50
U.K. £2.50
CANADA $4.50

0 790255 0

July

Two themes play a recurring role on *Hot Rod* covers this year. The iconic (and now 40-year-old) 1957 Chevy appears three times; so do participants from the magazine's street-car drag race series, now called the World's Quickest Street Car in a nod to the eighth-mile race distances. July's cover combines both trends in one with Tony Christian's 6-second Pro Street 1957 Chevy.

    The car has been a top street-car contender since the series' early days. Previous owner Stan Shaw earned a Top Ten spot at the 1994 Memphis shootout without nitrous or a blower, and Christian— with partners Jim and Randy Chappel, Richard Rainwater, and Darla Moore—bought the

Bel Air soon after. Christian won the Pro Street final at the 1995 Memphis shootout and earned enough points in the 1996 season to win the Pro Street championship, even though he didn't win in Memphis that year.

For the new season, "Tony Christian is gonna win it all," writes Feature Editor Rob Kinnan. "Don't believe it? Just ask him."

Christian's self-confidence is bolstered by his win at the first race of the year, a feat he accomplishes "with a car he feels is at a serious aerodynamic disadvantage to most of the others he routinely wastes," Kinnan writes.

Christian's car "is a '57 Chevy in silhouette only," a fiberglass body with Lexan windows draped over a full-tube chassis. Power comes from a 638-inch Reher-Morrison engine "with one or two Dominators (depending on the race) and loads of nitrous." Kinnan

1997

puts the engine's output at "1,100 hp without spray, and roughly 2,000 with both stages flowing." Coupled to the engine is a five-speed Lenco transmission and a Ford 9-inch housing with Strange 4.11:1 gears.

That's standard Pro Street stuff in these years, Kinnan admits. "It's what Tony does with it that makes a difference." In typical understated fashion, Christian explains, "Anybody can drive one of these cars. It's just now you separate the men from the boys, and it's all about how good you are."

Well, it's about the car too. "Growing weary of coaching his barn-door Bel Air to literally punch its way through the air, Christian bought a sleeker sheath," writes Kinnan, "a Camaro last raced by Mark Tate and Mike Matheos at Memphis in 1995. Christian feels the Camaro advantage will be 6 to 7 mph faster and .06 to .07 seconds quicker than the '57."

The switch is controversial, Kinnan admits. "The Bel Air is unique in Pro Street and enjoys immense popularity because of it. The Camaro probably won't enjoy this celebrity because it'll look like a current Pro Stock car. Frankly, we'd rather Tony stay with the '57 because it's our style, a traditional street machine with lots of reader appeal. But Tony's a racer and he wants to win."

Christian debuts the Camaro midseason and is true to his word: Despite missing the final race because of cancer surgery, he wins the year's Pro Street championship with a comfortable points lead.

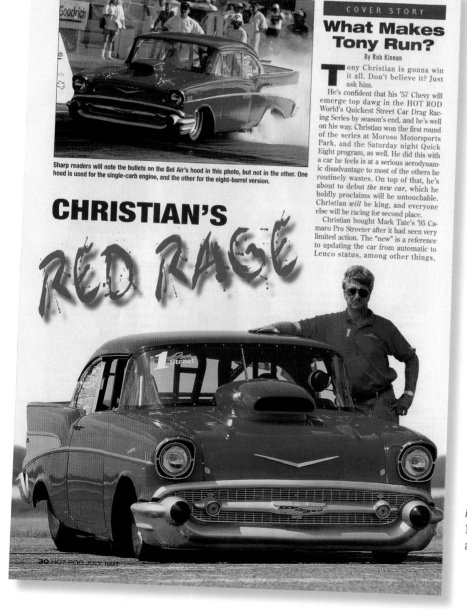

Photography: Rob Kinnan, Will Handzel & Scott Killeen

COVER STORY

What Makes Tony Run?

By Rob Kinnan

Tony Christian is gonna win it all. Don't believe it? Just ask him.

He's confident that his '57 Chevy will emerge top dawg in the HOT ROD World's Quickest Street Car Drag Racing Series by season's end, and he's well on his way. Christian won the first round of the series at Moroso Motorsports Park, and the Saturday night Quick Eight program, as well. He did this with a car he feels is at a serious aerodynamic disadvantage to most of the others he routinely wastes. On top of that, he's about to debut *the new car*, which he boldly proclaims will be untouchable. Christian *will* be king, and everyone else will be racing for second place.

Christian bought Mark Tate's '95 Camaro Pro Streeter after it had seen very limited action. The "new" is a reference to updating the car from automatic to Lenco status, among other things,

Sharp readers will note the bullets on the Bel Air's hood in this photo, but not in the other. One hood is used for the single-carb engine, and the other for the eight-barrel version.

CHRISTIAN'S RED RAGE

Hot Rod features Tony Christian's fast 1957 just before he transitions into a more aerodynamic Camaro.

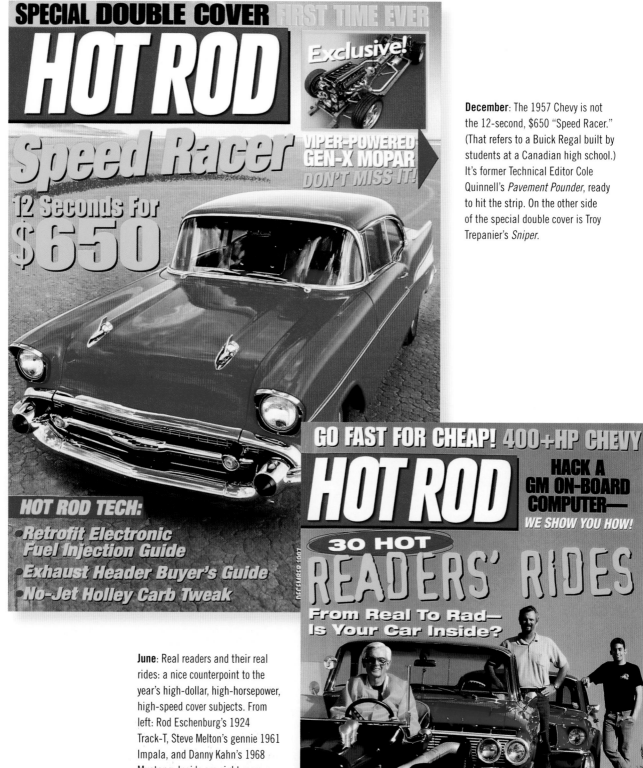

December: The 1957 Chevy is not the 12-second, $650 "Speed Racer." (That refers to a Buick Regal built by students at a Canadian high school.) It's former Technical Editor Cole Quinnell's *Pavement Pounder*, ready to hit the strip. On the other side of the special double cover is Troy Trepanier's *Sniper*.

June: Real readers and their real rides: a nice counterpoint to the year's high-dollar, high-horsepower, high-speed cover subjects. From left: Rod Eschenburg's 1924 Track-T, Steve Melton's gennie 1961 Impala, and Danny Kahn's 1968 Mustang. Inside are eight more pages of rides from around the world—literally.

January: Steve Gray's Camaro is a street hero; *Hot Rod's* new street car series launches.

February: Laughing-gas madness and the introduction of *Hot Rod TV* on TNN.

March: It's dramatic, but the gigabuck LE-1 *Groundfighter* is a big miss with the readers.

April: Mike Moran, the fastest man in Pro Street, with *Casper*, the fastest street car.

May: Boyd's latest braid blower is *RodZoom*, a phantom drop top built from a 1959 Impala.

August: Trucks are back, and the magazine kicks off its 50th anniversary countdown.

September: Larry Butler's *Zoomina* is one of 125 to make the long Power Tour® haul.

October: Best buys in hot parts include carbs, manifolds, clutches, mufflers, and spray.

November: Frank Currie's Shotgun-powered roadster chases Ken Zeller's blown and squeezed 'Vette.

1997

January

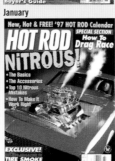

February

March

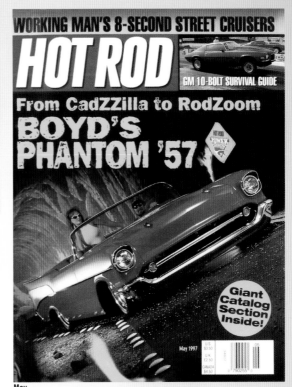

May

August

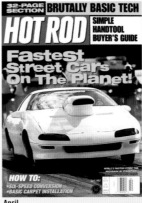

April

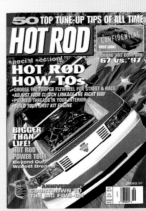

September

October

November

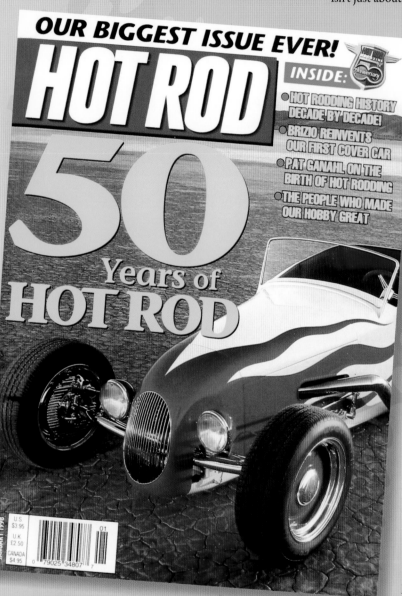

OUR BIGGEST ISSUE EVER!

HOT ROD

INSIDE:
- HOT RODDING HISTORY DECADE BY DECADE!
- BRIZIO REINVENTS OUR FIRST COVER CAR
- PAT GANAHL ON THE BIRTH OF HOT RODDING
- THE PEOPLE WHO MADE OUR HOBBY GREAT

50 Years of HOT ROD

JANUARY 1998
U.S $3.95
U.K £2.50
CANADA $4.95

0 79025 34807 7

01

January

The editors—especially Gray Baskerville—have been gearing up for *Hot Rod*'s 50th birthday for years, and the effort pays off in a massive, 226-page issue so full of golden anniversary ideas that they spill over into following issues for months to come. Yet *Hot Rod* isn't just about the past; it needs to stay current and even look ahead too. So the editors leave enough room in the issue to cover engine and drivetrain tech, quick street car racing, and other topics important to the present-day hot rodder.

Symbolic of that mix of old and new is the track-nose T on the cover. As Baskerville writes, it was Chip Foose who came up with the idea of putting a replica of *Hot Rod*'s first cover car—Regg Schlemmer's 1927 T-bodied track roadster—on the anniversary issue. At first it was going to be a duplicate of the Schlemmer T, "but then we had second thoughts," B'ville says. "We settled on a streeterized clone designed to be bad to the bone." Roy Brizio was tapped to build the car, which updated many of the original T's components. Instead of a flathead V-8, for example, the new car is powered by a dual-quad 302 Ford built by Edelbrock. Instead of gennie T bodywork, Brizio fashions the skin using a Wescott fiberglass body and Speedway Motors repro track nose. And instead of Schlemmer's distinctive yellow-with-black-flames paint scheme, *Hot Rod* colors—candy apple red flames over a white background—are chosen for the car.

No anniversary issue would be complete without a retrospective of the magazine's history, but this time the editors outdo themselves. Each writes a 10-to-12-page review of each decade in the magazine's history, while former Editor Pat Ganahl drafts a history of rodding itself, from its pre-war roots to 1948, when a young Bob Petersen recognizes an untapped market when he sees it. "He and a couple of partners quickly put together a new magazine devoted to these hot rods," Ganahl writes. "One source says Petersen was initially going to call it *Autocraft*, but decided to go with *Hot Rod*, a very bold move in 1948."

Even casual *Hot Rod* readers know how important Bonneville and the dry lakes are to the magazine's history, so it makes sense that each figures prominently in the issue's non-anniversary coverage. In "Haul in the Family," Baskerville writes about the twin-turbo Firebird being campaigned by "Jerry's kids": Jeff and Joe Kugel, sons of longtime land-speed racer Jerry Kugel. The boys are building the 'Bird to hit three bills, and they're close: Joe averages 295 at the SCTA World Finals.

Later in the issue, Will Handzel describes his "wild-eyed dream come true" of driving 200 miles per hour on the Muroc dry lake, thanks to his friends at BMR Racing and a borrowed 1932 five-window coupe. When he earns his time slip—202.93 miles per hour—he gets enough copies to "pass around to the BMR crew like $100 bills."

1998

The 50th anniversary gatefold cover sums up *Hot Rod*'s history from Regg Schlemmer's T to Brizio's modern recreation of that first cover car.

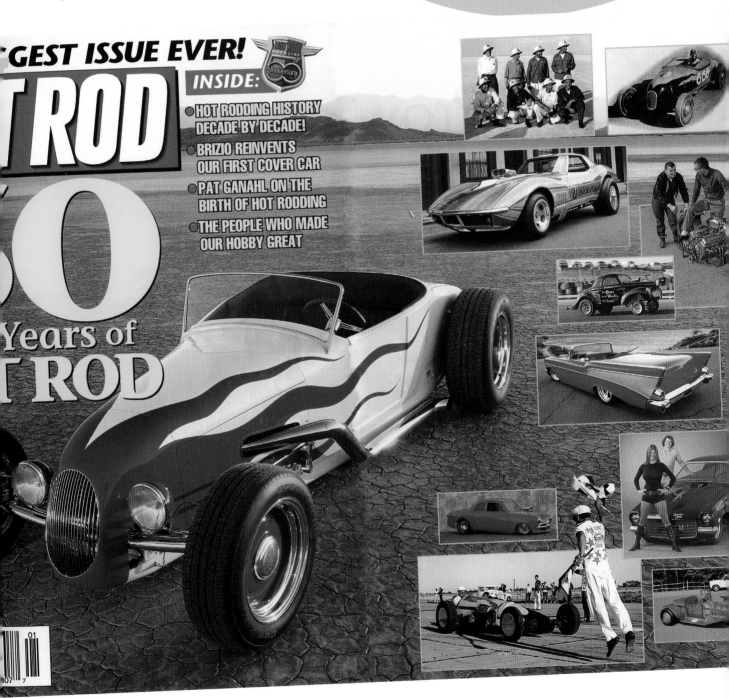

THE FUTURE OF CHEVY'S NEW V-8

HOT ROD
COOL CAMAROS!!!

- **HOT ROD'S NUMBER ONE**
- **LS1 402ci/530hp**
- **'82 GROUND-UP RESTOMOD**
- **725hp '94 ZL1**
- **510ci GEN IV**
- **'69 LT1 Ragtop**

CAMSHAFT TECH
- **CHOOSE THE RIGHT CAM**
- **THE BASICS & BEYOND**

HOW-TOS:
- **LIMITED-SLIP INST...**
- **4.6L MUSTANG BO...**

November: Vic Edelbrock's restoration of the *Red Car—Hot Rod*'s famous test Camaro— prompts a retelling of the legend by one who was there: former Editor Jim McFarland. "At the time, nobody fibbed about the Granddaddy of all *HRM* project cars, but there's a helluva lot we didn't tell you."

DIRT CHEAP! **10-20hp For $2!**

HOT ROD

BONUS SECTION!

24 PAGES OF WHEEL/TIRE TECH

Outlaw Streeters
Over 20 Bad-Ass Beasties!

PLUS

HOW TO...
- Install A B&M Blower
- Mount A Battery In The Trunk
- Bolt On A Sway Bar
- Convert Ford 351 To GM HEI Ignition

EXTRA POWER!
Street Performance Intake Manifolds

CROSS-COUNTRY BLOWN HEMI STREET ROD

Beyond 200MPH Lynwood Wood's Outlaw Street GTO

JULY 1998

U.S.A. $3.50
CANADA $4.50

0 790255 0   07

A PETERSEN PUBLICATION

July: The pop-the-chute-on-the-street trick has been done many times before, but Lynwood Wood's 200-mile-per-hour Outlaw Street GTO pulls it off with badass style. Down in the corner is Dave Rentsman, whose long-haul efforts on and off the Power Tour made him a hair-blown hero.

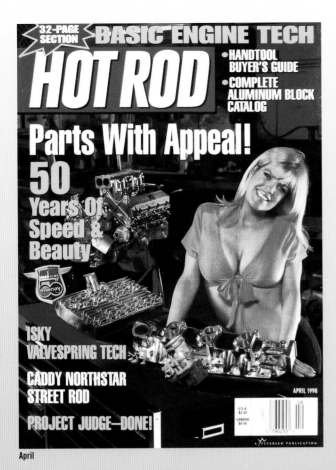

April

February

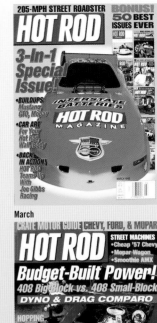

March

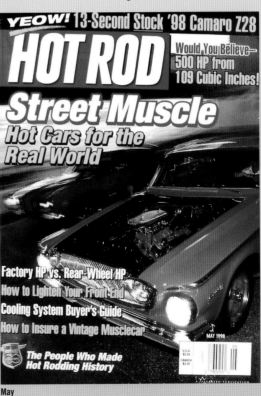

May

June

August

February: The Nitrous Demon purges his Dart, while golden anniversary stories keep on coming.

March: *Hot Rod* goes racing with Joe Gibbs; the 205-mile-per-hour roadster is Currie's from November 1997.

April: Not another swimsuit issue, but a retrospective of *Hot Rod*'s "Parts with Appeal" pinup pages.

May: Gary Wieman's 1962 Dart and Bob Griffith's 1969 Judge take it to the street.

June: The Chevy-heavy cover features a ZL1 Camaro shot by Editor McGonegal when both of them were younger.

August: The Rat versus Mouse debate again; inside, fastest street cars break the 200-mile-per-hour barrier.

September: Chuck Schroedl's 1965 Impala is not just torque-rich, it's a Power Tour® Long Hauler.

October: Model Jennifer Palmer has "Parts with Appeal," 1990s style. School librarians freak out.

December: Injection is nice, but inside Baskerville profiles rat rods. *Hot Rod Deluxe*, on deck.

September

October

December

1998

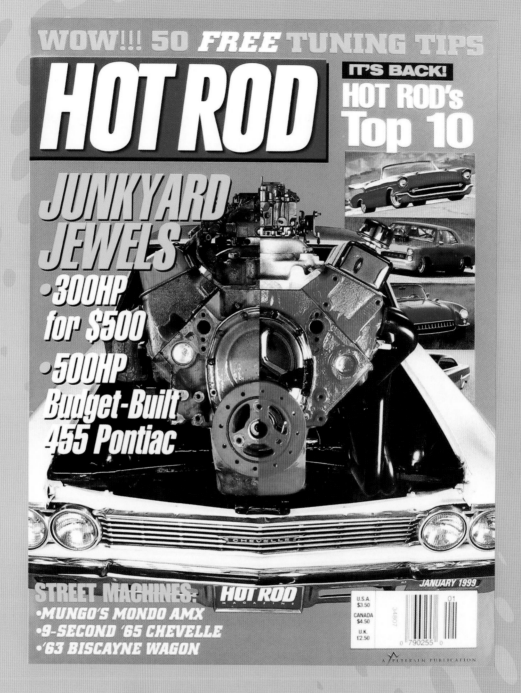

WOW!!! 50 FREE TUNING TIPS

HOT ROD

IT'S BACK!
HOT ROD's Top 10

JUNKYARD JEWELS
- **300HP for $500**
- **500HP Budget-Built 455 Pontiac**

STREET MACHINES:
- **MUNGO'S MONDO AMX**
- **9-SECOND '65 CHEVELLE**
- **'63 BISCAYNE WAGON**

HOT ROD MAGAZINE

JANUARY 1999

U.S.A. $3.50
CANADA $4.50
U.K. £2.50

0 790255

A PETERSEN PUBLICATION

January

Low-buck power has been a magazine staple for years, but the "Junkyard Jewels" theme gives it a new twist and proves to be a strong newsstand seller—so strong, in fact, that the blurb (and the engine) shows up again in August. Former Petersen staff photographer Jim Brown, now working as a freelancer, put the cover collage together with the "before" and "after" engine images imposed over the empty engine bay of Technical Editor Terry McGean's El Camino. (Also making his first appearance inside the issue is Steve Magnante's The Character alter-ego, white coat, nerd tape on the glasses, and all. We'll see him again soon.)

As Technical Editor Terry McGean writes in his "Getting Away With It" cover story, "Why do so many rodders feel that any and all performance engines require nothing less than the finest of whiz-bang, go-fast parts backed by a host of indestructible innards to qualify as a 'proper' powerplant? Do you really need that tungsten air-cleaner wing nut just to go to the local cruise? Does a decent streeter really need to make 800 hp and have the ability to withstand 8,000 rpm to be functional and enjoyable? And perhaps more importantly, does the entry-level hot rodder need a Kryptonite Visa card to join the ranks? We think not."

McGean's alternative is to build a 300-horse engine for $500, using as its foundation any of the "tons of sound, used engines out there just waiting to be plucked from heaps that have turned their last mile. Find one, freshen it, and then upgrade it with some low- and no-buck speed tricks for cheap thrills."

And he does just that, using a 350 V-8 pulled out of a 1976 Impala at his local Pick-Your-Part as his starting point. After cleaning and disassembly the motor proves sound, so he goes shopping for a budget cam and valvetrain, elects to reuse the stock heads (after a cleaning and three-angle valve job), rebuilds the Quadrajet, and mounts it on an aluminum intake he bought at a junkyard. After doing some tuning on the dyno the engine misses the 300-horsepower mark, but not by much. Peak power is 283 horses; "more impressive than output is the fact that after 25 pulls, many of which were back-to-back, our junkyard jewel never missed a beat." McGean's total expenditure is $533.

After a two-year absence, the "Top Ten Hot Rods" feature is "back by popular demand." Since 24 issues have elapsed since the last pick, the staff decides all two years are open for debate. Ultimately, they choose Frank Currie's 1932 roadster, which appeared in both the November 1997 and March 1998 issues, as the Hot Rod of the Year. The 70-year-old Currie "did what most of us considered mission impossible. He built the first show-go-Power Touring participant in history and drove it to the Bonneville Salt Flats where it was timed at 205 mph, and then he toured it to Detroit under its own power."

1999

TECH

GETTING AWAY WITH IT

Can We Build a 300hp Small-Block for $500?

By Terry McGean
Photography: Terry McGean

Why do so many rodders feel that any and all performance engines require nothing less than the finest of whiz-bang, go-fast parts backed by a host of indestructible innards to qualify as a "proper" powerplant? Do you really need that tungsten air-cleaner wing nut just to go to the local cruise? Does a decent streeter really need to make 800 hp and have the ability to withstand 8,000 rpm to be functional and enjoyable? And perhaps more importantly, does the entry-level hot rodder need a Kryptonite Visa card to join the ranks? We think not.

These questions spawned a challenge: Build a respectable street motor with a bargain price tag. But what's respectable? We felt that any engine that could theoretically propel a 3,300-pound car into the 13s would qualify, and a nice round 300 ponies should do it. What's cheap? We were stoked to do a 300 hp for $300 deal, but that proved a little too thrifty, so we set the high water mark at five bills. Of course, if you're pondering economical horsepower, you're probably already thinking small-block Chev, since the "As Low As..." catalog claims almost always cite the mouse motor pricing.

Outside of believing that it simply couldn't be done, some skeptics felt that attempting to make power on the cheap was just an unsound practice and claimed that we would be doing more harm than good by instructing readers to build their own grenades.

Tech Editor Magnante pulls out The Character to introduce the first "Junkyard Jewel" story. Turns out the concept wasn't nutty at all.

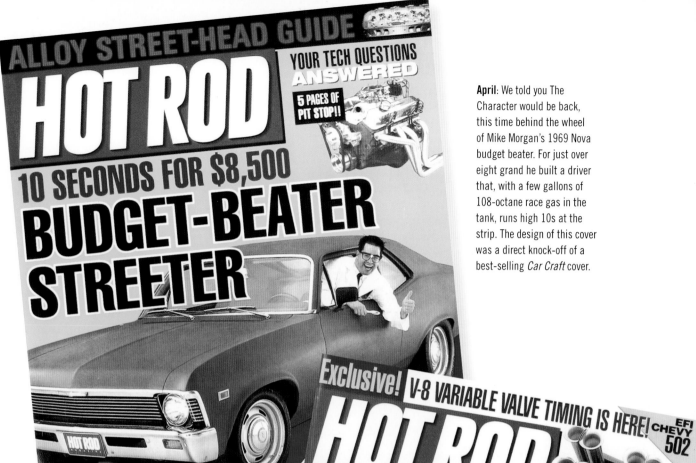

April: We told you The Character would be back, this time behind the wheel of Mike Morgan's 1969 Nova budget beater. For just over eight grand he built a driver that, with a few gallons of 108-octane race gas in the tank, runs high 10s at the strip. The design of this cover was a direct knock-off of a best-selling *Car Craft* cover.

July: The shot will be duplicated in other magazines to come using trick photography, but ace Petersen lensman Scott Killeen captures Mike Metz and his 10-second Mustang grabbing real air on a 70-mile-per-hour jump. And he had to do it more than once to get it right.

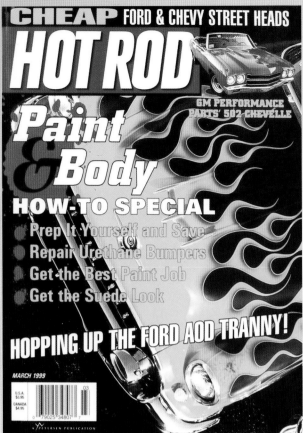

CHEAP FORD & CHEVY STREET HEADS

HOT ROD

GM PERFORMANCE PARTS' 502 CHEVELLE

Paint & Body

HOW-TO SPECIAL

- Prep It Yourself and Save
- Repair Urethane Bumpers
- Get the Best Paint Job
- Get the Suede Look

HOPPING UP THE FORD AOD TRANNY!

MARCH 1999

March

502 CHEVY: 700 FOOT-POUNDS, CLEAN & LEGAL

HOT ROD SPECIAL 16-PAGE MINI MAG HOW TO DRAG RACE

Big Street Cubes!!!

- Complete Stroker Kit Guide
- Cheap 500ci Mopar Wedge
- V-10 Challenger

POWER TOUR: EAST COAST INVASION

February

700HP PUMP-GAS BIG-BLOCK CHEVY

HOT ROD YIKES!! 3-VALVE CHEVY HEADS

20 PAGES OF **Street Machines!**

- '66 EFI GTO
- '64 LT5 VETTE
- '57 FORD NASCAR STOCKER
- '36 DODGE HUMPBACK
- '59 EL CAMINO
- '99 SILVERADO

17HP 5.0L ROCKER-ARM SWAP | AIRFLOW TESTING SECRETS | TORQUEFLITE LOW-GEAR SWAP

June

STREET MUSCLE: NITROUS, STROKERS, BLOWERS & TURBOS

HOT ROD POWER TOUR SURVIVAL GUIDE

POWER & SPEED SPECIAL!!!

- 1,000HP MUSTANG ROADSTER
- 200MPH TOP-SPEED SHOOTOUT
- HOT ROD'S 8-SECOND STREET CAR

FUEL INJECTED '57 OLDS | THE ART OF ENGINE BALANCING

May

BIG POWER SMALL BUCKS: NITROUS OXIDE

HOT ROD STREET TECH:
- BUILD A MODERN 12-BOLT
- CARB VERSUS EFI SHOOTOUT

JUNKYARD JEWELS

- 300 HP FOR $460
- 320 HP FOR $531
- 375 HP FOR $1,025

STREET MACHINES
- GENT'S COOL '69 RIV
- MODULAR '49 MERC RAGTOP
- PRO STREET '66 GRAND PRIX

August

February: Killeen again, snapping the GM Performance Parts 502 Chevelle on Power Tour East.

March: Flames over suede suck readers into the annual "Paint & Body" special.

May: When McGean drives Summit's 1,000-horsepower *QuickStang,* it's all "spinning tires, banging gears and giggling."

June: Heinrich Gerhardt's *Frankengoat* mixes computers and carbon fiber with vintage Pontiac tin.

August: The "Junkyard Jewel" returns and makes almost 400 horsepower for less than $1,500.

September: With overdrive and EFI, Danny Banh's Mustang runs 10s and gets 25 street mpg.

October: Brothers-in-law and Power Tourers Mark Moore and Kevin Harris in their on-the-ground Camaros.

November: Popular Swapular: "You need more motor, and we'll show you the way."

December: We hope no one fell for the "Last Issue" scam.

TOP 10 ENGINE QUESTIONS ANSWERED

HOT ROD

12 SECONDS and 20 MPG from your Car!

- PUMP-GAS SPECIAL!
- 940HP BLOWN BIG-BLOCK CHEVY
- 4.6L FLOW TEST
- '66 EL CAMINO PROJECT

September

YOU CAN BUILD IT! **HALF-PRICE HEMI**

HOT ROD HOW TO: UNDERSTAND DYNO TESTING CHASSIS & ENGINE

11 KEY BUYS! FOR YOUR STREET MACHINE

- CYLINDER HEADS
- NITROUS OXIDE
- GAS SHOCKS
- GEARS
- AND MORE!

WORLD'S FASTEST SMALL-BLOCK CHEVY

PROJECT '66 EL CAMINO: ENGINE/DRIVETRAIN

October

BOLT-ON POWER! BIG-BLOCK ALUMINUM HEAD GUIDE

HOT ROD

ENGINE SWAPS!

- INSTALLATION HOW-TOS
- PIGGYBACK ELECTRONICS
- HEADERS, ENGINE MOUNTS, LINKAGE, PANS, AND MORE!

November

SPECIAL COLLECTOR'S EDITION

LAST ISSUE OF THE 20TH CENTURY!

HOT ROD

INVASION OF THE CHEVY KILLERS!
500HP BIG-BLOCK SS IMPALA

THE future OF HOT RODDING

- EXPERTS SPILL THEIR GUTS
- HOT-PERFORMANCE TRENDS
- NEW DETROIT MUSCLECARS

THE ORIGINAL SIX-PACK DRAG TEST

BASIC TECH: UNDERSTANDING SPARK ADVANCE

DECEMBER 1999

December

1999

How do you keep readers interested in *Hot Rod* at the dawn of the new millennium, when the Internet and cable TV provide automotive instant gratification without subscription fees or trips to the newsstand?

One way is to let your staff off the leash. Technical Editor Steve Magnante sold Editor Ro McGonegal on some pretty wacky story ideas in 1999, and he continued to pitch outrageous concepts early in the decade. The Cadillac-powered Chevette on the April 2000 cover got people talking (opinions fell into the "Way cool" or "What were they thinking?" camps), as did Magnante's exploration of "Streetable Funny Cars" in May 2001 (which generated similar polarized opinions). Unfortunately, neither produced big results on the newsstand, though years later, when the street Funny Car trend did heat up, Magnante was credited with being far in front of the curve.

McGonegal also resurrected the swimsuit issue—sort of. By the mid-1990s the swimsuit theme had run its course as a reliable newsstand sales generator, and few models had appeared on the cover since. But McGonegal and Art Director Todd Westover gave it another shot with a retro-themed "Blacktop Burlesque" section for the April 2001 issue. The vintage-style pinups failed to spike newsstand sales, but for the next few years models became a regular part of the magazine's "Paint & Body" cover themes. And pinup models have been a cover mainstay for *Hot Rod Deluxe* since its successful rebirth in 2007. Like Magnante, McGonegal and Westover may have just been ahead of the curve by a few years.

The publishing company also tried to boost sales with issues that had multiple "collectible" covers. Many magazines, including *Hot Rod*, produce dedicated subscriber editions to accommodate the mailing label. The practice of putting different images on these subscriber covers was done regularly during the swimsuit-issue era to mollify school librarians. But looked at another way, if you put an image and blurbs on a subscriber edition that are different from the newsstand version—boom!—serious hobbyists have to buy one of each to own a complete collection of *Hot Rod* magazines. Cheesy? Maybe. But lots of magazines did it in the 2000s, and it gave the editors the opportunity to do some special things with that second cover, like tributes to Gray Baskerville in June 2002, Robert E. Petersen in August 2007, and Wally Parks in February 2008.

By far the biggest impact on newsstand sales came with Hot Rod's *comprehensive redesign in 2004.*

By far the biggest impact on newsstand sales came with *Hot Rod*'s comprehensive redesign in 2004. Editor-in-Chief David Freiburger pulled countless all-nighters with Primedia Creative Director Alan Alpanian to thoroughly rethink the magazine top to bottom, and the first redesigned issue in July was a huge newsstand success. Even better, the sales lift continued, proving the worth of the investment made in the package. Freiburger and Editor Rob Kinnan have since tuned up the redesign with Art Director Edwin Alpanian, giving the covers a bold, compelling look as the magazine moves into the 2010s and beyond.

The Pump Gas Drags and Drag Week (shown here) bring new life to the street-car racing concept.

Detroit starts building muscle cars again, and *Hot Rod* is right back in the thick of a horsepower war.

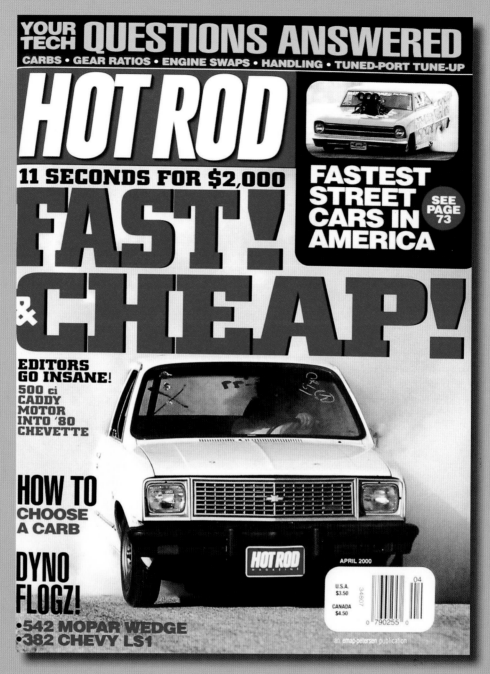

YOUR TECH QUESTIONS ANSWERED

CARBS • GEAR RATIOS • ENGINE SWAPS • HANDLING • TUNED-PORT TUNE-UP

HOT ROD

11 SECONDS FOR $2,000

FAST! & CHEAP!

FASTEST STREET CARS IN AMERICA SEE PAGE 73

EDITORS GO INSANE!
500 ci CADDY MOTOR INTO '80 CHEVETTE

HOW TO CHOOSE A CARB

DYNO FLOGZ!
•542 MOPAR WEDGE
•382 CHEVY LS1

APRIL 2000

U.S.A. $3.50
CANADA $4.50

34807
04
0 790255 0

an emap-petersen publication

April

From a graphic design standpoint there's nothing thrilling about Gray Baskerville's cover photo of a small white car almost lost in its own tire smoke. Sales-wise the issue isn't a hit either. So why is this the stand-out issue of 2000? Because everyone remembers the "Bad Seed" Chevette.

During production of the "Popular Swapular" engine-swap story for the November 1999 issue, one transplant idea that didn't make it to print was the notion of a 500-inch Cadillac engine in a Chevy Chevette. Technical Editor Steve Magnante, living his The Character persona, writes, "The thought of the smallest possible rear-wheel-drive car with the largest possible engine made us nuts. We had to try it."

Making it all possible—if not exactly probable—is the fact that "Southern California self-serve salvage yards are crawling with virtually every key ingredient for cheap, cheap, cheap! As a result, the total cash outlay is just over $2,000 (not counting labor)." That includes $200 paid for the 1980 Chevette and $150 for the 500-inch V-8 from a 1976 Coupe deVille.

"When contemplating such a bizarre swap, the question of exactly where to put the engine arises like the Loch Ness monster," Magnante admits. Too far forward and it's a "nose-heavy tire-smoker." Too far back and it's a "bumper-dragging wheelie fiend." The just-right approach is in between. "Our 'seat of the pants' sensibility said that if the carburetor was beneath the cowl, weight distribution ought to be acceptable." Turns out Magneto's seat is pretty accurate: The placement puts the Chevette's front/rear weight bias "within 15 pounds of the ideal 50/50 split." Making room for the V-8 in this beater "was easy thanks to the Sawzall demi-god."

Magnante knows the stock rear axle won't be up to the torque coming its way from the Caddy mill, so he swaps in a Mustang II 8-inch rear end and adapts the Chevette coils and panhard bar to the new housing, utilizing pickup truck leaf springs as lower control arms. "Crude as it is, this suspension setup is responsible for yanking the front tires and generating 1.6-second short times."

That's right. Others may call it a death trap, but Magnante calls the "psycho Scooter's" strip manners "flawless. It launches straight with an inch of daylight showing beneath the front tires before settling into a steady grin-inducing charge to the top end." At Los Angeles County Raceway the car's best ET is 12.335 at 107.633, which "equals a whopping 11.98 at sea level."

Eagle-eyed readers will also notice a small change to the cover that tips off bigger doings: The Petersen Publishing Viking helmet logo, stylized of late, has been replaced by the line, "an emap-petersen publication." The private equity firm that Robert E. Petersen sold his publishing company to in 1996 sold it in 1999 to British publisher emap. Within the next decade the company would be sold again—twice.

Hot Rod's editors have done some crazy things to go fast on the cheap, but Magnante's "Bad Seed" Chevette may be the craziest of all.

December: "1971 meets 2001" as the Hotchkis Performance gang swaps a spanking-new LS1 crate motor into a vintage Camaro. The dramatic burnout shot was staged at the magazine offices, hoping no one would notice. They did. "The security guys went nuts, the parking guys passed out."

August: B'ville goes to Oregon to shoot Steve Curry's Gasser-style Chevy, while Magnante finds a whole squadron of nose-high rodders in "The El Monte Air Force." A retrospective of the Ramchargers High & Mighty 1949 Plymouth C/Altered explains the roots of the nose-up attitude.

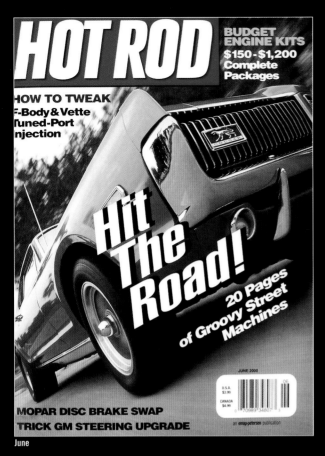

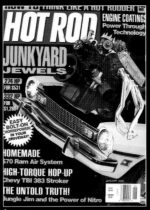
January

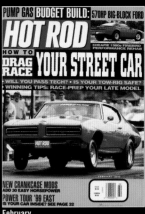
February

March

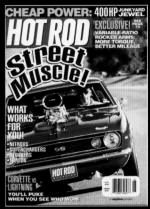
May

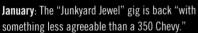
June

January: The "Junkyard Jewel" gig is back "with something less agreeable than a 350 Chevy."

February: Doug Hite's Real Street GTO gets readers warmed up for racing season.

March: "Flat broke" staff recycles a photo for the cover. "Praise the wonders of Photoshop."

May: Power adders, "once the provinces of truly paranoid street freaks," become the norm.

June: Bye-bye skyline blurb. *Hot Rod*'s logo moves to the very top of the cover.

July: Hemi? No, Northstar, one of the smog-legal late-model engine swaps inside.

September: Former Editor Jeff Smith drives his flaming El Camino through a tunnel near the Los Angeles Airport.

October: Troy's latest rad ride is the *Intruder*, "the sleekest '57 longroof Ford in existence."

November: A hot Camaro and Chevelle show off Chevy's new crate motors.

July

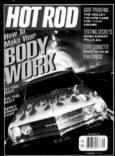
September

November

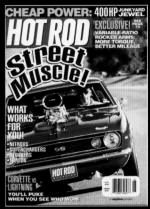
October

2000

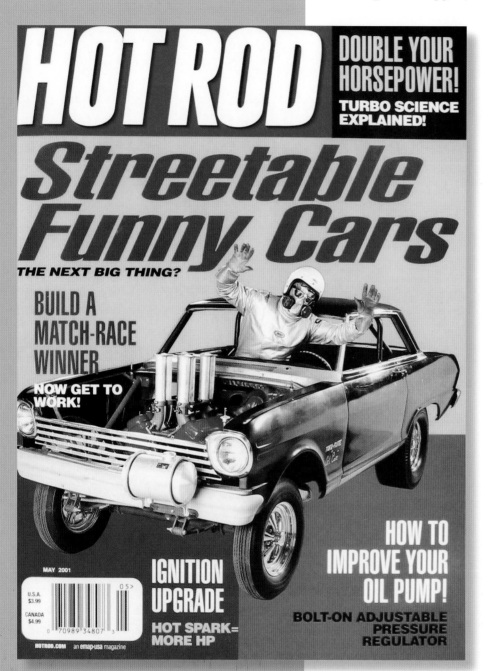

HOT ROD

DOUBLE YOUR
HORSEPOWER!
TURBO SCIENCE
EXPLAINED!

Streetable
Funny Cars

THE NEXT BIG THING?

BUILD A
MATCH-RACE
WINNER
NOW GET TO
WORK!

IGNITION
UPGRADE
HOT SPARK=
MORE HP

HOW TO
IMPROVE YOUR
OIL PUMP!
BOLT-ON ADJUSTABLE
PRESSURE
REGULATOR

May

Graphically, this cover's three-box design is a total rip-off of the April 1999 issue, which itself was a rip-off of a *Car Craft* cover. The photo, shot by freelancer Jim Brown, even features Technical Editor Steve Magnante acting goofy in a Nova again. But while the earlier cover explored going fast on the cheap, Magnante has far more ambitious plans this time: bringing the altered-wheelbase Funny Car look to the street.

Magnante likens hot rodding to a giant snowball, "picking up new trends and getting bigger all the time. Somewhere deep inside the snowball are the door-slammer Funny Cars of the '65–'67 era." These "mutated Super Stockers infected the nation with match race madness and paved the way for the modern flip-top fuel Funny Car." Magnante plans to pay tribute to those altered-wheelbase racers "by introducing the Match Bash building style," borrowing a term used by the NHRA to describe the Eliminator category for late-model match race hybrids. The idea is to "recreate that look and feel but with enough subtle upgrades to make it streetable." A side benefit: "Replicas can be based on battered, rusty and incomplete donors that might otherwise go to the crusher."

Magnante populates the article with a mix of vintage altered-wheelbase and Funny Car photos, contemporary shots of restored AWB cars, and the how-to steps that begin his Nova's transformation. Always thorough, Magnante delves into the technical reasons behind changing a car's wheelbase, using physics and math to demonstrate how a vehicle's center of gravity and weight balance can be shifted to great effect on the drag strip. "By sliding the chassis ahead under the body," he summarizes, "more weight can be brought to bear on the slicks for better bite and more effective use of available power. In 1965, Chrysler launched a fleet of 12 altered-wheelbase cars that took full advantage of center-of-gravity manipulation and *poof!*—the Funny Car was born."

Magnante's Nova won't just look like it goes fast, though. His plans call for a fuel-injected 502-inch Chevy big-block that potentially will propel the car into the high 10s at 120 miles per hour—"fast enough to earn respect." As he reasons, "Hey, if a tarmac-scraping Pro Streeter is valid, then a re-pop of an old-time Funny is fair game, too. The point is, there is no right or wrong way to go hot rodding."

Well, maybe. In mid-2001 readers aren't ready for Magnante's radical approach, and the issue sells poorly on the newsstand. A few years later, though, the craze catches heat, and Magnante—and *Hot Rod*—are, once again, setting trends rather than following. It just took a while for the rest of the rodding world to catch up.

Magnante dips into hot rodding's past elsewhere in the issue, too, writing a history of turbochargers and drag racing to accompany Technical Editor Terry McGean's explanation of turbo basics. "Turbocharging has lived in the world of brawny Detroit machinery for quite some time, and it is just as effective on a big motor as it is on a small one."

2001

"Match Bash" is Magnante's term for taking the altered-wheelbase Funny Car look to the street. He is way ahead of his time.

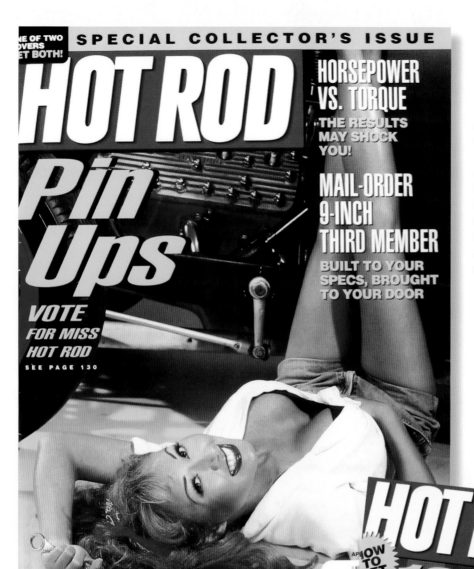

SPECIAL COLLECTOR'S ISSUE

HOT ROD

Pin Ups

VOTE FOR MISS HOT ROD

SEE PAGE 130

HORSEPOWER VS. TORQUE

THE RESULTS MAY SHOCK YOU!

MAIL-ORDER 9-INCH THIRD MEMBER

BUILT TO YOUR SPECS, BROUGHT TO YOUR DOOR

April: "Remember the swimsuit editions?" ask the editors. "For the past five years, people around here have been bugging us to do one . . . or something like it." Unfortunately, the retro-styled pinups don't move the newsstand needle. But *Hot Rod Deluxe* will adopt the style with great success a few years later.

U.S.A. $3.99
CANADA $4.99

HOT ROD

ELECTRONIC IGNITION UPGRADES!
EASY & QUICK

12 Seconds and 20 MPG

From Your Street Machine

THE TRUTH ABOUT PUMP GAS
ARE YOU GETTING YOUR $$$ WORTH?

REAL WORLD STOPPING POWER!
BIGGER BRAKES IN ABOUT AN HOUR

MARCH 2001

U.S.A. $3.99
CANADA $4.99

hotrod.com an emap usa magazine

March: Actually, what's inside this issue is more significant than the in-your-face Challenger. There's a—gasp!—Honda in the cover story. And Ro said it would never happen. But it does, and will again, soon. Hot rodding is changing. Should *Hot Rod* change with it?

HOT ROD
New
Old!

ANOTHER SMALL-BLOCK BUILDUP!
EASY 415 HP WITH YOUR 350 SHORT-BLOCK

MODERN INDUCTION
RETROFIT YOUR OLD ROD

SWAP GUIDE
WIRING HARNESSES FOR EFI CONVERTS

HOW-TO
HIGH-PRESSURE PLUMBING

NEW FEATURE!
HOT ROD REVISITED
SEE PAGE 42

FEBRUARY 2001

U.S.A. $3.99
CANADA $4.99

ORIGINAL RESTO
BACK FROM THE DEAD '40 COUPE

HOTROD.COM · an emap·usa magazine

February

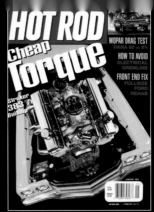

HOT ROD
Cheap *Torque*

MOPAR DRAG TEST
DANA 60 vs 8¾

HOW TO AVOID ELECTRICAL GREMLINS

FRONT END FIX
FULL SIZE FORD REHAB

Stroker 383 Buildup

January

HOT ROD
Cheaper *Faster*

EXCLUSIVE!
FORD FORTY-NINE

DETROIT'S NEW HOT ROD: WE'VE GOT THE INSIDE STORY

• NITROUS INSTALL
TWO SECONDS QUICKER FOR $300

• 10-SECOND LS1
NO BLOWER, NO NITROUS FACTORY SHORT-BLOCK

• LOW-BUCK NASCAR PARTS!
JEFF GORDON'S JUNK IS YOUR SECRET WEAPON

• SAVE YOUR BLOCK
REPAIR BEARING DAMAGE

July

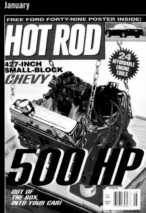

HOT ROD

FREE FORD FORTY-NINE POSTER INSIDE!

427-INCH SMALL-BLOCK CHEVY

24 AFFORDABLE ENGINE TOOLS

500 HP
OUT OF THE BOX, INTO YOUR CAR!

August

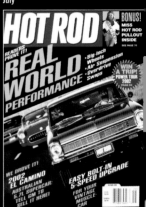

HOT ROD

BONUS!
MISS HOT ROD PULLOUT INSIDE
SEE PAGE 70

READERS PROVE IT!
REAL WORLD PERFORMANCE
• Big-Inch Wheels
• Air Suspension
• Overdrive Swaps

WIN A TRIP! POWER TOUR 2002

WE DROVE IT!
2002 EL CAMINO
AUSTRALIAN 5.7L SUPERCAR: TELL GM TO SELL IT HERE!

EASY BOLT-IN 5-SPEED UPGRADE
FOR YOUR VINTAGE MUSCLE CAR

September

HOT ROD

COLLECTOR'S ISSUE: 50 YEARS OF THE HEMI

WORLD'S FASTEST SMALL-BLOCK CAMARO

WIN A NEW HEMI!

JUNKYARD JEWEL 454
POWER PER DOLLAR
CAM · INTAKE · HEADS · BLOWER

289 FORD: 350 HP WITH A TWO-BARREL AND CHEAP GAS!

October

HOT ROD

FREE POSTER: CAMARO's 35th ANNIVERSARY
EXCLUSIVE
THE MUSCLE SEDAN IS BACK!
'03 MERCURY MARAUDER

PICK AND TUNE THE BEST
CAM & INTAKE
COMBOS

WIN A FREE 409 ASSEMBLY!

VIC EDELBROCK: INSIDE HIS NEW '57 CHEVY

SMOKEY YUNICK: TRIBUTE TO A LEGEND

PROWLER vs THUNDERBIRD: SHOWROOM-ROD SHOOTOUT

November

HOT ROD
25+

YOUR CAR FEATURED IN HOT ROD MAG

FREE MOVIE POSTER INSIDE:
"THE FAST AND FURIOUS"

IT'S OFFICIAL: CAMARO FINISHED? DEAD

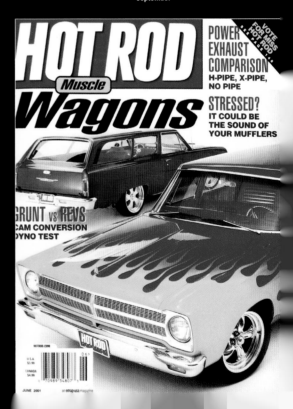

HOT ROD
Muscle *Wagons*

VOTE FOR MISS HOT ROD 2002

POWER EXHAUST COMPARISON
H-PIPE, X-PIPE, NO PIPE

STRESSED?
IT COULD BE THE SOUND OF YOUR MUFFLERS

GRUNT vs REVS
CAM CONVERSION DYNO TEST

HOTROD.COM

U.S.A. $3.99
CANADA $4.99

JUNE 2001 · an emap·usa magazine

Girls and engines (or engine parts) dominate *Hot Rod* covers in 2002, but this particular story is different. Not only does freelance photographer Jim Brown shoot the engine in an unusual head-on angle, but the story inside, about tuning a 383-inch small-block crate motor for maximum torque, generates discussion literally for years to come.

Editor-in-Chief David Freiburger describes making "500 lb-ft in Six Easy Steps" using a GM Performance Parts HT383 V-8. Out of the box the engine "is no slouch" despite its truck motor billing, but "just a few well-chosen add-ons can make it scream."

Step one is getting the engine out of the crate and running. Freiburger finds the engine "overdelivers on the dyno," producing 444 lbs-ft. of peak torque instead of the advertised 415. Step two, the addition of 1.6:1 rocker arms (which increases valve lift), raises torque output to 452.5 lbs-ft. Step three mounts an Edelbrock Performer RPM Air Gap intake manifold and sees torque rise to 466.6 lbs-ft. Step four exchanges the first-choice 625-cfm Road Demon carb for a 750 Speed Demon, and torque rises to 474.3 lbs-ft. Step five has the only non-bolt-on goods in the bunch: a new Comp Cams camshaft and valve springs, plus slightly thinner head gaskets to bump compression by half a point. The engine jumps to 493 lbs-ft. and changes character from "an ideal towing/daily driver engine to a hot rod engine." Freiburger calls the synthetic oil added in step six "the magic wand." Final result: 502.9 lbs-ft.

March

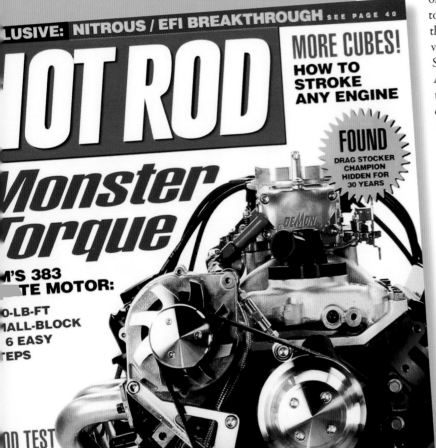

How do you make 500 lbs-ft. of torque from Chevy's 383-inch crate small-block? It's easy, says Freiburger.

2002

June: *Hot Rod* was into multiple "collector's edition" covers in 2002. Newsstand buyers got this high-dollar, 1,050-horsepower big-block; subscriber covers were a tribute to Gray Baskerville, who passed away in February. Inside was a feature on B'ville's 1932 roadster with recollections by "a few of his legion of pals."

January: "Ain't nothin' like carbs all over an engine," Freiburger writes. In reality, a single four-barrel carb works best on a street motor, but "duals and triples draw a crowd better than any lonely four-holer." This story tests 19 carbs and seven intakes on one small-block Chevy.

February: Subscribers and newsstand buyers get different vintage Camaro covers for the 350's anniversary.

April: Another two-cover month, both featuring Lisa Ligon, Miss Hot Rod 2002."

May: Hot Rod TV's shop helper Candace Clapp introduces best bolt-ons.

July: Bolt a blower on a crate Hemi and get 753 easy horsepower. Pricey? Yes.

August: *Hot Rod* loses another of its guiding lights with the passing of Ray Brock.

September: A publishing landmark: The first *Hot Rod* cover shot digitally.

October: Power Tour® goes huge. A two-page photo inside barely contains all 535 Long Haulers.

November: The aluminum ZL1 V-8 gets a new, fuel-injected life as a crate engine.

December: Mike Landi's 1955 is one of the "Top 10 Hot Rods of the Year."

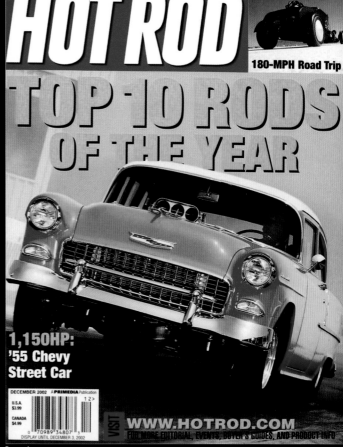

December

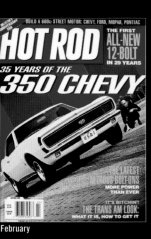

February

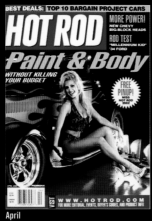

April

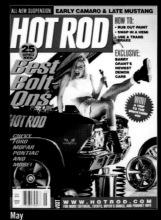

May

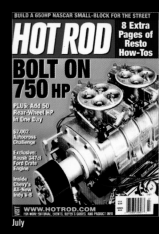

July

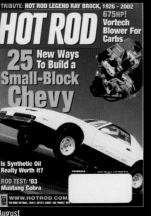

August

September

October

November

2003

Hot Rod's editors uniquely meld past and present for the magazine's 55th birthday. The embodiment of that theme is Larry Erickson's 1932 Chevy roadster, photographed by Randy Lorentzen. Erickson, whose day job is being Ford's chief designer for Mustang and Thunderbird and who penned four landmark hot rods, including *CadZZilla*, drew on influences from a number of historic rods

in the creation of his. "Instead of looking ahead, I was looking from overhead, seeing how cars from the past connected with the present and what combination of elements could make something unique," he says to Editor Ro McGonegal. The result is a "Potvin-blown, fully independent, ZF transaxle, '32 Chevy roadster" with a track nose and Boyd Coddington wheels like the "no-hole Halibrands that [Bob] Tindle had on the *Orange Crate* so many years ago."

McGonegal and Editor-in-Chief David Freiburger invite former Editor (and NHRA founder) Wally Parks to the magazine's photo archives to get Parks' firsthand recollections of *Hot Rod*'s past. "The SCTA and the NHRA might have perished were it not for *Hot Rod* magazine," Parks says in McGonegal's story. "The whole concept was like a dream. We had fun and weren't taking ourselves too seriously. How wholesome a thing it all was in the beginning."

Parks, nearly 90, has amazing recall. "He flipped through books loaded with images he'd either never seen or long forgotten," Freiburger writes, "and recalled details with clarity. Names, T-shirts, time slip numbers, cities. It was all right there."

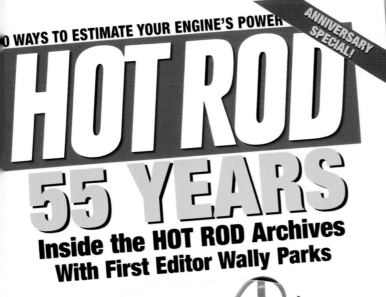

O WAYS TO ESTIMATE YOUR ENGINE'S POWER

ANNIVERSARY SPECIAL!

HOT ROD
55 YEARS
Inside the HOT ROD Archives
With First Editor Wally Parks

New
572ci
Chevy
pg. 42

450HP
Ford 390
Buildup

Larry
Erickson's
Heritage
Roadster

JANUARY 2003   A **PRIMEDIA** Publication

U.S.A. $3.99
CANADA $4.99

DISPLAY UNTIL JANUARY 7, 2003

VISIT WWW.HOTROD.COM: FOR MORE EDITORIAL, EVENTS, BUYER'S GUIDES, AND PRODUCT INFO

January

Wally Parks (left, with Mickey Thompson in 1960) visits the magazine's photo archive for a look back at *Hot Rod*'s history on its 55th anniversary.

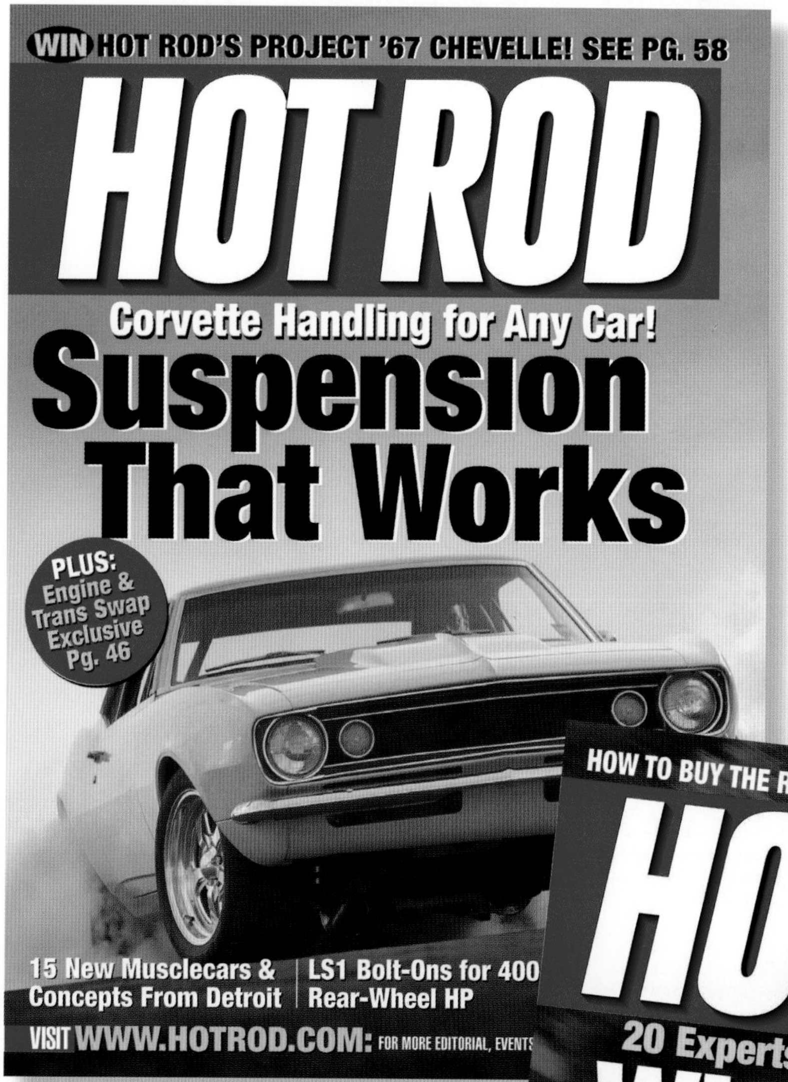

WIN HOT ROD'S PROJECT '67 CHEVELLE! SEE PG. 58

HOT ROD

Corvette Handling for Any Car!

Suspension That Works

PLUS:
Engine &
Trans Swap
Exclusive
Pg. 46

15 New Musclecars & Concepts From Detroit | **LS1 Bolt-Ons for 400 Rear-Wheel HP**

VISIT **WWW.HOTROD.COM:** FOR MORE EDITORIAL, EVENTS

HOW TO BUY THE RIGHT CRANK, RODS, AND PISTONS

POWER TOUR '03
TO JOIN SEE PG. 13

HOT ROD

20 Experts Reveal the Next Trends

What's Hot For 2003

FEBRUARY 2003 A **PRIMEDIA** Publication

U.S.A. $3.99

CANADA $4.99

0 2>

0 70989 34807 3

DISPLAY UNTIL FEBRUARY 4, 2003

5.0L Ford Focus!
Pg. 58

VISIT **WWW.HOTROD.COM:** FOR MORE EDITORIAL, EVENTS, BUYER'S GUIDES, AND PRODUCT INFO

May: Longtime readers will recognize the *Crusher Camaro*, the mid-1990s project car rescued from certain death at the hands of California's smog police. McGonegal brought the car back in the February issue, and it's now ready for its close-up. "Did I tell you it's *loud* and *insane?*" asks Freiburger.

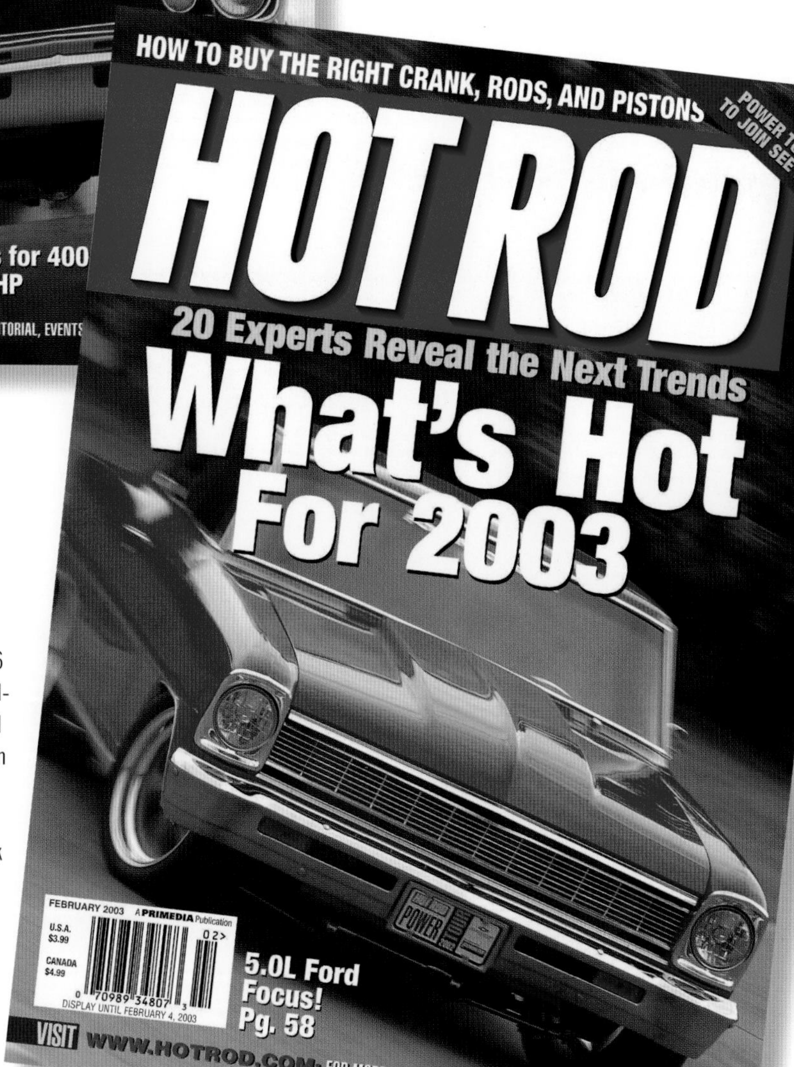

February: Ken La Fortune turned his "high school sweetheart" 1966 Nova into a "huge-cube, six-speed-bangin' perfect-10 cover car." And freelance photographer Wes Allison starts to make full use of digital photography's editable nature by perfecting slow-mo shots that look like they're going a million miles an hour.

2003

March: It's been a while since a Detroit stocker—even a prototype—made the cover.

April: Newsstand buyers get Mishell Thrope, Miss Hot Rod. Subscribers get a tamer 1940 Chevy.

June: You could win your dream engine, like "this mild-cammed 468-incher going in our '32."

July: Don Walsh's Pro 5.0 Mustang is among the "World's Fastest Cars."

August: Greg Smith's turbocharged 1967 Mustang sets the stage for the "Boost Shootout."

September: Touring? Street? Drag? It's all in the YearOne 1967 Chevelle.

October: More than 1,000 make the Power Tour® Long Haul® from Tennessee to Texas.

November: This blown 5.4 is the "baddest Ford V-8 ever." Wrapping it in the GT helps.

December: Three—count 'em—collectible covers this month, each with a different model and car.

March

June

July

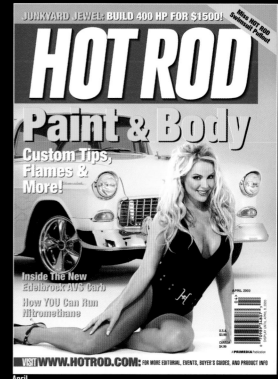

April

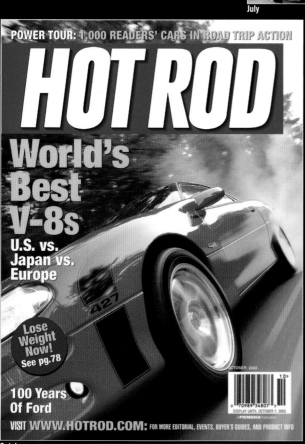

October

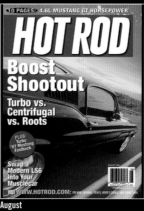

August

September

November

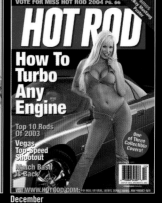

December

The cover shown reads:

TUNING THE NEW HOLLEY ULTRA SERIES CARBS

HOT ROD

GTO VS. THE IMPORT RACERS
SEE PG. 56

RECORD PRICES. MORE SPEED PARTS. WHAT'S DRIVING THE

MUSCLECAR BOOM

ULTIMATE INTAKE SHOWDOWN
WE TEST SIX EDELBROCK MANIFOLDS AND PROVE **WHICH ONE IS BEST FOR YOU**

FIND MORE @ HOTROD.COM
JULY 2004
USA $3.99 • CANADA $4.99

0 70989 34807 3
DISPLAY UNTIL JULY 6, 2004
07>

675 HORSE POWER
BUILD A 505ci FORD FE WITH ALL NEW PARTS

HOT ROD **WHERE IT ALL BEGAN**

A PRIMEDIA Publication

To hear company insiders tell it, this is the issue that saved *Hot Rod* magazine.

A revolving door of corporate owners after Robert Petersen sold the publishing company takes its toll. Too many managers try to influence the magazine's direction in too many different ways, blurring its focus. Plus, each time the company changes hands, operating budgets are cut, forcing the editors to work with fewer and fewer resources. Primedia, the current corporate parent, has trimmed so much that it becomes "the corporate entity that even readers love to hate," writes Editor-in-Chief David Freiburger in his Starting Line column.

All that changes when Craig Reiss, Primedia's chief creative officer, walks into Freiburger's office with an offer he can't refuse: Let's make *Hot Rod* all-new—rethought and repurposed from the ground up. Reiss offers additional pages, better paper stock, and cutting-edge graphic design, plus a big infusion of money to invest in the product. "He's in my office swearing we're going to birth the magazine that's hidden inside me," Freiburger explains in his column. "I'm gonna love it, he says—once the suffering is over."

Freiburger calls the redesign process "the best suffering of my career." This is not just a graphic patch job that's typical of magazine makeovers. "Paragraph by paragraph, image by image, we were challenged to ditch the hackneyed car-magazine conventions and confront our beliefs to perfect the editorial execution," Freiburger writes. "The corporate guys still don't know drag racing from drag queens, but they made us think deep to explain what hot rodding really means."

Primedia Creative Director Alan Alpanian heads up the visual end of the

---

Opposite Page: *Hot Rod* undergoes a complete overhaul in July, rethinking everything from its editorial focus to its graphic presentation. The reborn magazine is an immediate hit.

redesign process, crafting a look that's dramatically photo-intensive without losing the in-depth information readers have come to rely on. In fact, as part of the redesign, much of the tech-heavy material is given its own real estate in the magazine, a section called the "Hot Rod Garage," making it easy for gearheads to find and browse.

The cover that introduces the new look is a dynamic one: Lyle Owerko of Wonderlust.com photographs four muscle cars in tight formation as they exit Los Angeles' Third Street tunnel, representing the current explosion of interest in—and value of—1960s and 1970s muscle cars. Inside, former Editor Drew Hardin examines the elements making up the new muscle car boom, from fresh media attention in movies and music videos to the "stupid money" being paid for certain star cars at auction. "These cars are the SJ Duesenbergs of their era," says Craig

Jackson of the Barrett-Jackson auction company. "They are just as rare as the rarest classic cars." Which is why some—like Hemi 'Cuda convertibles—are in the $1 million range and climbing.

The makeover is an instant success. Newsstand sales make a big jump, and that momentum is sustained as readers respond not just to the new look, but also to the fresh article ideas coming from a revitalized editorial staff.

THE MUSCLECAR BOOM

Huge Prices. More Speed Parts Than Ever. Mopars as Pop Icons. America's Obsession With Musclecar Power Hits a Mid-'80s Frenzy

Suddenly, American muscle reigns anew. It seemed like the mid-'80s all over again during a recent Barrett-Jackson auction when a dozen musclecars sold for six figures a whack.

In the latest music video from Disney Channel actress-turned-singer Hilary Duff, her teen-heartthrob boyfriend shows up at her house not in an import, but in a '69 Camaro. Eddie Paul, who built cars for *The Fast and the Furious*, told us that

By Drew Hardin
Photography: Lyle Owerko/Wonderlust.com

THE LEGENDARY HEMI CHEVY 10-LITER IS BACK

HOT ROD

POWER TOUR
BIGGEST WEEK IN HOT RODDING

FINALLY, YOU CAN BUY AN ALL-NEW STEEL '69 CAMARO IN A CRATE. '67 MUSTANGS ARE NEXT. STREET MACHINES WILL LIVE FOREVER.

THIS CHANGES IT ALL

SHIPPING RECEIVING

FIND MORE @ HOTROD.COM
OCTOBER 2004
USA $3.99 • CANADA $4.99

"I WILL RUN 5s"
HOW MIKE MORAN WENT FROM STREET RACER TO BUILDER OF THE WORLD'S FASTEST DOOR-SLAMMER

HOT RO...

0 70989 34807 3   10 >
DISPLAY UNTIL OCTOBER 5, 2004
A PRIMEDIA Publication

October: Brand-new, all-steel 1969 Camaro bodies will free street machine builders from having to resurrect bent and rusted originals. It's the "street-rodification of the muscle car market," writes Freiburger, comparing Dynacorn's replica to the repop vintage Fords available to rodders. Lawyers will keep the Camaros in limbo for a year.

5 NEW CARS DETROIT MUST BUILD RIGHT NOW

HOT ROD

MORE POWER FROM YOUR K&N FILTER

PUMP GAS DRAGS

41 READERS' CARS.
93 OCTANE.
NO TRAILERS.
THE MOST LEGIT STREET CAR SHOOTOUT EVER.

EXCLUSIVE:
CHEVY GEN III V-8
THE SECRETS BEHIND THE MOST IMPORTANT PERFORMANCE ENGINE OF ITS TIME

August: "Real street cars. No trailers. 93 octane. A 33-mile drive in rush hour, then 9-second passes at 150-plus mph. Wheelstands, tire smoke and destruction. *Hot Rod*'s most legit shootout ever to find the fastest street car in America." Welcome to the Pump Gas Drags.

525HP MOD MOTOR
GETTING THE MOST OUT OF (CHEAP) '96-'03 MUSTANGS
HOT ROD WHERE IT ALL BEGAN

AUGUST 2004
USA $3.99 • CANADA $4.99

0 70989 34807 7   08 >
DISPLAY UNTIL AUGUST 10, 2004
A PRIMEDIA Publication

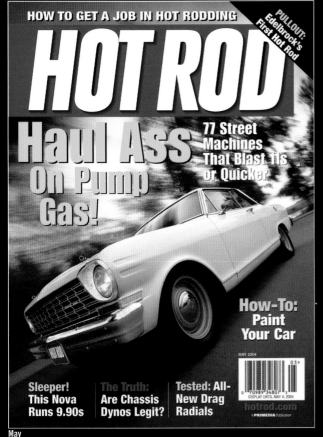

HOW TO GET A JOB IN HOT RODDING

HOT ROD

PULLOUT: Edelbrock's First Hot Rod

Haul Ass On Pump Gas!

77 Street Machines That Blast 11s or Quicker

How-To: Paint Your Car

MAY 2004

DISPLAY UNTIL MAY 4, 2004

hotrod.com A PRIMEDIA Publication

Sleeper! This Nova Runs 9.90s | The Truth: Are Chassis Dynos Legit? | Tested: All-New Drag Radials

May

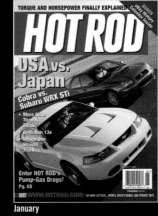

TORQUE AND HORSEPOWER FINALLY EXPLAINED

HOT ROD

USA vs. Japan

Cobra vs. Subaru WRX STi

• More Alike Than You Think; Both Run 13s
• Which One Should You Buy?

Enter HOT ROD's Pump-Gas Drags! Pg. 68

VISIT WWW.HOTROD.COM

January

300hp Daily Drivers: Chevy & Ford

HOT ROD

First Look! **The New Mustang**

Your 300hp GT Is Here

Ford Insiders Tell All

PLUS:
• Compare: Pro Stock vs. Pro Import
• Setup: All-New LS1 Heads
• New Project: '32 Ford Roadster

February

101 NEW SPEED PARTS AND HOT RODS FOR 2004

HOT ROD

Starsky & Hutch

Exclusive: We Drive The Torinos From The New Warner Bros. Movie

PLUS:
Engine Swap: 5.7L Hemi Into Your Musclecar
Secrets of the World's Quickest 4.6L Ford
First Ever: Texas Land Speed Race

March

JUNKYARD JEWELS: HIGH-TECH ENGINES FOR CHEAP

HOT ROD

125 Custom Paint Ideas

PLUS:
How To Paint Your Car
600hp Ford's 5.0L Is Back
Look: Jay Leno's 572ci Sleeper
Fast! 237-mph Dodge Charger

April

January: An import on the cover? Do we need to tell you it didn't sell?

February: A year ago we saw the retro-styled concept; here's the production Mustang.

March: Starsky's *Striped Tomato* Torino is back; a dozen are made for the movie.

April: All the right newsstand buzzwords: paint, "Junkyard Jewels," and a Miss Hot Rod poster.

May: The cars that weren't quite Pump Gas Drags material get their shot at fame.

June: GM doesn't want you to know that its ZZ572/720R *will* run on pump gas.

September: *Fear Factor* host Joe Rogan has Troy Trepanier build him a *Sick Fish*.

November: Speed parts that "forever altered the way hot rodders build hot rods."

December: The 50th anniversary of the U.S. Nationals brings hot rods back again.

WIN AN '04 MUSTANG MACH 1 BUILT BY HOT ROD

HOT ROD

Nastiest Crate Engines Yet!

• ZZ572: The Test GM Doesn't Want You To See
• 10 More Killers

PLUS:
Sign Up: Power Tour Is Coming | How-To: Basic Nitrous Tuning | All New: Three-Carb Induction

hotrod.com

June

'70 CHEVELLE MAKEOVER: FROM START TO FINISH

HOT ROD

NHRA DRAG RACING

HOTTEST PROJECTS

THE FEAR FACTOR HEMI CUDA LEADS OUR 20 MOST BADASS BUILD-UPS IN THE USA

TORQUE MONSTER

TOP FUEL FUNNY CAR

September

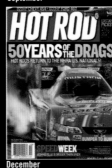

SHAVE CHEVY: S&T PRIMER FROM START TO FINISH

HOT ROD

50 YEARS OF THE DRAGS

HOT RODS RETURN TO THE NHRA U.S. NATIONALS!

SPEEDWEEK

BUMPER TO BUMPER

December

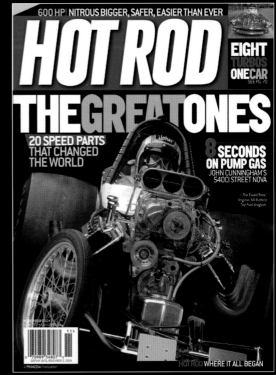

600 HP! NITROUS BIGGER, SAFER, EASIER THAN EVER

HOT ROD

EIGHT TURBOS ONE CAR SEE PG. 70

THE GREAT ONES

20 SPEED PARTS THAT CHANGED THE WORLD

8 SECONDS ON PUMP GAS JOHN CUNNINGHAM'S 540CI STREET NOVA

• The Ewald Bros.' Original '68 Buttera Top Fuel dragster

DISPLAY UNTIL NOVEMBER 2, 2004

A PRIMEDIA Publication

HOT ROD WHERE IT ALL BEGAN

November

2004

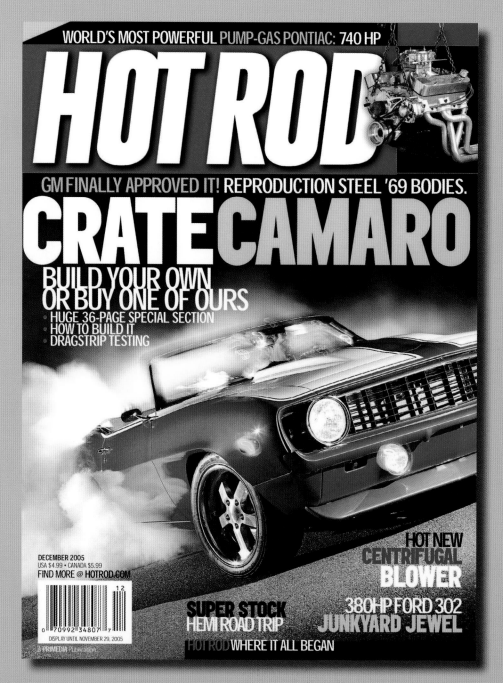

December

"That's not fake Photoshopped smoke you see coming from the Crate Camaro, and we've got the destroyed tires and roasted clutch disc to prove it." For a year, production of Dynacorn's Camaro-in-a-box had been tied up in legal issues. But Wes Allison's tire-frying cover shot announces that the bodies are in stock, and *Hot Rod* has built the first all-new 1969 Camaro in 36 years.

"The industry, the readers, and the restoration market came totally unglued when the October '04 issue hit the stands," writes Editor-in-Chief David Freiburger. Apparently, so did General Motors. Cease and desist orders went flying. The magazine was already deep into a major buildup—a project dubbed *Hot Rod 1*—to be unveiled at the 2004 SEMA auto industry trade show in Las Vegas. The legal wrangling nearly kept the Rally Green Camaro off the show floor, though when it did go on display it was shuffled off to a far corner and devoid of any Camaro badging.

In the ensuing months, the body manufacturer and the automaker reached an agreement, granting the new crate Camaros official GM licensing. With that hurdle cleared, the magazine was finally free to document *Hot Rod 1*'s construction.

Freiburger's opening story about the body shell answers two big questions right up front: "The price for a body from tailpanel to cowl and from floorpans to the windshield frame (no doors or trunklid) is $10,500, plus $495 for crating." And yes, "the sheetmetal is stamped in Taiwan." The new convertible bodies are made up of 850 separate stampings that are welded into 35 subassemblies and then shipped to Dynacorn, where they are robotically welded to GM production standards. The metal itself is "slightly thinner than the original but of a higher grade that is less brittle." The bodies are designed as stock replacements that are virtually identical to OE components, so they'll accept original and reproduction parts. In fact, "you can now buy every single part you need to assemble a complete car with nothing but brand-new parts," Freiburger writes.

And that's what *Hot Rod 1* is all about. From GM Performance Parts the magazine got a 510-horse ZL1 aluminum crate engine and backed it with a Keisler modified Tremec TKO-600 five-speed manual transmission. Detroit Speed & Engineering provided a Pro Touring–style suspension and subframe connectors, and Jim Barber's Classic Auto Restoration Service was tasked with the car's assembly. In all, "We worked 24-7 for a full week with 11 guys to finish the car in time for SEMA," Barber says.

No trailer queen, *Hot Rod 1* made the 2005 Power Tour Long Haul, where it performed flawlessly, says Barber. "It drives nice, and I was really surprised that it got decent gas mileage. We were driving it well over 80 a lot of the time, and it averaged 14.5 mpg." After the Power Tour, the Camaro went to Bradenton Motorsports Park, where it ran 12.69 at 109.64 miles per hour in 95-degree weather and on street tires.

Hot Rod builds a crate Camaro from Dynacorn, but legal issues put the project in jeopardy.

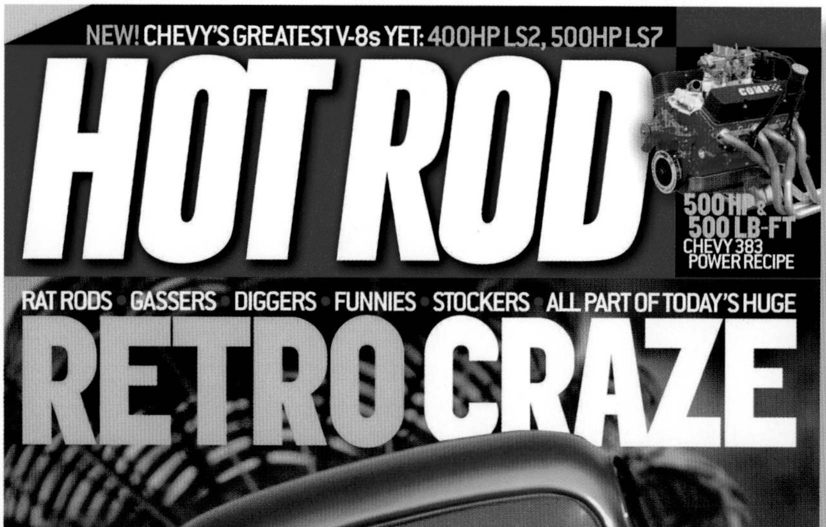

March: Old school is the new rule, and *Hot Rod* covers the retro trend from cackling front-engine dragsters to rat rods and the retro lifestyle. Randy Lorentzen shot the Stone, Woods & Cook Willys gasser for the cover, and that vintage Deist parachute was shredded in seconds.

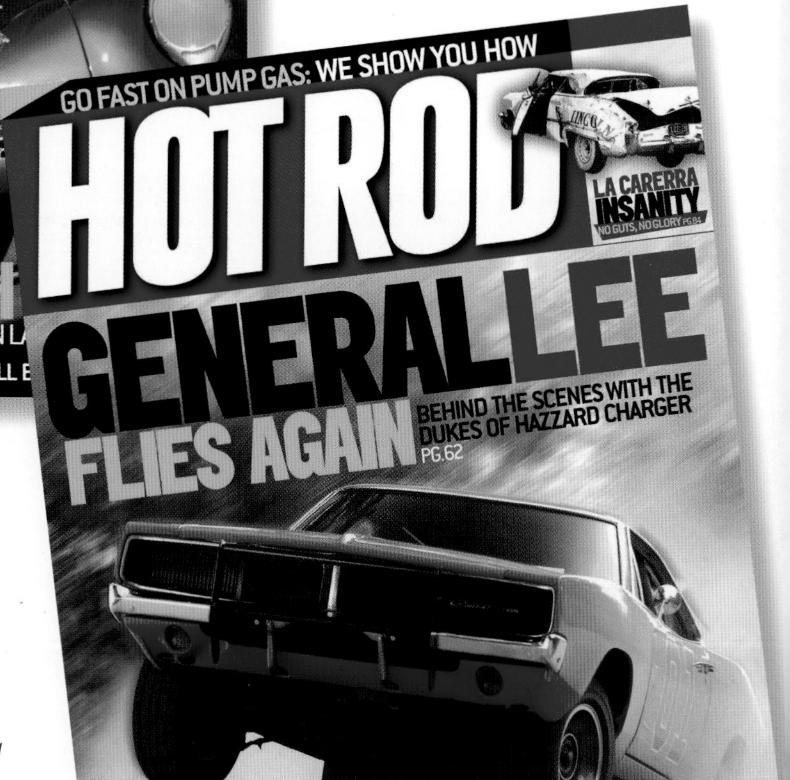

NEW! CHEVY'S GREATEST V-8s YET: 400HP LS2, 500HP LS7

HOT ROD

500HP & 500 LB-FT CHEVY 383 POWER RECIPE

RAT RODS · GASSERS · DIGGERS · FUNNIES · STOCKERS · ALL PART OF TODAY'S HUGE

RETRO CRAZE

MARCH 2005
USA $3.99 · CANADA $4.99

417-MPH
SETTING THE PISTON L...

HOT ROD WHERE IT ALL B...

A PRIMEDIA Publication

DISPLAY UNTIL MARCH 1, 2005

0 70989 34807 3

GO FAST ON PUMP GAS: WE SHOW YOU HOW

HOT ROD

LA CARERRA INSANITY
NO GUTS, NO GLORY PG.86

GENERAL LEE
FLIES AGAIN

BEHIND THE SCENES WITH THE DUKES OF HAZZARD CHARGER
PG.62

AUGUST 2005
USA $3.99 · CANADA $4.99
FIND MORE @ HOTROD.COM

HEMIS FOREVER!

- THE LEGEND OF THE CHRYSLER HEMI
- FIRST TEST: 5.7L HEMI CRATE ENGINE
- VINTAGE HEMI FUNNY CARS

HOT ROD WHERE IT ALL BEGAN

DISPLAY UNTIL AUGUST 9, 2005

0 70989 34807 3

A PRIMEDIA Publication

August: Freelancer John Pearley Huffman tags along with the second-unit crew to get the lowdown on the cars and stunts used in the new *Dukes of Hazzard* movie. It took 26 1968, 1969, and 1970 Chargers to play the *General Lee*. Thankfully, not all of them were completely wadded up.

January: Twelve-second Mustangs are cool, but Freiburger's quest for the Bonneville 200 MPH Club is compelling reading.

February: The *Overhaulin' Challenging Mopar* represents what's hot: big wheels, style, and reality TV.

April: A model with a spray gun—must be "Paint & Body" time again.

May: "Big Red is out of mothballs and ready to kick some Pro Touring tail."

June: Introducing Shelby's GT500 and Drag Week all in one issue. Whew!

July: Muscle cars revisited. Note the 'Cuda price tag. A year ago, $1 million was outrageous.

September: Pump Gas Drags produce two covers: Camaro for the newsstand, Mustang for subscribers.

October: These "real" hot rods are "built by regular guys without a truckload of cash."

November: Street-rod-style buildups of muscle cars are the Next Big Thing.

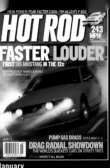

January

February

April

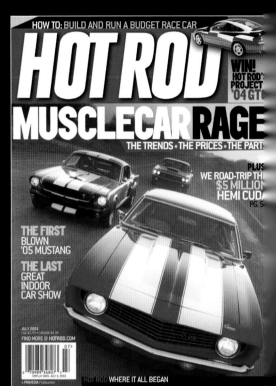

July

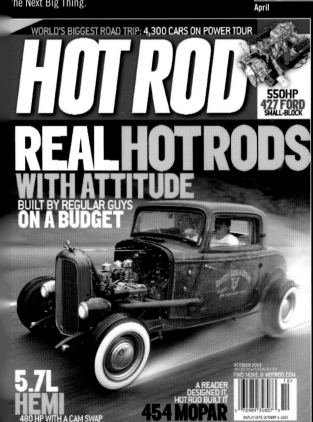

May

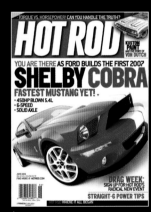

June

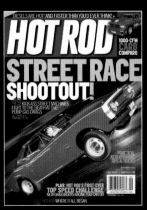

By 2006, just like in 1966, Ford has enjoyed a few years of having the pony car segment all to itself. But just like in 1966, that's about to change. At the North American International Auto Show in Detroit, Chevrolet and Dodge deliver exciting concept cars that could ignite a pony car war all over again.

Unlike the battle 40 years prior, though, it looks like Dodge's Challenger will be the first to take on the Mustang. That's partly due to the fact that, as of freelancer John Pearley Huffman's deadline, the Camaro concept hasn't been finished. The Camaro on the cover is a computer rendering of the finished car.

The Challenger, on the other hand, has a head start. Its foundation is the existing LX platform already underneath the Charger, Magnum, and 300. As Huffman explains, "The best thing about carrying all the LX stuff is that the Concept Challenger easily accommodates any engine Dodge wants to heave into it. And of course the engine that everyone wants to see in there is the Hemi." Dodge happily obliges, outfitting the concept with the 6.1L, 425-horsepower Hemi used in the Charger and 300C SRT8 models.

Like the 2005 Mustang, the Challenger concept is gloriously retro, evoking its 1970–1974 predecessors while at the same time improving on them. "Instead of merely recreating that car, the designers endeavored to build a Challenger most people see in their mind's eye," explains Advanced Vehicle Design VP Tom Tremont. It's a vehicle "without the imperfections, like the old car's tucked-under wheels, long front overhang and imperfect fits."

MUSCLECARS ARE HERE AGAIN
SPECIAL COLLECTOR'S ISSUE

26 PAGES OF DARE TO BE DIFFERENT HOT RODS

HOT ROD

10HP FOR $30
COOL TRICK FOR YOUR NEXT CAMSHAFT

GREAT COMEBACK

HEMI CHALLENGER FOR 2008

THE PONY CAR WAR IS ON! START PLANNING YOUR BUILDUP NOW. PG. 40

CAMARO RETURNS!

MARCH 2006
USA $3.99 • CANADA $4.99
FIND MORE @ HOTROD.COM
DISPLAY UNTIL FEBRUARY 21, 2006
A PRIMEDIA Publication

BOSS 429
BUILD ONE FROM A FORD 460

HOT ROD WHERE IT ALL BEGAN

March

The concept Camaro, on the other hand, doesn't recreate past designs as much as borrow elements from them—single headlamps on the edges of an egg-crate grille, the body's Coke-bottle shape, the slats in the rear fenders. "But the whole car is much sharper edged than the original," Huffman writes. "The design has facets much like Cadillac's current sedans. That results in a car that looks more aggressive than any factory '69 Camaro."

The fact that the Camaro isn't based on an existing platform is good news and bad. On one hand, it gives the designers freedom to "size and proportion it more freely than Dodge was with the Challenger," says Huffman. The Camaro's builders also have a whole lineup of Chevrolet products to use as powertrain sources and choose the 6.0L, 400-horsepower LS2 V-8 out of the Corvette.

The downside? Because the concept is "built around a hodge-podge conglomeration of parts from various GM lines," it isn't a car that's a "slam dunk for production like the Challenger," Huffman says. "But there is room for optimism. After all, when GM showed the Pontiac Solstice roadster as a concept at the '02 Detroit show, it was cobbled together in much the same way. Lightning can strike twice."

Just in case that happens, the editors include illustrations of hot-rodded Challengers and Camaros rendered by Thom Taylor, Steve Stanford, and Murray Pfaff to jump-start readers' imaginations.

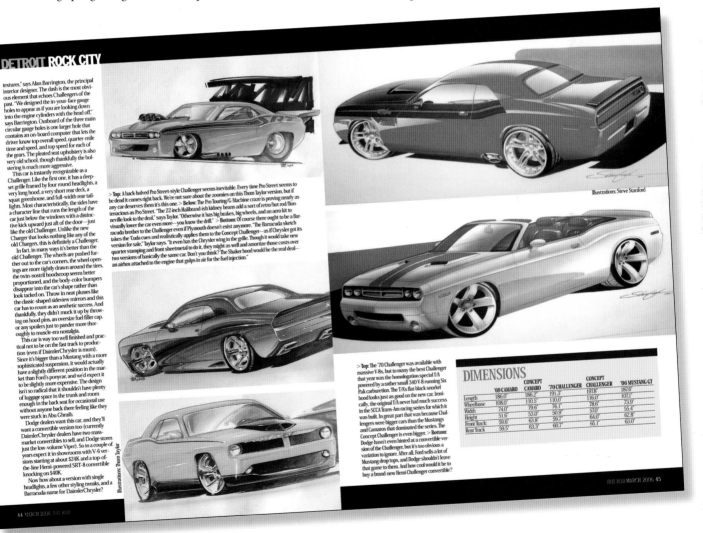

Hot Rod is all about cars *modified* for speed and beauty, so illustrators Thom Taylor and Steve Stanford visualize some hop-up ideas for the new Challenger.

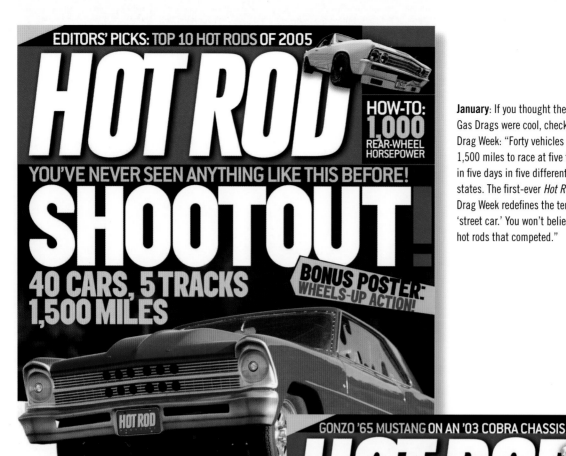

EDITORS' PICKS: TOP 10 HOT RODS OF 2005

HOT ROD

HOW-TO: 1,000 REAR-WHEEL HORSEPOWER

YOU'VE NEVER SEEN ANYTHING LIKE THIS BEFORE!

SHOOTOUT!

40 CARS, 5 TRACKS 1,500 MILES

BONUS POSTER: WHEELS-UP ACTION!

JANUARY 2006
USA $3.99 • CANADA $4.99
FIND MORE @ HOTROD.COM

BOLT-ON LS1 MUS...
5 STEPS TO 530 ...

HOT ROD **WHERE IT ALL BEGAN**

A PRIMEDIA Publication

DISPLAY UNTIL DECEMBER 27, 2005

January: If you thought the Pump Gas Drags were cool, check out Drag Week: "Forty vehicles driving 1,500 miles to race at five tracks in five days in five different states. The first-ever *Hot Rod* Drag Week redefines the term 'street car.' You won't believe the hot rods that competed."

August: Randy Lorentzen's cover setup at John Balow's Muscle Car Restorations merely hints at the cover story inside: A treasure trove of rare Chevys and countless engines, transmissions, fuel-injection systems, and other original and NOS parts collected since the 1950s by a Wisconsin man who stashed them in semi-truck trailers.

GONZO '65 MUSTANG ON AN '03 COBRA CHASSIS

HOT ROD

CARB VS. INJECTION POWER SHOOTOUT

RAREMUSCLE

UNCOVERED AFTER 30 YEARS!

21 TRUCKLOADS OF LS6 CHEVELLES, VETTES, CAMAROS, ENGINES, AND MORE

SEE THE INCREDIBLE STASH
READ THE AMAZING STORY PG.48

AUGUST 2006
USA $4.99 • CANADA $5.99

EASY RUST REPAIR
INSTALL NEW FLOORS WITH A $440 WELDER
PLUS: MORE DO-IT-YOURSELF BODYWORK BASICS

DISPLAY UNTIL JULY 18, 2006

FIND MORE @ HOTROD.COM
A PRIMEDIA Publication

700HP
500ci OLDSMOBILE
BIG DADDY ROTH KUSTOMS

HOT ROD **WHERE IT ALL BEGAN**

2 PULLOUT POSTERS

CAM INFO THAT COULD SAVE YOUR ENGINE

HOT ROD

HOW TO: PREP YOUR CAR FOR PAINT

RETRO NOW!

WILD '60s STREET MACHINES ARE BACK
13 CARS THAT PROVE IT
PG. 44

WAY COOL!
$5,700 SHOW-STOPPING ROADSTER

JUNE 2006
USA $4.99 • CANADA $5.99
FIND MORE @ HOTROD.COM
A PRIMEDIA Publication
DISPLAY UNTIL MAY 23, 2006

PINKS: HOTTEST CAR SHOW ON TV
600 HP: ALL-NEW BLOWER KIT
HOT ROD WHERE IT ALL BEGAN

une

HEMI SHOOTOUT. BEST HEADS-UP BATTLE IN THE NHRA

HOT ROD
NO FEAR BACK TO NICK

EXCLUSIVE: WE TEST GM'S BADDEST SMALL-BLOCK CRATE ENGINE, THE LS7
WICKED POWER!

TODAY'S MUST-HAVE POWERPLANT
• 540 HP OUT OF THE BOX
• 600+HP WITH A CAM & HEADERS
• PLUS: FIRST-EVER CARB INTAKE

ULTIMATE '57 MUSTANG FASTBACK
ROAD RACING FOR CHEAP: HOW TO WIN
HOW TO REBUILD A TOP-FUEL ENGINE IN AN HOUR

TOP 40 CAR MOVIES
WE REVIEW 'EM, RANK 'EM, AND TELL YOU WHERE TO GET 'EM

HOT ROD WHERE IT ALL BEGAN

February

HOW THEY BUILT IT: WORLD'S MOST SPECTACULAR CONCEPT CAR

HOT ROD

ALL-NEW HARDWARE THAT WILL BLOW YOUR MIND IN 2006
29 BREAKTHROUGH SPEED PARTS

ENGINE • SUSPENSION
BOLT-ONS • TOOLS • MORE
DON'T MISS THE 440CI SMALL-BLOCK MOPAR

HEMI 'CUDA OVERKILL
825 HP AND NOT ONE STOCK BODY PANEL

MORE CARS
• OVERHAULIN TV'S MACH 1
• NUTSO TWIN-TURBO COBRA

APRIL 2006
FIND MORE @ HOTROD.COM

BAM! YOUR ENGINE BLEW UP. HOW TO FIND OUT WHAT WENT WRONG!

HOT ROD WHERE IT ALL BEGAN

April

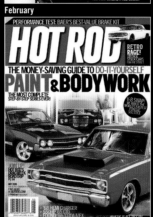

PERFORMANCE TEST: BAER'S BEST-VALUE BRAKE KIT

HOT ROD
RETRO RAGE!

THE MONEY-SAVING GUIDE TO DO-IT-YOURSELF
PAINT & BODYWORK
THE MOST COMPLETE STEP-BY-STEP SERIES EVER!

JOIN UP! HOT ROD'S V-8 SWAP SOURCE

'68 HEMI CHARGER FOUND: '65 'CUDA A/FX

HOT ROD WHERE IT ALL BEGAN

May

2 POSTERS INSIDE

HOW-TO: DO-IT-YOURSELF DENT REPAIR

HOT ROD

IT'S THE BADDEST MUSTANG EVER AND WE'VE GOT IT FIRST
'07 SHELBY

MORE EXCLUSIVES! GT500 SPEED PARTS & FORD'S NEW TURNKEY RACE CARS

•475+ HP
•0-60 IN 4.5 SEC.
•LOW 12s AT THE DRAGS

MAY 2006

816HP SMALL-BLOCK FORD!
PLUS: HOW DYNO TESTING CAN SAVE YOU TIME & MONEY

HOT ROD WHERE IT ALL BEGAN

July

February: GM's LS7 is "today's must-have powerplant." The see-through manifold is a clear-resin prototype.

April: 'Cuda overkill: "The owner says he's going to drive the wee out of it."

May: The scene at Barry White's Street Rod Repair Company starts this "Paint and Body" series.

June: The 13 1960s-style Gassers in the issue "all have loads of attitude."

July: The new GT500 "not only revives a legendary badge, but it kicks absolute butt."

September: Tom Nelson builds a 1,000-horsepower "daily driver" for Freiburger's *F-Bomb* Camaro.

October: Thirty-two hot projects plus thirty-two Pump Gas Drags cars plus one road race Boss.

November: *Transformer*'s Bumblebee is really—spoiler alert—mostly a GTO underneath.

December: The Factory Appearing Stock Tire (F.A.S.T.) drags: High 10s and big miles-per-hour.

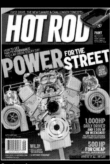

FIRST DRIVE: THE NEW CAMARO & CHALLENGER CONCEPTS

HOT ROD

POWER FOR THE STREET

1,000HP DAILY DRIVER
500 HP FOR CHEAP

HOT ROD WHERE IT ALL BEGAN

September

PAINT & BODY: BLOCK-SANDING TIPS FOR PERFECT SHEETMETAL

HOT ROD

64 TOP CARS!
32 STREET-SHOP MUSCLECARS IN ACTION!
+32 BEST PROJECT CARS IN AMERICA

HOT ROD WHERE IT ALL BEGAN

October

100+ CARS INSIDE

HOT ROD

TELL CHEVY HOW TO BUILD THE '09 CAMARO

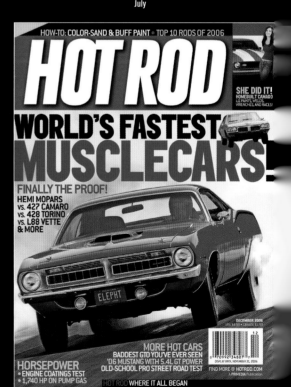

HOW-TO: COLOR-SAND & BUFF PAINT • TOP 10 RODS OF 2006

HOT ROD

SHE DID IT!
HOMEBUILT CAMARO
LIZ PAINTS, WELDS, WRENCHES, AND RACES!

WORLD'S FASTEST MUSCLECARS
FINALLY THE PROOF!

HEMI MOPARS
vs. 427 CAMARO
vs. 428 TORINO
vs. L88 VETTE
& MORE

ELEPHT

MORE HOT CARS
BADDEST GTO YOU'VE EVER SEEN
'06 MUSTANG WITH 5.4L GT POWER
OLD-SCHOOL PRO STREET ROAD TEST

HORSEPOWER
• ENGINE COATINGS TEST
• 1,740 HP ON PUMP GAS

DECEMBER 2006
USA $4.99 • CANADA $5.99
DISPLAY UNTIL NOVEMBER 21, 2006
FIND MORE @ HOTROD.COM
A PRIMEDIA Publication

HOT ROD WHERE IT ALL BEGAN

December

The August 2006 "Rare Muscle Uncovered" issue was a huge hit with readers—and just plain cool—so the editors revisit the topic with this "Barn Finds" special. "Contrary to what some may think, there are still hidden hot rod treasures out there just waiting to be discovered. We scoured the country and found 18 pages' worth of rescued musclecars, hot rods and race cars." Some of the cars in the section are true barn finds—those cars "unearthed after decades of neglect and outright memory loss. Others are still in the care of their original owners or builders but haven't seen the light of day for years."

To illustrate the subject, Randy Lorentzen sets up the cover photo in Editor-in-Chief David Freiburger's garage. The 'Cuda is Freiburger's latest acquisition, recently found in a Kentucky barn where it had sat since the transmission blew up in the early 1980s. How'd he locate it? By searching "barn find" on eBay Motors when he was looking for a cover car for this issue.

The Model A on the cover belongs to Tom McIntyre, though he tells Editor Rob Kinnan he feels more like its caretaker. "It will always be the Williams Brothers car," he says of the historic roadster, which Kinnan describes as "the most unbelievable barn find we've seen in a long time." This is not the first time the car has been in *Hot Rod*; back in December 1954 it earned a place in the magazine by smashing the B/Roadster record at Bonneville with a speed of 159 miles per hour. "It also did some drag racing and hill climbs," Kinnan writes, "but in '56 they put it away. The car sat in the Williams Brothers shop untouched

October

for 50 years until Tom found it, 100 percent original including the 1956 air in its Firestone Speedway tires."

McIntyre has no plans to restore the car, "drive it, or do anything but let his friends marvel at the history. And we're glad."

Every one of the found, exhumed, or in-storage cars in the section has a story to tell—archaeology writ in faded metal and checked rubber. There's Skip Kent's Hemi-powered Deuce dragster, stashed away for 40 years before Skip and his sons take on its rebirth; Dennis Sisco's Model A roadster, found "resting on its frame rails under a carport where it had been left to rot sometime in the late '60s"; Steve Atwell's Superbird, which Chrysler awarded to Richard Petty—then took back when Petty wanted cash instead; Rick Voegelin's Super Mod Camaro, a *Car Craft* project car built to race in

2007

1974 and still in Voegelin's barn; Al Kirschenbaum's 'Cuda, another magazine car built in the 1970s and parked in the 1980s; a Barracuda customized by Detroit's Alexander Brothers for car show duty and now in the hands of one of the original builder's sons; and more. So much more, in fact, that the editors compile 10 more pages of barn finds and survivors for the next month.

Not all barn finds are found in barns. Dennis Sisco's *Blue Racer* is more of a field find.

August: Two covers were produced for this issue. Newsstand buyers got YearOne's twenty-first-century reboot of the *Smokey and the Bandit* Trans Am; subscribers got the famous shot of Robert E. Petersen kneeling on 20 years of *Hot Rod* issues, in tribute to the passing of the magazine's founder.

March: In the latest reprise of the "Dare to be Different" cover theme, eight out-there rods are featured, including a Tucker, a 1935 Chevy street modified, a Rambler wagon, and even a jet-powered New Beetle. On the cover is Freiburger's *F-Bomb* Camaro, "the car that is bankrupting the editor-in-chief."

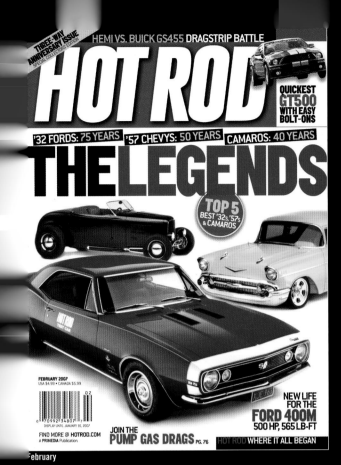

HEMI VS. BUICK GS455 DRAGSTRIP BATTLE

HOT ROD

QUICKEST GT500 WITH EASY BOLT-ONS

'32 FORDS: 75 YEARS   '57 CHEVYS: 50 YEARS   CAMAROS: 40 YEARS

THE LEGENDS

TOP 5 BEST '32s, '57s & CAMAROS

FEBRUARY 2007
USA $4.99 • CANADA $5.99

NEW LIFE FOR THE **FORD 400M** 500 HP, 565 LB-FT

JOIN THE **PUMP GAS DRAGS** PG. 76

DISPLAY UNTIL JANUARY 16, 2007
FIND MORE @ HOTROD.COM
A PRIMEDIA Publication   HOT ROD **WHERE IT ALL BEGAN**

February

AIR SUSPENSION IS HOT! 10 PAGES OF GREAT TECH

HOT ROD
THE NEW BOSS 302

28 REAL-WORLD POWER COMBOS
STREET & STRIP-PROVEN MUSCLECARS

TRUE STORIES OF **BONNEVILLE SPEED WEEK**

POST-PAINT TIPS & TRICKS

HOT ROD WHERE IT ALL BEGAN

January

ENGINE SWAPS: GM GEN III • FORD MOD • MOPAR 5.7 HEMI

HOT ROD
RACK & PINION CONVERSIONS FOR ANY CAR

'09 CAMARO CONVERTIBLE

GLORY DAYS!
650HP BLOWN VETTE • 600HP VIPER • 500HP SHELBY

NEW MINITUB KIT FOR '70-'81 CAMAROS

WHERE IT ALL BEGAN

May

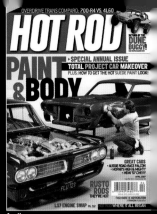

OVERDRIVE TRANS COMPARO: 700-R4 VS. 4L60

HOT ROD
THE DUNE BUGGY!

PAINT & BODY
› SPECIAL ANNUAL ISSUE
TOTAL PROJECT CAR MAKEOVER
PLUS: HOW TO GET THE HOT SUEDE PAINT LOOK!

GREAT CARS
• AUSSIE ROAD-RACE FALCON
• MOPAR'S HIGH & MIGHTY
• HEMI '57 CHEVY

RUSTO RODS THEY'RE HOT!

LS7 ENGINE SWAP   HOT ROD WHERE IT ALL BEGAN

April

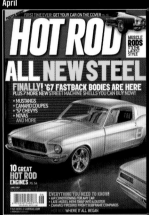

FIRST TIME EVER! GET YOUR CAR ON THE COVER

HOT ROD
MUSCLE RODS IT'S THE LATEST STYLE

ALL NEW STEEL
FINALLY! '67 FASTBACK BODIES ARE HERE
PLUS 7 MORE NEW STREET MACHINE SHELLS YOU CAN BUY NOW!
• MUSTANGS
• CAMARO COUPES
• '57 CHEVYS
• NOVAS
• AND MORE

10 GREAT HOT ROD ENGINES

EVERYTHING YOU NEED TO KNOW!
• AIR CONDITIONING FOR ANY CAR
• LATE-MODEL HEMI SWAP INTO ANY CAR
• CAMARO/FIREBIRD FRONT SUBFRAME COMPAROS

FIND MORE @ HOTROD.COM   HOT ROD WHERE IT ALL BEGAN

June

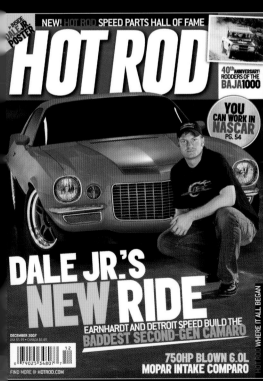

INSIDE DALE JR. POSTER   NEW! HOT ROD SPEED PARTS HALL OF FAME

HOT ROD

40TH ANNIVERSARY! RODDERS OF THE **BAJA 1000**

YOU CAN WORK IN NASCAR PG. 54

DALE JR.'S NEW RIDE
EARNHARDT AND DETROIT SPEED BUILD THE **BADDEST SECOND-GEN CAMARO**

DECEMBER 2007
USA $5.99 • CANADA $6.99

FIND MORE @ HOTROD.COM

750HP BLOWN 6.0L MOPAR INTAKE COMPARO

HOT ROD WHERE IT ALL BEGAN

December

600HP STROKER SMALL-BLOCK MOPAR BUILDUP

HOT ROD
PONTIAC 1,728 NOVA

FOOSE COUPE!
CHIP'S MOST RADICAL PROJECT YET

& YOU CAN BUY 1 of 50

GET A GOOD PAINT JOB FOR $98

• TWIN-BLOWN FASTBACK
• TROY TREPANIER'S LATEST, TOO!

WHERE IT ALL BEGAN

July

EXTREME MAKEOVER: '57 CHEVY PRO STREETER

HOT ROD
HEADER DESIGN TIPS

WE TEST 'EM
POWER PARTS!

EASY BOLT-ON SPEED FOR TODAY'S HOT V-8s

• DIRT-CHEAP 5.0 MUSTANG
• TRI-TRAIN CAM
• S4 FAWN BLED
HOMEBUILT TURBO CARS

WHERE IT ALL BEGAN

September

10 PAGES OF AMAZING BARN FINDS & SURVIVORS

HOT ROD
86 ROAD PROVEN MOPAR POWER TOUR

SPECIAL LOW-BUCK ISSUE

BODYWORK MAKEOVER
HOW TO DO IT AT HOME IN ONE WEEK!

WHERE IT ALL BEGAN

January: "Real-World Power Combos" from Drag Week; the Mustang ran 12.27 at 105 miles per hour.

February: Hot rodding's icons celebrate milestones; *Hot Rod* presents the five best of each.

April: GTO and Mustang on the outside; inside the *F-Bomb* gets its suede paint.

May: "If your car isn't packing 500 hp, you'd better get back on the porch."

June: This fastback Mustang is just one of a growing number of new steel reproduction bodies.

July: *Hemisfear* is wild. The $98 paint job? Rustoleum laid on with a roller. Seriously.

September: Bolt-on power for modern Ford, Dodge, and Pontiac muscle.

November: Low-buck bodywork and barn finds that wouldn't fit in the October issue.

December: Dale Earnhardt Jr. grew up wanting to be on the cover of *Hot Rod*.

2007

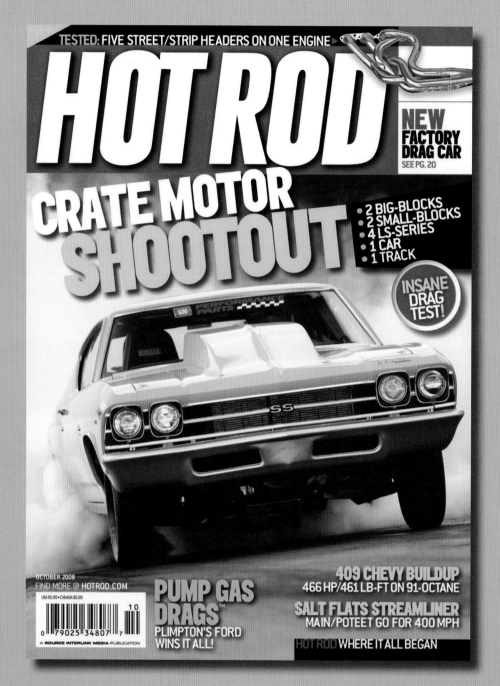

October

"Just where this scheme was first hatched nobody seems to remember, but it has hotel bar written all over it." So begins Detroit Editor Bill McGuire's story on one of the most epic tests in *Hot Rod*'s history, the "Jumbo Crate Motor Comparo of Death!"

OK, maybe not to the death. But McGuire accurately describes the notion as a "track thrash of heroic proportions. One would have to be crazy to even suggest such a thing." But suggest they did, and the gearheads at GM Performance Parts "not only liked the idea, they loved it. Turns out they are as crazy as we are." GMPP puts together a team of wrenches, racers, and fabricators and also supplies the test mule: a real-deal 1969 SS396 Chevelle modified to be safe, consistent, and easy to work on at the track. Its Corvette Millennium Yellow paint is perfect for Wes Allison's boiling-the-hides cover photo.

The team tests two engines per day for four days. Out of the gate, the 7.0L, 505-horsepower LS7 sets the bar with a best of 10.781 at 120.33 miles per hour. Even more dramatic, on the very first launch the car's front wheels head straight for the sky. "I guess the chassis is working fairly well," says Mike Copeland, a GM Performance Division project manager who's heading up the test.

Next up is GMPP's 6.2L, 430-horsepower LS3, about half the price of the LS7, which turns a best of 11.333 at 114.23 miles per hour. The first small-block, the 5.3L, 327-horsepower LS327/327, stops the clocks at 12.354 at 105.67 miles per hour—"pretty stout for a truck motor, and a dinky one at that." Another small-block, the 350ci, 355-horse ZZ4 350, is just a tenth slower at 12.447 at 105.67. The 383-inch, 425-horse ZZ383 "sits at the top of GMPP's 383 crate motor lineup" and delivers a best of 11.705 at 111.71 miles per hour.

Back in big-block territory comes the ZZ427/430, with a displacement (the first number) and power rating (the second) that echo the mighty aluminum L88 from the 1960s but with an iron block and a tamer compression ratio. Its best run is 11.351 at 115.94 miles per hour. The LS7's number looks unapproachable until the "bruiser of our ensemble" is stabbed into the Chevelle: the ZZ572/720R, with its big mechanical roller cam and thirst for 110-octane race fuel. "Too much motor and not enough tire" is the verdict, despite a test-best 10.217 at 128.98 miles per hour. The final engine, the LSX 454, is the only one that gives the crew trouble, but it still turns in a respectable 10.754 at 120.333 miles per hour, despite misfire issues and the wrong rear gear.

"We know we didn't extract the full potential from any of these crate engines," McGuire admits, "but that was never the goal." The back-to-back tests, with as many variables minimized as possible, enable readers to see "where each engine measures up in comparison with the others. We got that done, with useful accuracy if not full scientific rigor."

Eight engines, four days, one well-flogged Chevelle. GM Performance Parts puts its crate motors to the test.

ENGINE TECH

THE JUMBO CRATE MOTOR COMPARO OF DEATH!

One Car. One Dragstrip. Four Days. Eight Crate Engines From GM Performance Parts. We Tested Them and Here Are the Results.

By Bill McGuire

Photography: Wes Allison, Bill McGuire, and Mike Yoksich

THE PLAN

Just where this scheme was first hatched nobody seems to remember, but it has hotel bar written all over it. It must have been after a long, beautiful day on the road on Power Tour" or on top of 14 hours of sensory overload at the SEMA show in Las Vegas. When the HOT ROD staff is spooled up into a state of giddy exhaustion and the second round of beverages has been ordered—only then can a story idea as extreme as this one begin to make sense.

The high concept: Take a truckload of crate engines and race-test them all in the same car, at the same time, on the same dragstrip. Yeah, right. Get real. Such a project would require a track thrash of heroic proportions. The logistics alone are a nightmare. It would demand far more time and budget than one feature could ever justify; meanwhile, any one of a zillion little things could go wrong and crash the whole stupid plan. One would have to be crazy to even here is the truly weird part: We pitched the idea to the gearheads at General Motors Performance Parts, Lisa Reffett and Dr. Jamie Meyer, and they bought it, the fools. They not only liked the idea, they loved it. Turns out they are as crazy as we are.

As the plan was fine-tuned over the ensuing months, the inventory of engines we proposed to flog was trimmed from more than 20 (insane) to approximately a dozen (a bit redundant) to eight. In the view of GM Performance Parts, that number provided a nice representative cross section of the engines in its catalog. There are two traditional Chevy small-blocks, two hairy big-blocks, and four versions of the engine family that GMPP believes represents the future of enthusiast performance, the LS small-block series. The engines ranged in displacement from 323 to 572 ci and from 327 to 720 hp. So there is something for everyone here, and as they say, everybody likes something. Here's our complete report.

January: For *Hot Rod*'s 60th anniversary, the editors name the most influential hot rods of all time. Number 1? The *General Lee*, which has "influenced more people to get into cars, or at least pay attention to them, than any other car." Responses swamp the mailroom and email inboxes.

February: An issue with two covers: Newsstand buyers get Jack Hodson's "Homebuilt Hero" 1967 Camaro, while subscribers get vintage Wally Parks. The magazine pays tribute to Parks, whose unwavering dedication to our industry shaped *Hot Rod*, the NHRA, and so much more. Also, Freiburger "pulls the chute" to work online, leaving Editor Kinnan to run the show.

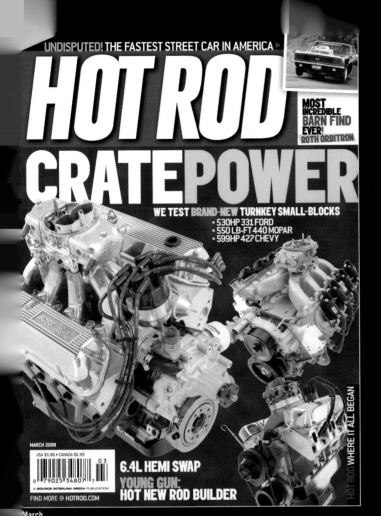

2008

March: Dyno testing turnkey, 500-plus-horsepower crate engines from Ford, GM, and Mopar.

April: *Hot Rod* finally gets its hands on a production Challenger. "Believe the hype."

May: Inside are 125 steps to perfect paint, from stripping to wet sanding.

June: Editors drive the snot out of seven hot rods to reveal their unique characteristics.

July: Personal—and usually hidden—car collections that make all drool.

August: The restomod GTO is painted in an appropriately named Hurst Gold hue.

September: Nostalgia Funny Cars are back, and are they hot! Too hot!

November: Need more power and better economy? Fuel injection the answer for any car.

December: Danny Thompson conjures the spirit of his father with Mustangs at Bonneville.

March

April

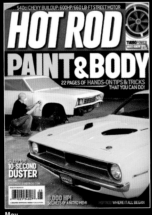

May

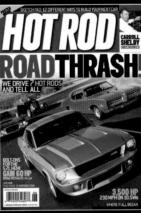

June

July

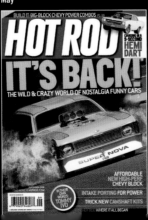

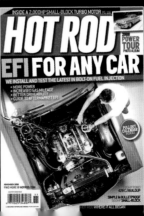

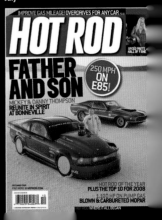

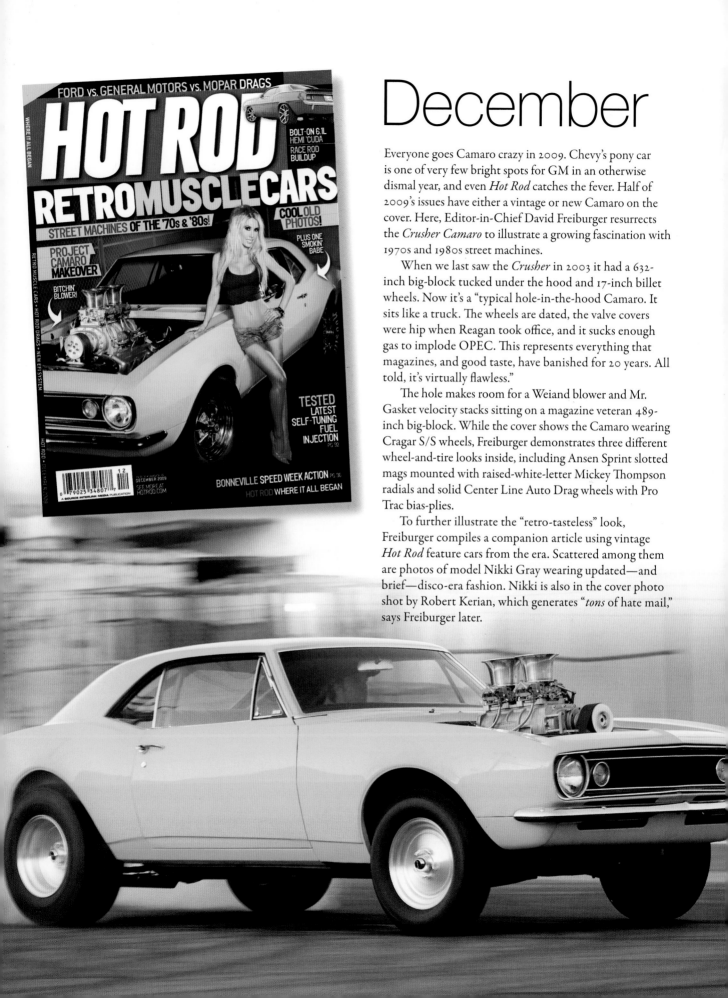

December

Everyone goes Camaro crazy in 2009. Chevy's pony car is one of very few bright spots for GM in an otherwise dismal year, and even *Hot Rod* catches the fever. Half of 2009's issues have either a vintage or new Camaro on the cover. Here, Editor-in-Chief David Freiburger resurrects the *Crusher Camaro* to illustrate a growing fascination with 1970s and 1980s street machines.

When we last saw the *Crusher* in 2003 it had a 632-inch big-block tucked under the hood and 17-inch billet wheels. Now it's a "typical hole-in-the-hood Camaro. It sits like a truck. The wheels are dated, the valve covers were hip when Reagan took office, and it sucks enough gas to implode OPEC. This represents everything that magazines, and good taste, have banished for 20 years. All told, it's virtually flawless."

The hole makes room for a Weiand blower and Mr. Gasket velocity stacks sitting on a magazine veteran 489-inch big-block. While the cover shows the Camaro wearing Cragar S/S wheels, Freiburger demonstrates three different wheel-and-tire looks inside, including Ansen Sprint slotted mags mounted with raised-white-letter Mickey Thompson radials and solid Center Line Auto Drag wheels with Pro Trac bias-plies.

To further illustrate the "retro-tasteless" look, Freiburger compiles a companion article using vintage *Hot Rod* feature cars from the era. Scattered among them are photos of model Nikki Gray wearing updated—and brief—disco-era fashion. Nikki is also in the cover photo shot by Robert Kerian, which generates "*tons* of hate mail," says Freiburger later.

2009

June: This is the only engine cover of the year, and what an engine: Nelson Racing's "latest 1,700hp, billet-laden, twin-turbo, 427ci eye candy." Its home is the "world's cleanest third-gen Camaro," writes Freiburger, who is back in his editor-in-chief role after a 15-month stint on the World Wide Web.

August: Hemi Road Runner? Cool. All-new Cammer motor? Very cool. Drag-race AMCs? Actually, compared to some of the other "Dare to be Different" rods inside, they're almost mainstream. All three are street-driven cars that turn mid-6s in the eighth-mile, roughly equivalent to low to mid-10s in the quarter.

Facing page: Freiburger brings back the *Crusher Camaro* with a 1980s makeover. "Happy days are here again."

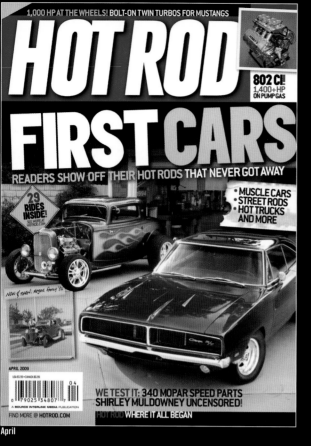

April

January

February

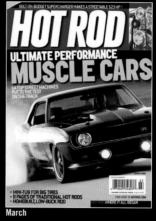

March

July

September

October

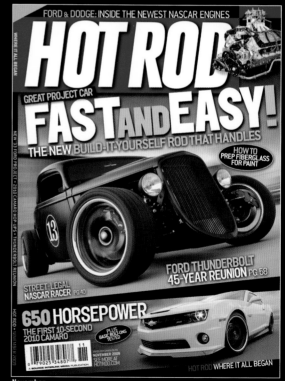

November

January: The old-timey dude-car-garage setup is back, with a girlfriend this time.

February: The LS7 Camaro and Grand Am racer are two of the four "radical Camaros inside."

March: The Ringbrothers took a mild Camaro project and turned it into the awesome *Razor*.

April: *Hot Rod* finds nearly 30 "first cars" that are still in the owners' hands.

May: A Camaro, 1957 Gasser, and Bonneville roadster are just some of the barn finds inside.

July: *Hot Rod* reviews the new Camaro—"I want one"—and gives one away too.

September: "GM closes the book on 84 years of Pontiac performance."

October: Vinyl wrap sets this Impala on fire; the Power Tour snarls traffic in seven cities.

November: Factory Five's rod kit "will handle and stop as well as a modern supercar."

2009